I0032829

GENDER EQUALITY AND SOCIAL INCLUSION IN SOUTH ASIA

AN ASSESSMENT FOR ACTION

DECEMBER 2023

ADB

ASIAN DEVELOPMENT BANK

Creative Commons Attribution 3.0 IGO license (CC BY 3.0 IGO)

© 2023 Asian Development Bank
6 ADB Avenue, Mandaluyong City, 1550 Metro Manila, Philippines
Tel +63 2 8632 4444; Fax +63 2 8636 2444
www.adb.org

Some rights reserved. Published in 2023.

ISBN 978-92-9270-329-5 (print); 978-92-9270-330-1 (electronic); 978-92-9270-331-8 (ebook)
Publication Stock No. TIM230354-2
DOI: http://dx.doi.org/10.22617/TIM230354-2

The views expressed in this publication are those of the authors and do not necessarily reflect the views and policies of the Asian Development Bank (ADB) or its Board of Governors or the governments they represent.

ADB does not guarantee the accuracy of the data included in this publication and accepts no responsibility for any consequence of their use. The mention of specific companies or products of manufacturers does not imply that they are endorsed or recommended by ADB in preference to others of a similar nature that are not mentioned.

By making any designation of or reference to a particular territory or geographic area, or by using the term "country" in this publication, ADB does not intend to make any judgments as to the legal or other status of any territory or area.

This publication is available under the Creative Commons Attribution 3.0 IGO license (CC BY 3.0 IGO) https://creativecommons.org/licenses/by/3.0/igo/. By using the content of this publication, you agree to be bound by the terms of this license. For attribution, translations, adaptations, and permissions, please read the provisions and terms of use at https://www.adb.org/terms-use#openaccess.

This CC license does not apply to non-ADB copyright materials in this publication. If the material is attributed to another source, please contact the copyright owner or publisher of that source for permission to reproduce it. ADB cannot be held liable for any claims that arise as a result of your use of the material.

Please contact pubsmarketing@adb.org if you have questions or comments with respect to content, or if you wish to obtain copyright permission for your intended use that does not fall within these terms, or for permission to use the ADB logo.

Corrigenda to ADB publications may be found at http://www.adb.org/publications/corrigenda.

Note:
In this publication, "$" refers to United States dollars.

On the cover: WUA members (Boriyazar) meeting with the Project committee at Salehmatha, Chhattisgarh. Chhattisgarh irrigation development project funded by ADB (photo by Rakesh Sahai).

Cover design by Josef Ilumin.

CONTENTS

Tables, Figures, and Boxes   vi

Currency Equivalents   viii

Abbreviations   ix

Executive Summary   xi

I.   **Setting the Context: Gender Equality and Social Inclusion in South Asia**   **1**

      A.   Introduction   1

      B.   Gender Equality and Social Inclusion Situation in the Six Countries: An Overview 11

II.   **Gender Inequality in South Asia: Issues and Responses**   **25**

      A.   Introduction: Definitions   25

      B.   Status of Gender Equality Across the South Asia Department's
            Developing Member Countries   25

      C.   Policy Analysis   32

      D.   Gender Equality Features of South Asia Department Projects   35

      E.   Good Practices and Lessons Learned   40

      F.   Conclusions and Way Forward   44

III. **Old Age in South Asia: Issues and Responses**   **49**

      A.   Introduction: Definition   49

      B.   Status of Older People in South Asia Department Developing Member Countries   49

      C.   Policy Analysis   55

      D.   South Asia Department Projects Aiming to Benefit Older People   56

      E.   Good Practices in Responding to the Issues of Older People   58

      F.   Conclusions and Way Forward   60

IV.   **Disability in South Asia: Issues and Responses**   **63**

      A.   Introduction: Definitions   63

      B.   Status of People with Disabilities in the Six South Asia Department   63
           Developing Member Countries

      C.   Policy Analysis   69

      D.   South Asia Department Projects Aiming to Benefit People with Disabilities   71

      E.   Good Practices in Responding to Disability Issues   72

      F.   Conclusions and Way Forward   74

V.   **Social Identity in South Asia: Issues and Responses**   **79**

      A.   Introduction: Definitions   79

      B.   Status of People with Disadvantaged Social Identities   79

      C.   Policy Analysis   90

      D.   South Asia Department Projects Aiming to Benefit Disadvantaged   92
           Social Identity Groups

      E.   Good Practices in Responding to Disadvantaged Social Identity Issues   93

      F.   Conclusions and Way Forward   94

VI.   **Diverse Sexual Orientation, Gender Identity and Expression,**   **97**
      and Sex Characteristics in South Asia: Issues and Responses

      A.   Introduction: Definitions   97

      B.   Status of People with Diverse Sexual Orientation and Gender Identity   98
           and Expression in the Six South Asia Department Developing Member Countries

      C.   Policy Analysis   104

      D.   South Asia Department Projects Aiming to Benefit Individuals   105
           with Diverse Sexual Orientation and Gender Identity

      E.   Good Practices in Responding to the Issues of Individuals with Diverse Sexual   105
           Orientation and Gender Identity

      F.   Conclusions and Way Forward   108

VII. **Geographic Location and Income Poverty in South Asia: Issues and Responses**   **111**

      A.   Introduction: Definitions   111

      B.   Status of the Geographically Excluded and Income Poor   112

      C.   Policy Analysis   117

D. South Asia Department Projects Aiming to Benefit People   119
    in Difficult Geographic Locations and the Income Poor

E. Good Practices in Responding to the Issues of People   122
    in Difficult Geographic Locations and the Income Poor

F. Conclusions and Way Forward   124

VIII. **Young Age and Migrant Status in South Asia**   **127**

A. Introduction   127

B. Disadvantaged Youth   127

C. Migrant Workers in India and Maldives   131

D. South Asia Department Projects Aiming to Benefit Disadvantaged Youth   136
    and Migrant Workers

E. Good Practices in Responding to the Issues of Disadvantaged Youth   137
    and Migrant Workers

F. Conclusions and Way Forward   141

IX. **Overview of the Assessment Results and Action Points**   **145**

A. Overview of the Assessment Results   145

B. Way Forward: 10-Point Guide for Designing and Operationalizing 146
    Gender Equality and Social Inclusion Programs

APPENDIXES

1 List of Reviewed Projects of the Asian Development Bank's South Asia Department   151
2 United Nations Treaty Ratification Status of South Asia Department Countries   153
3 Definitions of Disability   155
4 Definitions and Population of Different Social Identities   156

TABLES, FIGURES, AND BOXES

TABLES

1.1	The South Asia Department's Adaptation of the Three Pillars of the "Leave-No-One-Behind" Framework of the Department for International Development of the United Kingdom	6
1.2	Excluded and Vulnerable Groups in ADB Member Countries in South Asia	7
1.3	Key Demographic Indicators, 2020	11
1.4	Life Expectancy at Birth and Infant Mortality Rate by Sex, 2020	12
1.5	Age Dependency Ratio and Working Age Population, 2020	13
1.6	Human Development Index, 2018–2019	15
1.7	Gross Domestic Product Growth Rate, 2019–2020	16
1.8	Overview of Types of Historical Exclusion	18
1.9	Fundamental Rights of Individuals Guaranteed by the Countries' Constitutions	19
1.10	Overview of Existing National Policy and Institutional Framework	20
2.1	Gender Development and Inequality Indexes	26
2.2	Education-Related Indicators by Sex, 2021	27
2.3	Labor force Participation and Unemployment Rates in 2019 and 2021 by Sex	28
2.4	Employment and Income Indicators for Women	29
2.5	Indicators Related to Women's Participation and Decision-Making and Gender-based Violence	30
2.6	Some Key Acts and Policies for Gender Equality of the Six Countries in South Asia	33
3.1	Key Indicators Related to Older People	50
3.2	Old Age Dependency Ratio, 2019 and 2050	50
3.3	Percentage of People Age 65 and Older, Living Arrangements	51
3.4	Social Security Allowances and/or Pension Schemes for Older People	52
3.5	Statistics on Abuse of Older People	54
3.6	Key Acts and Policies for Older People	55
4.1	Disability Prevalence Rates	64
4.2	Statistics on Educational Attainment of People with Disabilities	65
4.3	Economic Indicators for People with Disabilities in Selected Developing Member Countries	66

4. 4   Key Acts and Policies for People with Disabilities   69

4.5   Assessment of 34 South Asia Department Projects using ADB's Disability Inclusion   75
        Marker System, 2021

5. 1   Health and Education Data of India, Disaggregated by Social Identity Groups   81

5. 2   Acts and Policies for Social Identity Groups   90

6.1   Policies and Acts for People with Diverse Sexual Orientation, Gender Identity   104
        and Expression, and Sex Characteristics in Selected Countries

7.1   Exclusionary Geographical Locations   111

7. 2   Rural Population, Poor Population, and Rural and Urban Poor Population   113

7. 3   Key Acts and Policies for Geographically Excluded People   117

7. 4   Key Acts and Policies for Poverty Alleviation   118

8.1   Key Acts and Policies for Disadvantaged Youth   131

8. 2   Key Acts and Policies for Migrant Workers in India and Maldives   134

FIGURES

1. 1   Key Definitions   4

1. 2   Dimensions of Exclusion and Vulnerability   5

1. 3   Population by Sex, 2020   12

1. 4   Poverty Trends Prior to the COVID-19 Pandemic   14

1. 5   Multidimensional Poverty Prior to the COVID-19 Pandemic   14

1. 6   Distribution of Aid Commitment to Gender Equality and Women's Empowerment   22
        from Development Assistance Committee Members, 2019

BOXES

1. 1   ADB Strategy 2030: Operational Priority 1 and Operational Priority 2   2

1. 2   Impact of COVID-19 on Women and Excluded and Vulnerable Groups   17

1. 3   Common Gender Equality and Social Inclusion Framework of International   21
        Development Partners Group in Nepal

2. 1   The Gendered Impact of Masculinity   31

4. 1   Making Work Environment More Conducive for People with Disabilities   67

6. 1   Legal Status of People with diverse Sexual Orientation, Gender Identity   99
        and Expression, and Sex Characteristics in South Asia Department Developing
        Member Countries

CURRENCY EQUIVALENTS

Currency equivalent for $1.00 are as follows:

Country	As of 15 May 2023
Bangladesh	Tk105
Bhutan	Nu81.84
India	₹81.84
Maldives	Rf15
Nepal	NRs130.75
Sri Lanka	SLRs319.68

Source: United Nations Treasury. Operational Rates of Exchange.

ABBREVIATIONS

ADB	Asian Development Bank
CEDAW	Convention on the Elimination of All Forms of Discrimination Against Women
CHT	Chittagong Hill Tracts
COVID-19	coronavirus disease
CSO	civil society organization
DAC	Development Assistance Committee
DFID	Department for International Development of the United Kingdom
DMC	developing member country
EGM	effective gender mainstreaming
FGD	focus group discussion
GAP	gender action plan
GBV	gender-based violence
GDP	gross domestic product
GEN	gender equity theme
GESI	gender equality and social inclusion
GNHC	Gross National Happiness Commission
GRB	gender-responsive budgeting
HDI	Human Development Index
IPSA	initial poverty and social analysis
LGBT	lesbian, gay, bisexual, and transgender
LNOB	leave no one behind
MPI	Multidimensional Poverty Index
MSMEs	micro, small, and medium-sized enterprises
NITI Aayog	National Institution for Transforming India
NGO	nongovernment organization
OECD	Organisation for Economic Co-operation and Development
OM	operations manual
OP1	operational priority 1

OP2	operational priority 2
OPHI	Oxford Poverty and Human Development Initiative
PMAY	Pradhan Mantri Awas Yojana
SARD	South Asia Regional Department
SDG	Sustainable Development Goal
SGE	some gender elements
SOGIESC	sexual orientation, gender identity and expression, and sex characteristics
TA	technical assistance
UN	United Nations
UN Women	United Nations Entity for Gender Equality and the Empowerment of Women
UNDP	United Nations Development Programme
UNFPA	United Nations Population Fund
UNICEF	United Nations Children's Fund

EXECUTIVE SUMMARY

The Asian Development Bank (ADB) South Asia Department (SARD) identified the need to develop an evidence-based gender equality and social inclusion (GESI) framework to strengthen its current initiatives to operationalize Strategy 2030, particularly operational priority 1 (OP1) (addressing remaining poverty and reducing inequalities) and operational priority 2 (OP2) (accelerating progress in gender equality), in South Asia. To inform the SARD GESI framework, a study to assess the GESI context in its six developing member countries (DMCs)—Bangladesh, Bhutan, India, Maldives, Nepal, and Sri Lanka—was conducted. This report presents the results of this assessment.

Assessment Objectives and Dimensions of Exclusion and Vulnerability

The assessment covered (i) the status of women and excluded and vulnerable groups; (ii) their agency or capability to recognize and claim their rights and influence decisions that affect their lives; (iii) national laws and policies to promote and protect their rights and welfare; (iv) assessment of the GESI mainstreaming elements and good practices of selected ADB SARD projects that benefit women and excluded and vulnerable groups; (iv) initiatives of other development actors (i.e., government, civil society organizations [CSOs], and international development partners) to promote the empowerment and inclusion of women and excluded and vulnerable groups; and (v) ADB's potential areas of action.

SARD identified the following dimensions of exclusion and vulnerability across its six DMCs: (i) gender; (ii) age (older people and disadvantaged youth); (iii) disability; (iv) social identities (e.g., caste, ethnicity, and religion); (v) sexual orientation, gender identity and expression, and sex characteristics (SOGIESC); (vi) geographic location; (vii) income status; and (viii) migrant status. Recognizing that different identities intersect or overlap and impact the extent of inequality, exclusion, and vulnerability (or power and advantage) that people or groups of people experience, SARD commits to responding to intersectional inequalities experienced by women and disadvantaged groups who are disproportionately represented in the poorest and most excluded groups in SARD DMCs.

Gender Equality and Social Inclusion Analytical Frameworks

The study used two GESI analytical frameworks to assess ADB SARD's and other stakeholder groups' responses to the situation of women and excluded and vulnerable groups: (i) the GESI mainstreaming framework, which analyzes the extent of integration of the GESI agenda in policies, institutional arrangements, programs, budgets, and monitoring and evaluation; and (ii) three pillars of the "Leave-No-One-Behind" (LNOB) framework of the former Department for International Development of the Government of the United Kingdom (DFID) (now the Foreign, Commonwealth and Development Office): (a) Understand for action, which is to identify barriers to GESI and analyze the capacities of women and excluded and vulnerable groups to claim their rights and promote GESI; (b) Empower for change, which is to promote the livelihood, voice, and social empowerment of women and excluded and vulnerable groups; and (c) Include for opportunity, which is to promote the GESI-suitability of the physical environment, such as infrastructures, technologies, and spaces, and the GESI-responsiveness of the social environment, such as shifts in social and gender norms and practices, health services, educational curricula, and the political environment (e.g., governance policies, structures, and systems that would reduce discrimination and promote inclusion and equality).

The assessment employed a qualitative research methodology. The data collection methods were (i) review of secondary data, available documents, and studies on GESI in the six SARD DMCs (secondary data collected included relevant statistical data); (ii) virtual focus group discussions (FGDs) with (a) government representatives responsible for enforcing laws related to GESI and implementing GESI programs in the country, (b) representatives of CSOs working with the excluded and vulnerable groups, (c) representatives of the excluded and vulnerable groups themselves, (d) international development partners, and (e) ADB officers based at resident missions and headquarters; and (iii) key informant interviews with experts and individual ADB-financed project officers.

The selection criterion for the participants (individuals and organizations) of the FGDs or stakeholder consultations was experience working with (i) excluded and vulnerable groups, (ii) national governments, and (iii) ADB. Of the 500 participants in the 122 consultations (FGDs and key informant interviews), 50% were women, about 50% were associated with CSOs (including beneficiary groups), 26% were ADB project officers (including from executing agencies and/or implementing agencies), 11% were government officials, 9% were representatives of international development agencies, and 3% were subject matter experts.

Overall, 34 projects of ADB SARD were selected to inform the assessment, of which 19 were analyzed from a sector perspective and 15 were assessed for good practices and lessons. Both sets of projects were analyzed based on a review of key project documents and consultations with the respective project teams. The overall selection criteria of these projects were (i) Gender categorization—the projects should be categorized gender equity theme (GEN) or effective gender mainstreaming (EGM) in the ADB project categorization system; projects categorized some gender elements (SGE) were included if a DMC had no projects categorized GEN or EGM in any of the three sectors; (ii) projects experiencing success in implementing gender and/or GESI elements to identify factors contributing to success; and (iii) projects experiencing challenges in implementing gender and/or GESI elements to identify barriers to success.

The assessment of the situation and responses (including ADB's responses) related to gender, older people, disability, SOGIESC, geographic location, and income poverty covered all six DMCs, while the assessment of social identity groups concentrated on four DMCs (Bangladesh, India, Nepal, and Sri Lanka), where exclusion based on caste, ethnic, and religious identities exists. Only the India Resident Mission, Bhutan Resident Mission, and GESI team in Maldives included an assessment of disadvantaged youth, and only India and Maldives included an assessment of migrant workers.

Summary of Findings

The assessment of the situation of different disadvantaged groups identified the following general concerns:

- Evidence shows that, in the six DMCs, the most disadvantaged are women. Among the excluded and vulnerable groups, the most disadvantaged are poor people and people with diverse SOGIESC. Discriminatory practices, entrenched in social norms, have constrained them from accessing available services, resources, and opportunities.

- Men and individuals with diverse SOGIESC of disadvantaged groups, especially those with disability and belonging to excluded social identity groups, experience intersectional inequality, exclusion, and vulnerability as well. In line with the LNOB principles, development interventions need to address their conditions, too. Men also have a role to play in promoting women and girls' empowerment.

- The six countries have favorable laws and policy frameworks for GESI. Ministries and institutional arrangements to implement these laws and policies have been established and are functional in each country. However, effective policy implementation has been a challenge across all DMCs. Also, many of these laws and policies do not explicitly address the overlapping discrimination that women and girls of disadvantaged groups and other excluded and vulnerable groups (e.g., older people, people with disabilities, minority social identity groups, people with diverse SOGIESC, income poor people, people in difficult geographic locations, and migrants) face because of their intersecting disadvantaged identities.

- The government and CSOs in the six DMCs, with their many years of work on gender and development, have exemplary practices and have developed their competencies in gender mainstreaming. Many also have good practices related to the social inclusion needs of other disadvantaged groups.

- ADB SARD's contributions and competencies are more concentrated on gender equality with a focus on women's empowerment. Responses to the inequality and exclusion issues of other disadvantaged groups, such as older people, people with disabilities, minority ethnic groups and/or castes, disadvantaged youth, and vulnerable migrant workers, are limited. SARD has no program or project responding to the issues of individuals with diverse SOGIESC. This also implies limited interventions on the intersectional inequalities, exclusion, and vulnerabilities experienced by women and girls of these disadvantaged groups.

- The assessment of ADB SARD projects and stakeholder initiatives along the LNOB framework suggests an unbalanced focus on the three pillars. As designing programs along all these three pillars ensures a holistic or comprehensive response to inequality, exclusion, and vulnerability, this point is worth noting. For instance, while initiatives in line with the "empower for change" pillar need further strengthening (as they are critical to achieving GESI), equal attention and action are also required on the other two pillars: "understand for action" and "include for opportunity."

- In view of these concerns, social and gender analysis to inform the GESI features of SARD projects needs to include the identification and examination of the manifestations of intersectional inequalities, exclusion, and vulnerability experienced by the projects' targeted beneficiaries, in addition to the assessment of gender inequality experienced by women and poverty experienced by disadvantaged social groups in general.

Way Forward: 10-Point Guide for Designing and Operationalizing the South Asia Department's Gender Equality and Social Inclusion Programs and Projects

The assessment of good practices of SARD and stakeholder organizations in the six DMCs provides a list of action points to consider in designing and operationalizing GESI programs and projects. Some of these points are lessons (from success factors and challenges encountered), and some are affirmations of current practices. These lessons reiterate the importance of a GESI mainstreaming and transformative approach, which cuts across the three pillars of the LNOB framework.

Point 1: Mainstream GESI in program or project design and operational frameworks and tools rather than treat it as a separate added activity.

A.   Pillar 1: Understand for Action

Point 2: Identify the disadvantaged groups (as defined in this assessment report) in program or project areas and consult them on how they can benefit and/or can be adversely affected by a proposed program or project. Integrate their views into the project's GESI features.

Point 3: Use participatory and reliable methods in collecting disaggregated data or information about the disadvantaged groups in ethical ways that do not place them into more vulnerable situation.

B.   Pillar 2: Empower for Change

Point 4: In designing the GESI features of a project, consider the distinct empowerment needs of women, girls, men, and boys experiencing overlapping exclusion and vulnerabilities due to their intersecting disadvantaged identities (e.g., age, disability, social identity, SOGIESC, geographic location, income status, and migrant status).

Point 5: Incorporate skills development and capacity building in project design and interventions, as it helps address the livelihood difficulties experienced by women and excluded and vulnerable groups.

Point 6: Organize or strengthen self-help groups that can provide a common platform for women's and excluded and vulnerable groups' empowerment.

Point 7: Enhance the accountability of service providers for GESI.

C.   Pillar 3: Include for Opportunity

Point 8: Develop the awareness and sensitivity of communities and service providers to the GESI needs of women, girls, and excluded and vulnerable groups to challenge discriminatory gender and social norms and address the structural inequalities that create stigma and discrimination.

Point 9: Incorporate GESI elements in infrastructure design as they enhance the infrastructure's utility and GESI impact on women, girls, and disadvantaged groups.

Point 10: Seek government buy-in and collaboration, and build on existing institutional mechanisms.

I. SETTING THE CONTEXT: GENDER EQUALITY AND SOCIAL INCLUSION IN SOUTH ASIA

A. Introduction

Background and Objectives of the Assessment

1.   The Asian Development Bank (ADB) has long been committed to gender equality and social inclusion (GESI). It approved its Policy on Gender and Development in 1998 and strengthened this commitment when it published operations manual (OM) section C2 on gender and development in 2010.[1] In 2004, it approved OM section C1 on poverty reduction,[2] and in 2010 OM section C3 on the incorporation of social dimensions in ADB operations.[3]

2.   ADB further affirmed this strong commitment to GESI through its Strategy 2030, which envisions a prosperous, inclusive, resilient, and sustainable Asia and the Pacific with seven operational priorities (OPs).[4] Of the seven OPs, operational priority 1 (OP1) focuses on reducing inequalities and operational priority 2 (OP2) focuses on achieving gender equality (Box 1.1). Furthermore, ADB's Corporate Results Framework (2019–2024), which tracks the indicators for measuring progress against the seven OPs, has many complementary indicators for OP1 and OP2, indicating that a harmonized approach can produce greater GESI results.

3.   To operationalize Strategy 2030, particularly OP1 and OP2, in South Asia, ADB's South Asia Department (SARD) identified the need to develop an evidence-based strategy to strengthen its current GESI-related initiatives. Hence, SARD engaged the consulting firm PricewaterhouseCoopers Pvt. Ltd. (India) to assess the GESI context in its six developing member countries (DMCs)—Bangladesh, Bhutan, India, Maldives, Nepal, and Sri Lanka.[5]

---

[1]   ADB. 2010. Gender and Development in ADB Operations. *Operations Manual.* OM C2/BP. Manila.
[2]   ADB. 2004. Poverty Reduction. *Operations Manual.* OM C1/BP. Manila.
[3]   ADB. 2010. Incorporation of Social Dimensions Into ADB Operations. *Operations Manual.* OM C3/BP. Manila.
[4]   ADB. 2018. *Strategy 2030: Achieving a Prosperous, Inclusive, Resilient, and Sustainable Asia and the Pacific.* Manila.
[5]   The engagement of the consulting form was through the support of ADB. 2019. *Technical Assistance for Supporting the Operational Priority 1 Agenda: Strengthening Poverty and Social Analysis.* Manila. This report presents the results of the assessment done by the consulting firm.

Box 1.1: ADB Strategy 2030: Operational Priority 1 and Operational Priority 2

- **Operational priority 1** is "addressing remaining poverty and reducing inequalities," whereby ADB commits to supporting human development and social inclusion.
- **Operational priority 2** is "accelerating progress in gender equality," whereby ADB commits to support targeted operations to empower women and girls, and gender mainstreaming that directly narrows gender gaps.

ADB = Asian Development Bank.
Source: ADB. 2018. *Strategy 2030: Achieving a Prosperous, Inclusive, Resilient, and Sustainable Asia and the Pacific.* Manila. p. 14.

The assessment covered (i) the status of women and excluded and vulnerable groups; (ii) their agency or capability to recognize and claim their rights and influence decisions that affect their lives; (iii) GESI features of ADB SARD projects;[6] (iv) initiatives of development actors, i.e., ADB, government, civil society organizations (CSOs), and international development partners, to promote the empowerment and inclusion of women and excluded and vulnerable groups; and (v) ADB's potential areas of action based on (i) to (iv). Because of the differential reality of inequalities and exclusion in the South Asia region, SARD developed a common GESI framework in line with Strategy 2030, drawing lessons from SARD projects and the experiences of key stakeholders in the DMCs.

Gender Equality and Social Inclusion Conceptual Framework

4.   ADB's commitment to social inclusion builds on its efforts toward gender equality and women's empowerment. To define its perspective on "social inclusion," SARD draws from an ADB study that views *social exclusion as a cause and consequence of capability deprivation in different forms* (e.g., to find employment, live a minimally decent life, interact with others without shame, participate in governance, be educated, and decide one's own life path) and unravels the nature of capability deprivation for a better understanding of social exclusion and appropriate actions.[7] Some of the key concepts brought forward by the study are as follows:

(i)   Social exclusion is a **relational deprivation** such that some are deprived while others are not; hence, it is an issue of inequality.

(ii)   **Deprivation is involuntary**, in contrast, for example, to fasting-induced hunger, which is voluntary.

(iii)   Deprivation may be **constitutively relevant**, i.e., it is unacceptable in itself, such as malnutrition, unemployment, and lack of participation in governance, or **of instrumental importance**, e.g., landlessness leads to poverty of farmers but not of all people; disability leads to poverty in an unfriendly social environment. This point also differentiates social exclusion from vulnerability in that vulnerable groups are at risk of deprivation because of their situation.

(iv)   Deprivation could be **active** (i.e., deliberate in policies and programs) or passive (i.e., unintentional because of, for example, lack of resources to reach poor people in remote areas).

---

[6]   In 2019, the country director of the India Resident Mission (now director general of SARD) requested SARD to take stock of the GESI situation in SARD DMCs and its initiatives to address the barriers to GESI faced by women and excluded and vulnerable groups. Corporate technical assistance (TA) (Vice President [Operations 1] TA funds) was used to conduct this stocktaking.

[7]   A. Sen. 2000. Social Exclusion: Concept, Application, and Scrutiny. *Social Development Papers.* No. 1. Manila: ADB.

(v)   **"Unfavorable inclusion"** is an attempt to include but on unequal terms (e.g., unequal wage for work of equal value, unequal participation in decision-making, insensitivity to the distinct conditions of women and other disadvantaged groups).

(vi)   The people most likely to be left behind by development are those facing **"intersectional inequalities"** based on multiple disadvantaged identities and situations.[8]

5.   Hence, SARD's social inclusion initiatives aim to primarily focus on women and girls who experience overlapping social exclusion and vulnerability because of their intersecting disadvantaged social identities, such as gender; age (older women and disadvantaged girls); disability; social identity (ethnicity or caste); sexual orientation, gender identity and expression, and sex characteristics (SOGIESC); income status; and geographic location. Responding to these other sources of exclusion and vulnerability necessarily brings one's attention to other people, including nonbinary individuals, who experience intersecting disadvantages too. Thus, to SARD, the advancement of gender equality cannot be divorced from the pursuance of social inclusion, with the concept of intersectionality serving as their link. Figure 1. 1 presents the definitions of these concepts in the SARD GESI framework.

6.   Based on the application of these concepts in the context of South Asia and recognizing the need to strengthen the GESI focus and impacts of its operations, SARD identified the following dimensions of exclusion and vulnerability across its six DMCs: (i) **gender**;[9] (ii) **age** (older people and disadvantaged youth); (iii) **disability**; (iv) **social identities** (e.g., caste, ethnicity, and religion);[10] (v) diverse **SOGIESC**;[11] (vi) **geographic location**; (vii) **income status**; and (viii) **migrant status**.[12] This list is not exhaustive and may be expanded to include other dimensions of exclusion and vulnerability in the DMCs, such as occupations (e.g., marginal farming and fishing, traditional salt panning, manual sewage cleaning) in the future.

---

[8]   The most enduring forms of identity-based inequalities are ascribed from birth, such as race, caste, and ethnicity, and persist over generations. The compounding quality of this form of disadvantage is captured by the term "intersecting inequalities." N. Kabeer. 2016. "Leaving No One Behind": The Challenge of Intersecting Inequalities. In International Social Science Council; Institute of Development Studies; and United Nations Educational, Scientific and Cultural Organization. *World Social Science Report, 2016: Challenging Inequalities, Pathways to a Just World*. Paris. pp. 55–58.

[9]   Gender refers to the social attributes and opportunities associated with being male and female and the social relationships between women and men and girls and boys. United Nations Entity for Gender Equality and the Empowerment of Women (UN Women). Concepts and definitions. SARD broadens the definition of gender equality to cover nonbinary groups.

[10] In this report, social identity, such as caste, ethnicity, tribe, and class, refers to the collective identity of people or group with whom people identify themselves based on shared origin or characteristics and values.

[11] People with diverse SOGIESC in this report cover lesbian, gay, bisexual, transgender, queer, and intersex individuals and others with diverse gender identities. Lesbian describes a woman who predominantly has romantic, emotional, and/or physical attraction to other women; and gay describes a man who predominantly has romantic, emotional, and/or physical attraction to other men. Bisexual describes people who have romantic, emotional, or physical attraction to person(s) of the same and different sex or gender. A transgender individual refers to a person whose sex assigned at birth does not match their gender identity, while intersex is an umbrella term that refers to people possessing one or more physical sex characteristics that fall outside the traditional conceptions of male or female bodies. Some intersex characteristics are identified at birth, while others may be discovered later in life. Queer is an umbrella term for people with diverse SOGIESC and is also used to refer to individuals who are in the process of questioning or determining their sexual orientation and/or gender identity or who do not identify with the binary sex and gender identities and LGBTI. C. Cortez, J. Arzinos, and C. De la Medina Soto. 2021. *Equality of Opportunity for Sexual and Gender Minorities*. Washington, DC: World Bank; and American Psychiatric Association. 2019. The 'Q' in LBGTQ: Queer/Questioning. *APA Blogs*. 11 December.

[12] Certain groups of people are "vulnerable" rather than "excluded" when deprivations are a result of a particular situation that reduces their ability to withstand shocks and their disadvantage or risk of disadvantage is situational rather than based on their more deeply embedded social identity. International Development Partners Group, Nepal–GESI Working Group. 2017. *A Common Framework on Gender Equality and Social Inclusion*. Kathmandu.

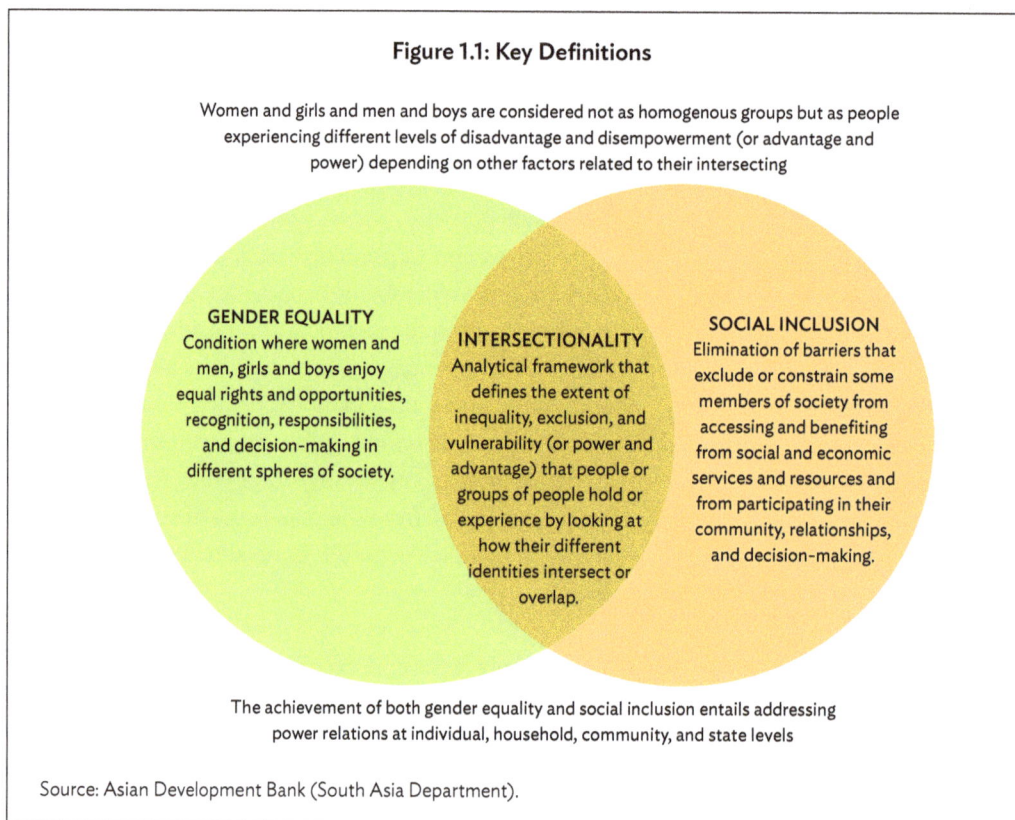

Figure 1.1: Key Definitions

Women and girls and men and boys are considered not as homogenous groups but as people experiencing different levels of disadvantage and disempowerment (or advantage and power) depending on other factors related to their intersecting

GENDER EQUALITY
Condition where women and men, girls and boys enjoy equal rights and opportunities, recognition, responsibilities, and decision-making in different spheres of society.

INTERSECTIONALITY
Analytical framework that defines the extent of inequality, exclusion, and vulnerability (or power and advantage) that people or groups of people hold or experience by looking at how their different identities intersect or overlap.

SOCIAL INCLUSION
Elimination of barriers that exclude or constrain some members of society from accessing and benefiting from social and economic services and resources and from participating in their community, relationships, and decision-making.

The achievement of both gender equality and social inclusion entails addressing power relations at individual, household, community, and state levels

Source: Asian Development Bank (South Asia Department).

7.   The intersectionality framework highlights the issue of **intersecting inequalities and disadvantages**, in which experience of exclusion increases or worsens for those who belong to multiple disadvantaged groups or identities. Intersecting inequalities and disadvantages result in numerous legal, economic, social, or cultural barriers and reinforce the exclusion of certain individuals and groups.[13] Among those experiencing intersecting inequalities in South Asia, women and girls belonging to disadvantaged groups (e.g., older women and disadvantaged girls), people with disabilities, excluded social identity groups (ethnic groups or castes), people with diverse SOGIESC, and those in vulnerable geographic locations and belonging to income-poor households are disproportionately represented in the poorest and most excluded groups in SARD DMCs. In addition, they experience discrimination because of dominant patriarchal norms in the private and public realms (Figure 1. 2).[14]

8.   The discourse on gender equality recognizes men and boys' crucial role and responsibility as partners, stakeholders, and co-beneficiaries in reducing gender disparities and achieving a more gender-equal society. Along with women and other groups, men have an important role in creating a just and fair world and transforming the systems that give them an unjust share of power.[15] Moreover, all men are not equal, and some men are disadvantaged by their social identity (caste, ethnicity, and religion) or SOGIESC. The social inclusion-related

---

[13]   D. Chaplin, J. Twigg, and E. Lovell. 2019. Intersectional Approaches to Vulnerability Reduction and Resilience-Building. *Resilience Intel.* No. 12.

[14]   This analysis of the intersecting inequalities experienced by women and girls in South Asia is based on an initial study done by SARD in 2021. The results of this earlier study are integrated in this report.

[15]   D. Olowu. 2011. Mainstreaming Women, Equating Men: Charting an Inclusionary Approach to Transformative Development in the African Decade for Women. *Law, Democracy and Development.* Vol. 15.

discussion in this GESI assessment report demonstrates that men of excluded groups (e.g., Dalits in Nepal, scheduled castes and scheduled tribes in India, the income-poor, and those in remote geographically difficult locations) are also marginalized, though not to the same extent as their women counterparts.

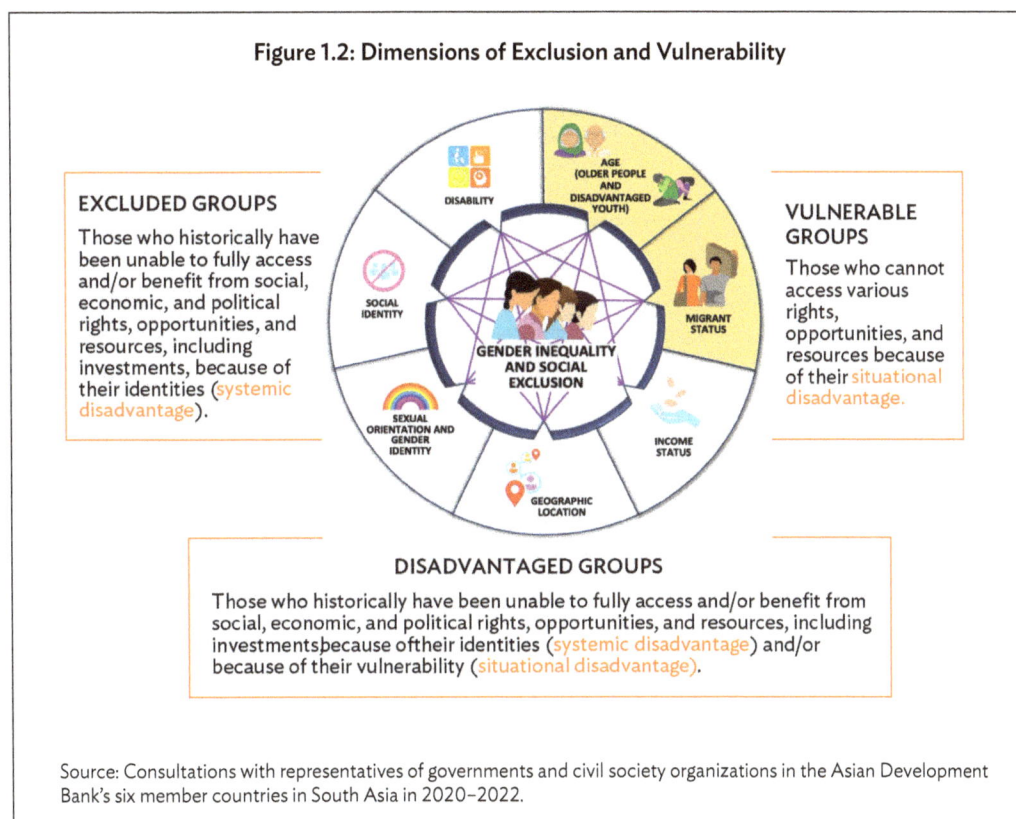

Figure 1.2: Dimensions of Exclusion and Vulnerability

EXCLUDED GROUPS

Those who historically have been unable to fully access and/or benefit from social, economic, and political rights, opportunities, and resources, including investments, because of their identities (systemic disadvantage).

VULNERABLE GROUPS

Those who cannot access various rights, opportunities, and resources because of their situational disadvantage.

DISADVANTAGED GROUPS

Those who historically have been unable to fully access and/or benefit from social, economic, and political rights, opportunities, and resources, including investments because of their identities (systemic disadvantage) and/or because of their vulnerability (situational disadvantage).

Source: Consultations with representatives of governments and civil society organizations in the Asian Development Bank's six member countries in South Asia in 2020–2022.

Gender Equality and Social Inclusion Analytical Framework

9.   This assessment merged the following frameworks for its analytical framework:

(i)   **GESI mainstreaming framework** that lists the following organizational components as areas where GESI should be integrated and made a core agenda: (a) policies that aim to address barriers to GESI in the organization's internal and external operations; (b) institutional arrangements that locate responsibilities for ensuring the implementation and achievement of GESI objectives; (c) programming and budgeting directed at supporting the achievement of GESI objectives; and (d) a monitoring and reporting system that captures GESI results, including challenges encountered and lessons learned.

(ii)   **Three pillars of the "Leave-No-One-Behind" (LNOB) framework** of the former Department for International Development of the Government of the United Kingdom (DFID):16 (a) understand for action (i.e., identify barriers to GESI and

---

16   DFID is now the Foreign, Commonwealth and Development Office of the Government of the United Kingdom.

analyze the capacities of women and excluded and vulnerable groups to claim their rights and promote GESI); (b) empower for change (i.e., promote the livelihood, voice, and social empowerment of women and excluded and vulnerable groups); and (c) include for opportunity (i.e., promote the GESI-suitability of the physical environment, such as infrastructures, technologies, and spaces, and the GESI-responsiveness of the social environment, such as shifts in social and gender norms and practices, gender-based violence levels, health services, and educational curricula; and the political environment, such as governance policies, structures, and systems that would reduce discrimination and promote inclusion and equality). The framework also responds to the transformative agenda of OPs 1 and 2 of Strategy 2030.

10.   The GESI mainstreaming framework and the LNOB framework were used for the assessment of 19 selected projects of SARD in three sectors: (i) energy, (ii) transport, and (iii) water and other urban infrastructure and services. The LNOB framework was used to (i) analyze the key objectives of government policies for each of the disadvantaged groups covered in this assessment, (ii) classify the good practices of 15 selected projects of SARD, and (iii) list SARD's potential next actions according to the participants of the stakeholder consultations.

11.   Table 1.1 presents SARD's adaptation of the three pillars of the LNOB framework. In this adaptation, while both "empower for change" and "include for opportunity" encompass laws, policies, institutional arrangements, and programs, the focus of their analysis and responses are different. "Empower for change" aims to improve the situation of women and excluded and vulnerable groups by developing their capability to, among others, access economic resources and opportunities; improve their livelihood; participate in decision-making and leadership

Table 1.1: The South Asia Department's Adaptation of the Three Pillars of the "Leave-No-One-Behind" Framework of the Department for International Development of the United Kingdom

Domains	Understand for Action	Empower for Change	Include for Opportunity
Purpose	Identify barriers to GESI and analyze the capacities of women and excluded and vulnerable groups to claim their rights and promote GESI based on disaggregated data and evidence	Promote the livelihood, voice, and social empowerment of women and excluded and vulnerable groups	Ensure the GESI-responsiveness of the social, political, and physical environment, including infrastructures, technologies, resources, and services
Questions for Analysis	• Who is excluded and vulnerable? • Why are they excluded and/or vulnerable? • What are the barriers to their access to services, resources, and opportunities? • What are their resources and capability in removing these barriers?	What laws, policies, institutional arrangements, strategies, programs, and projects contribute or can contribute to: • Livelihood and/or resource empowerment • Voice empowerment • Social empowerment (improving individual and collective social capital)	• Changing harmful formal and informal norms and practices • Making public infrastructures, facilities, spaces, workplaces, and services an enabling environment for GESI

GESI = gender equality and social inclusion.

Source: Asian Development Bank (South Asia Department), patterned from S. Herbert. 2019. Leaving No One Behind: Perspectives and Directions from DFID Multi-Cadre Conferences. *K4D Emerging Issues Report*. Brighton, United Kingdom: Institute of Development Studies.

at different levels (e.g., family, community organizations, workplace, and local and national governance structures); and prepare and respond to natural and human-induced disasters. On the other hand, "include for opportunity" aims to change the physical and social infrastructures, systems, structures, norms, and practices that perpetuate gender inequality and social exclusion.

Gender Equality and Social Inclusion Assessment Focus and Methodology

12. The assessment focused on seven causes of exclusion and vulnerability in the six DMCs: (i) gender;[17] (ii) old age; (iii) disability; (iv) social identities (ethnicity, caste, and religion); (v) diverse SOGIESC; (v) geographic location and income poverty; (vi) migrant status (for India and Maldives); and (vii) young age (particularly disadvantaged youth) (for Bhutan, India, and Maldives) (Table 1. 2).[18]

Table 1. 2: Excluded and Vulnerable Groups in ADB Member Countries in South Asia

DMC	Women	Older People	PWD	Ethnic or Caste Group	Religious Minorities	SOGIESC	Geographic Location	Income-Poor	Migrant Status	Young Age
Bangladesh	✓	✓	✓	✓	✓	✓	✓	✓	–	–
Bhutan	✓	✓	✓	✓	–	✓	✓	✓	–	✓
India	✓	✓	✓	✓	✓	✓	✓	✓	✓	✓
Maldives	✓	✓	✓	–	–	–	✓	✓	✓	✓
Nepal	✓	✓	✓	✓	✓	✓	✓	✓	–	–
Sri Lanka	✓	✓	✓	✓	✓	✓	✓	✓	–	–

✓ = covered in the assessment; – = not applicable or not included in the assessment; ADB = Asian Development Bank; DMC = developing member country; PWD = people with disabilities; SOGIESC = people with diverse sexual orientation, gender identity and expression, and sex characteristics.

Source: Consultations with representatives of governments and civil society organizations in ADB DMCs in South Asia.

13. The assessment of GESI in SARD's operations focused on three sectors: (i) energy, (ii) transport, and (iii) water and other urban infrastructure and services. To understand how well SARD is addressing the barriers to GESI, the assessment of its selected projects under these three sectors was in four areas: (i) policies, (ii) institutions, (iii) programming and budgeting, and (iv) monitoring and reporting. Additionally, selected projects were also assessed to identify good practices and lessons learned in mainstreaming GESI in SARD's operations.

---

[17] While feedback from in-country consultations suggest that gender equality should be inclusive of people with diverse sexual orientations and gender identities, global and national data on gender remain in binary form. Hence the discussion on gender (in Chapter 2) follows the binary concept of women and men. A separate chapter is devoted to the assessment of the various forms of exclusion faced by people with diverse SOGIESC in the six DMCs. The GESI assessment of disadvantaged youth and migrant workers is incomplete as these two dimensions of vulnerability were not covered in the assessment of SARD projects.

[18] In Bhutan and Maldives, low-skilled migrants are acknowledged as "socially excluded" especially since the coronavirus disease (COVID-19) pandemic, but conceptually they are vulnerable rather than excluded because their experience of disadvantage is because of their migrant situation (which could be temporary) and not their identity. Migrants from remote areas, income-poor families, and women migrants are socially excluded and vulnerable.

14.   The assessment employed a qualitative research methodology. The data collection methods were:

(i)   review of secondary data, available documents, and studies on GESI in the six SARD DMCs (secondary data included relevant statistical data);

(ii)   virtual focus group discussions (FGDs) with (a) government representatives responsible for enforcing laws related to GESI and implementing GESI programs in the country, (b) representatives of CSOs working with the excluded and vulnerable groups, (c) representatives of the disadvantaged groups, (d) international development partners, and (e) ADB offices based at resident missions and headquarters; and

(iii)   key informant interviews with experts and officers or staff of ADB-financed projects.

15.   The selection criterion for the participants (individuals and organizations) of the FGDs was experience working with (i) excluded and vulnerable groups, (ii) national governments, and (iii) ADB. Of the 122 consultations held, 83 were key informant interviews. The rest were FGDs with project teams, CSOs, or community members from different disadvantaged groups. Of the 500 participants of the 122 consultations, 50% were women, about 50% were associated with CSOs (including excluded and vulnerable groups), 26% were ADB project officers (including executing agencies and/or implementing agencies), 11% were government officials, 9% were representatives of various international development agencies, and 3% were subject matter experts.[19]

16.   The objectives of the stakeholder consultations were to (i) validate the assessment's GESI conceptual and analytical frameworks (understand for action, empower for change, and include for opportunity) and information on the GESI situation and national policies and institutional mechanisms drawn from secondary data and reviewed documents; and (ii) get to know their organizational responses to the GESI issues, including their good practices. The participants' analyses of the GESI contexts in six DMCs are integrated in the discussion of the situation, and some of their initiatives are included in the discussion of good practices.

17.   Overall, 34 projects of ADB SARD were selected to inform the assessment, of which 19 were analyzed from a sector perspective and 15 were assessed for good practices and lessons. Both sets of projects were analyzed based on a review of key project documents[20] and consultations with the respective project teams (Appendix 1 contains the list of projects).

[19]   A total of 498 people participated in the discussions, comprising 58 government representatives, 132 ADB project officers, 246 representatives from CSOs and/or nongovernment organizations (NGOs), 46 internally displaced persons, and 16 key resource persons. Maldives had the highest number of participants from the government (26), India had more ADB project officers (58) and project officers from international development agencies (23), and Nepal had more participants from CSOs.

[20]   Secondary document review covered the document types available on the ADB website: report and recommendation of the President, initial poverty and social analysis (IPSA), summary poverty reduction and social strategy, project administration manual, and social monitoring report. Consultations were with project senior management, officers, gender specialists, and other project staff as relevant.

18.   The 19 projects assessed for sector analysis were selected based on the following criteria:

(i)   **Sector categorization.** The projects were from three sectors: energy, transport, and water and other urban infrastructure and services.

(ii)   **Gender categorization.** The projects should be categorized gender equity theme (GEN) or effective gender mainstreaming (EGM).[21] Projects categorized some gender elements (SGE) were included if a DMC had no projects categorized GEN or EGM in any of the three sectors.

(iii) **Projects experiencing success in implementing gender and/or gender equality and social inclusion elements.** This was to identify factors contributing to success. GESI teams in each DMC were consulted to satisfy this criterion.

(iv)   **Projects experiencing challenges in implementing gender and/or gender equality and social inclusion elements.** This was to identify barriers to success. GESI teams in each DMC were consulted to satisfy this criterion.

19.   Of the 19 projects (2 GEN, 14 EGM, and 3 SGE), 5 belonged to the energy sector, 6 to the transport sector, and 8 to the water and other urban infrastructure and services sector. The 15 projects (11 EGM and 4 GEN) selected to identify good practices and lessons were recommended by the GESI teams in each DMC based on criteria (iii) and (iv) in para. 18.

20.   The assessment followed a participatory and iterative approach recognizing the need for periodic inputs and guidance from SARD GESI teams in the ADB headquarters and resident missions to ensure that the GESI assessment addresses their information needs and is consistent with Strategy 2030.

Limitations

21.   The limited availability of disaggregated data, especially about people with diverse SOGIESC, and evidence about intersecting inequalities experienced by different groups of people was a constraint. Data disaggregated by all variables like gender; social identity (caste, ethnicity, religion); income; and disability were not readily available in any country. The lack of information about staff diversity, work plan budgets, human resource and/or personnel policies, and organizational culture in projects limited the institutional and budget analysis of the sector projects.[22]

22.   Because of the coronavirus disease (COVID-19) pandemic, only virtual consultations were conducted, which may have inhibited some stakeholders from fully participating. However,

---

[21] ADB's four-tier gender categorization system defines the extent of gender features in the project design. At the highest level is the GEN category, where the project's design and monitoring framework has at least one gender performance indicator at the outcome level and at least one gender performance indicator in 50% of the design and monitoring framework outputs. Next to GEN is EGM, which is not required to have a gender indicator at the outcome level but should have at least one gender indicator in 50% of the design and monitoring framework outputs. Each project categorized GEN and EGM, except for results-based or policy-based loans, is required to have a gender action plan (called a GESI action plan in some projects). After EGM is some gender elements (SGE), which has gender indicators in less than 50% of the design and monitoring framework outputs. The last is no gender elements, which has no gender performance indicators in the design and monitoring framework. All projects, including those that are categorized no gender elements, are required to integrate gender considerations in the project's social safeguards framework and/or plan. ADB. 2021. *Guidelines for Gender Mainstreaming Categories of ADB Projects.* Manila.

[22] This was because of the complexity of separating government counterparts' policies and/or processes and the project-specific arrangements. Additionally, detailed workplans with budgets were part of government budgets and not in a suitable format with detailed activities for a GESI analysis.

the consulting firm was able to leverage its network and support the key beneficiaries in participating fully, wherever possible. The firm used several measures to make the consultations as accommodating as possible. Some of these measures included the following:

(i)   The use of local language to allow for an open discussion with all participants, especially disadvantaged group members. The documentation of the consultations was translated into English for this report.

(ii)   When disadvantaged group members faced difficulty managing the virtual platform, the consulting firm team and the CSO representatives supported them to ensure their participation. For the income-poor target group, the CSOs working with them ensured their presence in the consultations.

(iii) Special accommodation was made for people with disabilities joining the consultations. For instance, in the meeting for Sri Lanka, a sign language interpreter was present. Further, provisions were made for sharing images of the different icons with visually impaired participants before or after the consultations to include their insights.

(iv)   There were delays in consultations with the government because of the COVID-19-related lockdowns. However, with the support of ADB resident missions' GESI teams, the consulting firm completed most planned consultations.

(v)   There were variations in response rates across countries (e.g., stakeholders declining the meeting request, nonresponses). However, stakeholders from each category of excluded and vulnerable groups were covered. Where alternative representatives of stakeholder groups were needed, the consulting firm assessment team sought the approval of the resident mission GESI team.

Organization of the Report

23.   This report has nine chapters:

(i)   The **first chapter** provides an overview of the GESI assessment: background and objectives, conceptual and analytical frameworks, methodology, general GESI situation, and overview of policy mandates for all covered disadvantaged groups in the six DMCs and development partners involved in GESI in the region.

(ii)   The **second to eighth chapters** are on the covered dimensions of exclusion and vulnerability in the six DMCs: (a) gender; (b) old age; (c) disability; (d) social identities (ethnicity, caste, and religion); (e) diverse SOGIESC; (vi) geographic location and income poverty; and (f) young age (particularly disadvantaged youth) and migrant status. The chapter on gender is richest in content because of the availability of sex-disaggregated data on various socioeconomic indicators and the presence of more related initiatives and good practices of SARD and other stakeholders, given their many years of work on gender inequality compared to other social exclusion issues. Each chapter provides (a) an analysis of the situation of a disadvantaged group, including their experiences of intersecting inequalities, and related government policies; (b) an assessment of SARD's and other stakeholders' responses; and (c) SARD's potential next actions, according to the participants in stakeholder consultations held for this assessment.

(iii) The ninth **chapter** provides a summary of the general findings and lessons.

B.   Gender Equality and Social Inclusion Situation in the Six Countries: An Overview

Key Development Indicators

Demography

24.   The six SARD DMCs constitute 20.6% of the world's population in 2021, with the highest population in India accounting for 18% of the world's population.[23] The population growth rates in Bangladesh, Maldives, and Nepal in 2020–2021 were higher than the world's average of 1.01% in 2020 and .86% in 2021 (Table 1.3).[24]

Table 1.3: Key Demographic Indicators, 2020

DMC	Population Growth (%)		Sex Ratio (at Birth)	Male to Female Population Ratio
	2020	2021	2020	2020
Bangladesh	1.14	1.15	1.05	1.02
Bhutan	0.66	0.64	1.04	1.13
India	0.96	0.80	1.10	1.08
Maldives	1.95	1.36	1.07	1.73
Nepal	1.77	2.31	1.07	0.85
Sri Lanka	0.53	1.07	1.04	0.92

DMC = developing member country.

Note: The male-to-female population ratios were computed using the sex-disaggregated population data of the World Bank Group. A ratio of (i) 1 means an equal number of males and females in the population, (ii) greater than 1 means there are more males, and (iii) less than 1 means there are more females.

Sources: World Bank. Open Data. Population growth (annual %) (accessed 4 May 2022); and World Bank. Open Data. Sex ratio at birth (male births per female births) (accessed 4 May 2022).

25.   The sex ratio in the six DMCs in 2020 showed more male births than female births across these countries (Table 1. 3).[25] The lower proportion of female births has been attributed to strong son preference, which has made practices like sex-selective abortions and neglect of female children common across the region.[26] However, in 2020, based on the population data of the World Bank Group (Figure 1. 3), there were more females than males in the populations of Nepal and Sri Lanka. In Bangladesh and India, the proportion of females in the population was slightly higher than that of female births. In Maldives, the proportion of females in the population is significantly lower than the proportion of female births.[27]

---

[23]   United Nations Department of Economic and Social Affairs, Population Division. World Population Prospects 2022 (accessed 3 April 2023). Computed from the data files for Annual Population by Age Groups—Both Sexes.

[24]   World Bank. Open Data. Population growth (annual %) (accessed 4 May 2022).

[25]   World Bank. Open Data. Sex ratio at birth (male births per female births) (accessed 4 May 2022). A sex ratio of 1 means an equal number of male to female births, a sex ratio of more than 1 means more male births, and a sex ratio of less than 1 means more female births.

[26]   C.Z. Guilmoto. 2005. *Sex-Ratio Imbalance in Asia: Trends, Consequences and Policy Responses.* Paris: United Nations Population Fund (UNFPA).

[27]   World Bank. Open Data. Population, female (% of total population) (accessed 4 May 2022).

Figure 1.3: Population by Sex, 2020
(%)

	Female	Male
Bangladesh	49.4	50.6
Bhutan	46.9	53.1
India	48.0	52.0
Maldives	36.6	63.4
Nepal	54.2	45.8
Sri Lanka	52.1	47.9

■ Female   ■ Male

Source: World Bank. Open Data. Population, female (% of total population) (accessed 4 May 2022).

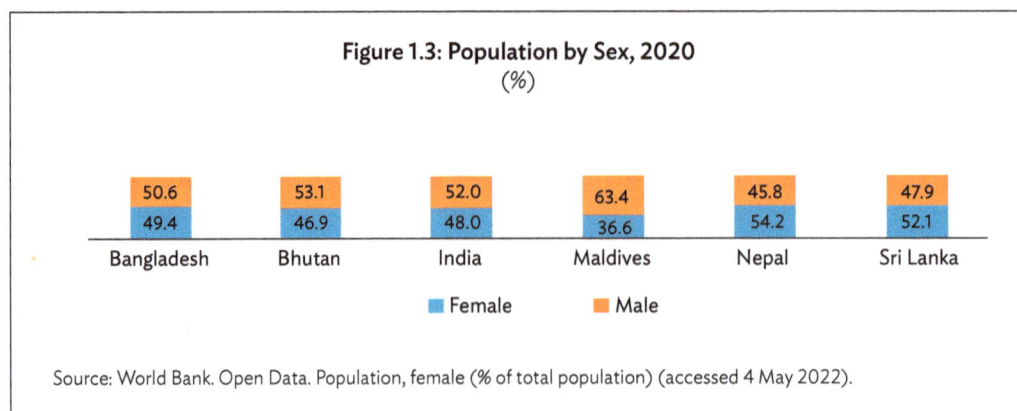

26.   The decreased proportion of males in the population—despite their higher proportion at birth—could be attributed to the higher female life expectancy and higher male infant mortality rate (Table 1.4 In 2020, life expectancy was more than 69 years for all six DMCs, with Sri Lanka having the highest life expectancy of 77 years. In all six DMCs, the life expectancy of females was higher than males, and the male infant mortality rate was higher than the female infant mortality rate.

Table 1.4: Life Expectancy at Birth and Infant Mortality Rate by Sex, 2020

DMC	Life Expectancy Birth (years)			Infant Mortality Rate (deaths per 1,000 live births)			Fertility Rate (births per woman)
	Total	Female	Male	Total	Female	Male	
Bangladesh	72.9	74.9	71.1	24.3	22.7	25.9	2.0
Bhutan	72.1	72.5	71.7	23.2	20.9	25.3	1.9
India	69.9	71.2	68.7	27.0	26.8	27.2	2.2
Maldives	79.2	81.0	77.8	5.5	5.0	6.0	1.8
Nepal	71.1	72.5	69.5	23.6	21.4	25.7	1.8
Sri Lanka	77.1	80.4	73.8	5.9	5.3	6.5	2.2

DMC = developing member country.

Sources: World Bank. Open Data. Life expectancy at birth, total (years) (accessed 4 May 2022); and World Bank. Open Data. Mortality rate, infant (per 1,000 live births) (accessed 4 May 2022).

27.   The age dependency ratio is the number of dependents—children (ages 0 to 14) and older people (ages 65 and above)—for every 100 people of working age (ages 15 to 64). The six DMCs' dependency ratios in Table 1. 4suggest that for every 100 people of working age, there are 47 dependents in Bangladesh, 45 in Bhutan, 48 in India, 30 in Maldives, 53 in Nepal, and 53 in Sri Lanka. Of the population aged 15–64 in five DMCs (except in Maldives), women and men comprise an almost balanced proportion (Table 1. 5).

28.   The rising life expectancy and decreasing fertility rates indicate that the six DMCs have been witnessing a demographic transition and earning demographic dividends in the form of higher population productivity.[28]

[28]   D.E. Bloom, D. Canning, and L. Rosenberg. 2011. Demographic Change and Economic Growth in South Asia. *Program on the Global Demography of Aging Working Paper Series.* No. 67. Boston: Harvard School of Public Health.

Table 1.5: Age Dependency Ratio and Working Age Population, 2020

DMC	Age Dependency Ratio	Percentage of Working Age Population (15–64 Years)		
		Total (% of total population)	Female (% of total)	Male (% of total)
Bangladesh	47.0	68.0	49.6	50.4
Bhutan	45.1	68.9	46.2	53.8
India	48.7	67.3	47.9	52.1
Maldives	30.2	76.8	33.0	67.0
Nepal	53.0	65.4	56.3	43.7
Sri Lanka	53.7	65.1	52.0	48.0

DMC = developing member country.

Sources: World Bank. Open Data. Age dependency ratio (% of working-age population) (accessed 9 May 2022); World Bank. Open Data. Population, total (accessed 9 May 2022); and World Bank. Open Data. Population ages 15-64, total (accessed 9 May 2022).

National Economy

29.   Five of the six DMCs were classified by the World Bank Group as lower-middle-income counties while Maldives was classified as an upper-middle-income country.[29] Before the start of the global COVID-19 pandemic in 2020 and the economic crisis in Sri Lanka in 2022, all the DMCs experienced unprecedented economic growth, with most growing by more than 5% throughout the period, making it the second-fastest-growing region in the world. Bangladesh, Nepal, Bhutan, and Maldives exhibited strong economic growth in 2019 because of remittances from abroad, gross capital formation, growing importance of the service sector, and sustained economic reforms.[30]

30.   With this high economic growth, the six South Asian countries made great strides in reducing poverty before the COVID-19 pandemic. In Bangladesh, the Multidimensional Poverty Index (MPI), which reflects the multiple deprivations that poor people experience in education, health, and living standards, decreased from 0.344 in 2004 to 0.198 in 2014[31] and 0.104 in 2019.[32] In Bhutan, the MPI declined from 0.175 in 2010 (footnote 31) to 0.050 in 2012 and further to 0.023 in 2017.[33] India decreased its MPI from 0.283 in 2005–2006 to 0.123 in 2015–2016 (footnote 31). The MPI of Maldives decreased from 0.018 in 2009[34] to 0.003 in 2016–2017 (footnote 31). Nepal's MPI declined from 0.350 in 2006 (footnote 34) to 0.148 in 2016 (footnote 31) to 0.074 in 2019 (footnote 32). Sri Lanka had an MPI of 0.021 in 2003 (footnote 34), which decreased to 0.009 in 2016.[35]

[29] World Bank. Open Data. GDP growth (annual %) (accessed 4 May 2022).
[30] M.M. Rahman, R.H. Rana, and S. Barua. 2019. The Drivers of Economic Growth in South Asia: Evidence from a Dynamic System GMM Approach. *Journal of Economic Studies*. 46 (3). pp. 564–577. Bingley, United Kingdom.
[31] United Nations Development Programme (UNDP) and Oxford Poverty and Human Development Initiative (OPHI). 2019. *Global Multidimensional Poverty Index 2019: Illuminating Inequalities*. New York. pp. 18–20. Sri Lanka is not on the list of studied countries.
[32] UNDP and OPHI. 2021. *Global Multidimensional Poverty Index 2021: Unmasking Disparities by Ethnicity, Caste and Gender*. New York.
[33] Government of Bhutan, National Statistics Bureau and OPHI. 2017. *Bhutan: Multidimensional Poverty Index 2017*. Thimphu.
[34] UNDP. 2011. *Human Development Report 2011—Sustainability and Equity: A Better Future for All*. New York.
[35] Government of Sri Lanka, Department of Census and Statistics. 2019. *Global Multidimensional Poverty in Sri Lanka*. Battaramulla, Sri Lanka. The MPI of Sri Lanka in 2016 was 0.011 (footnote 32).

31.   However, despite this significant progress, the Global Multidimensional Poverty Index 2019 suggested that the six SARD DMCs were trailing other countries in the region before the pandemic (footnote 31). More than one-third of the multidimensionally poor in the world live in Bangladesh, Bhutan, India, and Nepal. Figure 1.4 and Figure 1.5 show that while poverty rates had fallen in 2008 to 2019, more than one-fifth of the population in Nepal, Bangladesh, and India continued to live below the national poverty line. The MPI (Figure 1.5) also suggests that more than one-third of the population in all six DMCs experienced multidimensional poverty, higher in rural than urban areas and unequal among age groups, with children suffering the most.

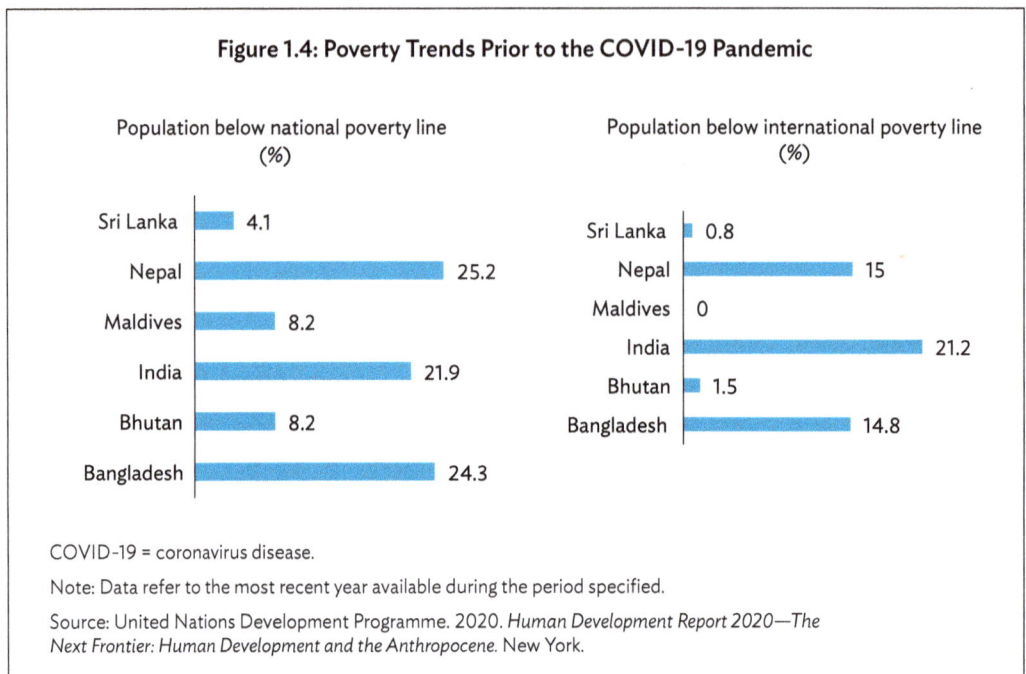

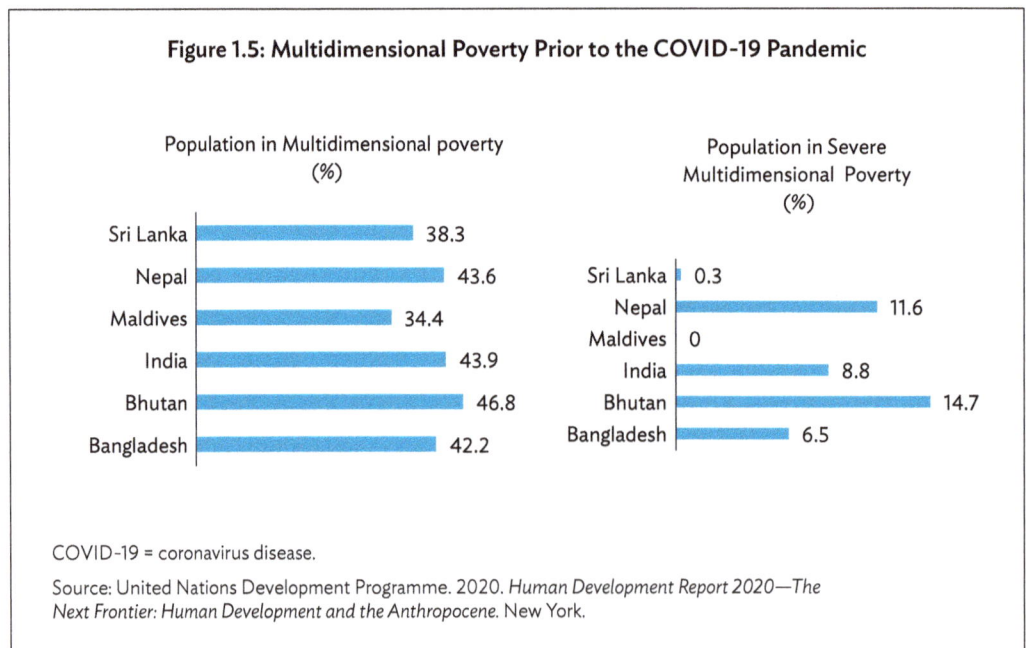

Figure 1.4: Poverty Trends Prior to the COVID-19 Pandemic

Population below national poverty line (%)

Country	%
Sri Lanka	4.1
Nepal	25.2
Maldives	8.2
India	21.9
Bhutan	8.2
Bangladesh	24.3

Population below international poverty line (%)

Country	%
Sri Lanka	0.8
Nepal	15
Maldives	0
India	21.2
Bhutan	1.5
Bangladesh	14.8

COVID-19 = coronavirus disease.

Note: Data refer to the most recent year available during the period specified.

Source: United Nations Development Programme. 2020. *Human Development Report 2020—The Next Frontier: Human Development and the Anthropocene.* New York.

Figure 1.5: Multidimensional Poverty Prior to the COVID-19 Pandemic

Population in Multidimensional poverty (%)

Country	%
Sri Lanka	38.3
Nepal	43.6
Maldives	34.4
India	43.9
Bhutan	46.8
Bangladesh	42.2

Population in Severe Multidimensional Poverty (%)

Country	%
Sri Lanka	0.3
Nepal	11.6
Maldives	0
India	8.8
Bhutan	14.7
Bangladesh	6.5

COVID-19 = coronavirus disease.

Source: United Nations Development Programme. 2020. *Human Development Report 2020—The Next Frontier: Human Development and the Anthropocene.* New York.

Human Development

32.   In 2018–2019, there were improvements in life expectancy, adult literacy rate, and other indicators in the six countries at varying stages of progress. Sri Lanka (with a rank of 72) and Maldives (with a rank of 95) were in the high human development category. The other four countries (Bangladesh, Bhutan, India, and Nepal) were in the medium human development category. The Human Development Index (HDI), which is a measure of achievements in health (life expectancy at birth), education (expected years and mean years of schooling), and income (gross national income per capita) of each DMC in 2019, is in Table 1.6. The HDI ranking included 189 countries and territories as of 2019.

Table 1.6: Human Development Index, 2018–2019

DMC	HDI Rank		HDI Value	
	2018	2019	2018	2019
Bangladesh	135	133	0.614	0.632
Bhutan	134	129	0.617	0.654
India	129	131	0.647	0.645
Maldives	104	95	0.719	0.740
Nepal	147	142	0.579	0.602
Sri Lanka	71	72	0.780	0.782

DMC = developing member country, HDI = Human Development Index.

Source: United Nations Development Programme. 2020. *Human Development Report 2020—The Next Frontier: Human Development and the Anthropocene.* New York.

33.   However, indicators on improving access to health, education, and other basic services do not indicate the quality of access that is needed to achieve a decent standard of living. The following observations indicate that although the six countries have made significant improvements in enhancing the access to services of their populations, the issue of quality remains.

(i)   **Quality of health services.** The quality of health services needs improvement across DMCs. For instance, fewer than 10 physicians and fewer than 20 hospital beds are available per 10,000 people in Bangladesh, Bhutan, Nepal, and India, well below the world average of 16 physicians and 27 beds per 10,000 people. Lost health expectancy (the relative difference between life expectancy and healthy life expectancy, expressed as a percentage of life expectancy at birth) is also higher than the world average in these four DMCs.[36]

(ii)   **Quality of education.** The pupil–teacher ratio (defined as the number of students who attend a school divided by the number of teachers in the school) is higher in Bangladesh (30), Bhutan (35), and India (33) than the world average (24), indicating high pressures on teaching personnel. A total of 50% of primary school teachers in Bangladesh and 30% in India do not have any formal training in teaching (footnote 36).

[36]   UNDP. 2020. *Human Development Report 2020—The Next Frontier: Human Development and the Anthropocene.* New York.

(iii) **Digital divide.** Internet access, which, especially in the post-pandemic world, is important for ensuring the continuity of education, remains poor in five of the DMCs, barring Maldives. For instance, a meager 4% of primary schools in Bangladesh and 12% in Sri Lanka have internet facilities. A report on the Unified District Information System for Education for 2021–2022 of the Government of India Ministry of Education showed that only 24.5% of all public and private schools in India in 2020–2021 and 33.9% in 2021–2022 had access to internet facilities.[37]

(iv) **Quality of water and sanitation.** In Bangladesh, India, and Nepal, close to 10% of the population does not have access to drinking water from improved drinking sources and does not use improved sanitation facilities (footnote 36).

Impact of the COVID-19 Pandemic

34. The economic growth achieved in 2019 and prior years was reversed during the COVID-19 pandemic, when the countries locked down to prevent the spread of the virus. As shown in Table 1.7, all six DMCs experienced a significant decrease in gross domestic product (GDP) growth rate in 2020 (from 2019), with only Bangladesh retaining a positive growth rate. Bhutan and Maldives, which economically rely on the tourism industry, were the worst affected in South Asia. India's GDP contracted by 7.3% from 2020 to 2021 because of nationwide lockdowns to contain the pandemic.[38] The decreased economic growth has resulted in increasing levels of poverty and unemployment, threatening decades of hard-won development gains while exacerbating existing inequalities in the impacted countries. There are groups of people across the six SARD DMCs who, even before the pandemic, faced multiple barriers in accessing available resources, accessing development opportunities, and participating in the community because of various barriers arising from discriminatory social norms and practices. Box 1.2 presents evidence of the impact of the pandemic on women and other disadvantaged groups in the region.

Table 1.7: Gross Domestic Product Growth Rate, 2019–2020
(%)

DMC	GDP Growth Rate 2019	GDP Growth Rate 2020
Bangladesh	8.15	3.51
Bhutan	5.76	(10.01)
India	4.04	(7.25)
Maldives	6.88	(33.50)
Nepal	6.66	(2.09)
Sri Lanka	2.26	(3.57)

( ) = negative, DMC = developing member country, GDP = gross domestic product.

Note: Number in parentheses means negative rate.

Source: World Bank. Open Data. GDP growth (annual %) (accessed 4 May 2022).

---

[37] Government of India, Ministry of Education, Department of School Education and Literacy. *Report on the Unified District Information System for Education PLUS (UDISE+), 2021-2022: Flash Statistics.* Delhi. p. 25.

[38] Government of India, Ministry of Statistics and Programme Implementation. 2022. First Advance Estimates of National Income, 2021–22. News release. 7 January.

Box 1.2: Impact of COVID-19 on Women and Excluded and Vulnerable Groups

- There was a sharp increase in crimes against women during lockdowns. In Nepal, 1,669 domestic violence cases were registered in March 2020 through a toll-free helpline service. Similarly, in India, an estimated 300,000 women experienced domestic violence and abuse during the lockdown period.[a]

- In Bangladesh, 80% of people with disabilities could not work, and 85% experienced job insecurity during the pandemic. About 49% of people with disabilities in the country reported not having access to all the necessary personal protective equipment for themselves, their families, or support workers.[b] In addition, people with disabilities encountered challenges in accessing social security and additional funding as a result of the unprecedented crisis.[c]

- About 400 million residents of India, including migrant workers, were negatively affected by the lockdown as reported by the International Labour Organization.[d] Many remote pockets and villages of Bangladesh were unable to receive any pandemic relief because of being geographically excluded.[d] Many indigenous groups in Gaibandha, Oraon, Pahariya, and Santal reported being in a situation of starvation.[e]

- During the COVID-19 crisis, the concerns of people with diverse SOGIESC have intensified. Apart from the incidence of homophobic attacks, stay-at-home directives increased their exposure to domestic violence. Moreover, the pandemic has caused a loss of income and livelihood among people with diverse SOGIESC working in the informal sector in South Asia.[d]

- Older people were adversely affected, as the travel restrictions and lockdowns limited their access to routine and preventive checkups, creating more risk of mortality and morbidity for this group.[f]

COVID-19 = coronavirus disease; SOGIESC = sexual orientation, gender identity and expression, and sex characteristics.

[a] G.Y. Gurol and G. Luchsinger. 2021. *Overview: In South Asia, COVID-19 Deepens Gender Disparities.* United Nations Entity for Gender Equality and the Empowerment of Women Asia Pacific.
[b] i2i Innovation to inclusion. 2020. *Impact of COVID-19 on the Lives of People with Disabilities: Insight and Stories from Bangladesh and Kenya.*
[c] Christian Blind Mission Global Disability Inclusion. 2021. *Experiences of Persons with Disabilities in the COVID-19 Pandemic: Bangladesh, Bolivia and Nigeria.* 21 June.
[d] The South Asia Collective. 2020. The Impact of COVID-19 on South Asia's Marginalised. *Online Bulletin.* April.
[e] Office of the United Nations High Commissioner for Human Rights. 2020. *COVID-19 and the Human Rights of LGBTI People.*
[f] R.L. Solano. 2021. Sri Lanka must Increase Its Efforts to Protect and Promote the Human Capital of the Elderly. End Poverty in South Asia. *World Bank Blogs.* 1 October.

Source: Asian Development Bank (South Asia Department).

Exclusion and Vulnerability Dimensions in the Region

35.   In each of the six SARD DMCs, there are groups of people who have limited access to development opportunities and face exclusion based on their gender; social identity (caste, ethnicity, religion); disability; income; geographic location; SOGIESC; and vulnerability based on age. Table 1. 8 presents an overview of the challenges to social inclusion in the six countries and uses the traffic light colors to indicate whether the challenges are high (orange) or low (yellow) because of the extent of sociocultural embeddedness of discriminatory social norms, or if no formal or legal exclusion (green) exists.

Table 1.8: Overview of Types of Historical Exclusion

Bases of Exclusion		Bangladesh	Bhutan	India	Maldives	Nepal	Sri Lanka
OLD AGE		Financial dependency, health issues, mental health					
DISABILITIES		Considered a curse, lack of disabled-friendly infrastructure, low education, limited employment options					
SOCIAL IDENTITIES	Caste	Within Hindus		Scheduled castes, other backward classes, and denotified and nomadic tribes		Dalits	Tamils and some Sinhala groups
	Ethnicity	Tribal groups Chittagong Hill Tracts Southern plains		Pastoral communities / Scheduled tribes and particularly vulnerable tribal groups		Adivasi Janajatis, Madhesis	Sri Lankan Tamils Tamils of Indian origin
	Religion	Hindu minorities		Minority religious groups		Muslims	Christian, Hindu, and Muslim minorities
SEXUAL ORIENTATION, GENDER IDENTITY AND EXPRESSIONS, AND SEX CHARACTERISTICS		Same-sex sexual activities punishable by law	Same-sex sexual activities not punishable by law		Same-sex sexual activities punishable by law	Same-sex sexual activities not punishable by law	Same-sex sexual activities punishable by law
		Third gender legally recognized	Third gender legally recognized			Third gender legally recognized	
GEOGRAPHIC LOCATION		Rural–urban Wetlands (Haors)	Rural–urban Difficult terrain		Outer atolls Rural–urban	Rural–urban Difficult terrain	Rural–urban–estate Northern and Eastern provinces
INCOME POVERTY		Poor settlements, marginalized groups					

DNT = denotified tribe, PVTG = particularly vulnerable tribal group.

Note: The color code indicates the degree of the challenges: orange for a high level of challenge because of the extent of the sociocultural embeddedness of discriminatory social norms and practices, yellow for a lower level of challenge, green for no formal legal exclusion, and white for not applicable. Young age (disadvantaged youth) and migrant status are not reflected in this table as they were assessed only in some developing member countries.

Source: Consultations with representatives of governments and civil society organizations in the Asian Development Bank's six member countries in South Asia in 2020–2022.

Policy Mandates and Institutional Arrangements for Gender Equality and Social Inclusion in Developing Member Countries

36.   There are strong policy commitments in the six DMCs to protect the fundamental rights of individuals and for nondiscrimination. A brief review of the constitution of each DMC (Table 1. 9) reveals several articles protecting and promoting the rights of women, older people, people with disabilities, social identity groups (ethnic, tribal, and caste groups), people in geographically difficult areas, and people living below the poverty line. The Constitution of the Republic of Maldives guarantees rights and freedoms to all people in a manner that is not contrary to any tenet of Islam. However, the rights of the SOGIESC community are not universally guaranteed in the six countries.

Table 1.9: Fundamental Rights of Individuals Guaranteed by the Countries' Constitutions

DMC	Fundamental Rights of Individuals Guaranteed and Nondiscrimination on the Grounds of
Bangladesh	Religion, race, caste, sex, or place of birth
Bhutan	Race, sex, language, religion, politics, or any other status
India	Religion, race, caste, sex, age, mental or physical disability, place of birth, or any of these
Maldives	Race, national origin, skin color, sex, age, mental or physical disability, political or other opinion, property, birth or other status, or native island
Nepal	Class, caste, region, language, religion, gender and sexual minorities, and all forms of caste-based untouchability
Sri Lanka	Race, religion, language, caste, sex, political opinion, place of birth, or any of these

Source: Extracted from the constitutions of the six countries.

37.   The DMCs have various national policies that seek to safeguard the rights of the excluded and vulnerable groups. The institutional mechanisms for the different groups are functional and, in most cases, comprise nodal government agencies responsible for designing, implementing, and monitoring programs for the identified excluded groups. Table 1.10 provides an overview of which countries have policies and institutional frameworks for the different categories.

38.   Most SARD countries have ratified the principal international human rights instruments and are obligated to implement the prescribed standards through appropriate national laws and policies. For instance, all SARD member countries are signatories of the Convention on the Elimination of All Forms of Discrimination Against Women (CEDAW) (Appendix 2 provides the ratification status of treaties relevant to GESI for the six countries).

39.   All SARD DMCs also support Agenda 2030 with its pledge of reducing inequalities and ensuring that no one is left behind, and the Sustainable Development Goals (SDGs) that incorporate these objectives. Hence, all six DMCs are formally committed to addressing gender issues (SDG 5: achieve gender equality and empower all women and girls) and reducing inequalities (SDG 1: no poverty, and SDG 10: reduce inequality within and among countries). Complying with SDG 5 implies achieving gender equality by "ending all forms of discrimination against all women and girls everywhere," while SDG 1 includes ensuring that "by 2030, all men and women, in particular poor and vulnerable groups, have equal rights to economic resources, as well as access to basic services, ownership and control over land and other forms of property, inheritance, natural

Table 1.10: Overview of Existing National Policy and Institutional Framework

Category	Bangladesh P	Bangladesh IF	Bhutan P	Bhutan IF	India P	India IF	Maldives P	Maldives IF	Nepal P	Nepal IF	Sri Lanka P	Sri Lanka IF
Gender	✓	✓	✓	✓	✓	✓	✓	✓	✓	✓	✓	✓
Old age	✓	✓	X***	✓	✓	✓	✓	✓	✓	✓	✓	✓
Disability	✓	✓	✓	✓	✓	✓	✓	✓	✓	✓	✓	✓
Social Identities												
Ethnicity and caste	✓	✓	✓	✓	✓	✓	-	-	✓	✓	✓	✓
Religion	✓	✓	X	X	✓	✓	✓#	✓	✓	✓	✓	✓
Sexual Orientation, Gender Identity and Expressions, and Sex Characteristics												
Sexual orientation,	X*	X	✓**	X	✓**	✓	*	*	✓	✓	X*	X
Gender identity and expressions,	✓	✓	✓	X	✓	✓	X	X	✓	✓	✓	✓
Sex Characteristics	X	X	X	X	✓#a	✓#a	X	X	✓#a	✓#a	X	X
Geographic location	✓	✓	✓	✓	✓	✓	✓	✓	✓	✓	✓	✓
Income poverty	✓	✓	✓	✓	✓	✓	✓	✓	✓	✓	✓	✓

✓ = government has laws or policies for the category; X = there are no government policies for the category; # = for Muslims and the Ministry of Islamic Affairs; * = same-sex sexual activities punishable by law; ** = same-sex sexual activities not punishable by law, gender identities recognized; *** = policy being discussed; - = not applicable because of absence of ethnic groups and castes in the country; = intersex groups; P = policy, IF = institutional framework.

Notes:
1. Bangladesh Penal Code section 377 states, "Whoever voluntarily has carnal intercourse against the order of nature with any man, woman or animal shall be punished with imprisonment for life, or with imprisonment of either description for a term which may extend to ten years and shall also be liable to fine." Government of Bangladesh, Legislative and Parliamentary Affairs Division. Laws of Bangladesh. 1860. *The Penal Code, 1860.*
2. Maldives Penal Code Section 411 punishes "unlawful sexual intercourse" and "unlawful sexual contact." This provision carries a maximum penalty of 8 years' imprisonment and 100 lashes. "A person commits an offense if: (2) he engages in sexual intercourse with a person of the same sex." Government of Maldives. *Law No 6/2014 Penal Code.* Malé. Quoted in Human Dignity Trust. Country Profile: Maldives. The law cannot be directly cited as it is in the local language.
3. Sri Lanka Chapter 19 Penal Code Section 365 states, "Whoever voluntarily has carnal intercourse against the order of nature with any man, woman, or animal, shall be punished with imprisonment of either description for a term which may extend to ten years, and shall also be punished with fine and where the offence is committed by a person over eighteen years of age in respect of any person under sixteen years of age shall be punished with rigorous imprisonment for a term not less than ten years and exceeding twenty years and with fine and shall be ordered to pay compensation of an amount determined by court..." Sections 365A and 399 also have provisions that criminalize same-sex relations and impersonation, which impacts transgender people Government of Sri Lanka, Ministry of Justice. *Penal Code Consolidated.* Colombo.
a   As defined in the Transgender Persons (Protection of Rights) Act, 2019 of India, and included in the Circular by the Ministry of Home Affairs, Nepal, Registration No. 180/2069/70, issued on 20 January 2013.

Source: Extracted from the constitutions and official websites of nodal agencies of the six countries.

resources, appropriate new technology, and financial services, including microfinance."[39] SDG 10 calls to "empower and promote the social, economic and political inclusion of all, irrespective of age, sex, disability, race, ethnicity, origin, religion or economic or other status," thus envisaging a socially inclusive society.

[39]   UNDP. The SDGs in Action: What are the Sustainable Development Goals?

40.   The constitutions, policy and legal frameworks, and international instruments (e.g., Convention on the Elimination of All Forms of Discrimination Against Women, Convention on the Rights of Persons with Disabilities, International Convention on the Elimination of all Forms of Racial Discrimination, Convention on the Rights of the Child, etc.) provide a strong foundation upon which to directly promote, fulfill, and protect the rights of women and disadvantaged groups' in SARD's six member countries. The principle of gender equality is enshrined in the constitution of each of the SARD DMCs and is reflected in their various gender-specific policies. As a result, there is now a common understanding of the idea, rationale, and mechanisms of achieving gender equality. However, emphasis on social inclusion remains limited in the six countries. There are separate policies for some of the different categories of excluded groups, and DMCs have varying levels of experience working on issues related to these groups. Still, there has been less work on addressing intersecting inequalities (as evidenced by a lack of such policies or interventions) across all six DMCs.

41.   In Nepal in 2006, the World Bank and DFID conducted a study on gender, caste, and ethnic exclusion in Nepal, and in 2012 produced a series of monographs on gender and exclusion in seven sectors.[40] In 2017, the International Development Partners Group adopted a common GESI framework (Box 1.3), which defines GESI as "a concept that addresses unequal power relations experienced by people on the grounds of gender, wealth, ability, location, caste/ethnicity, language and agency or a combination of these dimensions. It focuses on the need for action to rebalance these power relations, reduce disparities and ensure equal rights, opportunities and respect for all individuals regardless of their social identity."[41]

Box 1.3: Common Gender Equality and Social Inclusion Framework of International Development Partners Group in Nepal

The practice in Nepal has demonstrated that the understanding of gender equality and social inclusion (GESI) as a mindset, process, and set of desired outcomes, a way of doing development with a focus on ensuring that no one is left out of development programs and government services that are intended to be universal is useful and can be practically applied. The Theory of Change, adopted by development partners in Nepal in the Common GESI framework, states that people and institutions influence each other, and the people who are dominant (men and advantaged social groups) have stronger influence on the distribution of institutional resources/benefits than women and minority groups. To move towards inclusion from this state of inequality and exclusion, the livelihood and voice empowerment of excluded and vulnerable groups need strengthening along with shifts in policies and formal and informal systems, which constrain these groups' access to resources and benefits.

GESI = gender equality and social inclusion

Source: IDPG Nepal–GESI Working Group. 2017. *A Common Framework on Gender Equality and Social Inclusion*. Kathmandu, Nepal.

---

[40] World Bank and DFID. 2006. *Unequal Citizens: Gender, Caste and Ethnic Exclusion in Nepal—Executive Summary*. Kathmandu; and ADB. *Sectoral Perspectives on Gender and Social Inclusion*. Manila.
[41] The International Development Partners Group copied this definition of GESI from the Government of Nepal, Ministry of Health and Population. 2013. *Operational Guidelines for Gender Equality and Social Inclusion Mainstreaming in the Health Sector*. Kathmandu. p. 1.

Brief Overview of Development Partner and Civil Society Efforts on Gender Equality and Social Inclusion

42.   Several external development partners—international governments, multilateral, bilateral agencies, and international nongovernmental organizations (NGOs)—support the six countries.[42] While poverty reduction and capability enhancement are always overarching goals of aid, the Organisation for Economic Co-operation and Development (OECD) and Development Assistance Committee (DAC) agreed in 1998 that a focus on gender equality and women's empowerment is necessary to enhance the development effectiveness of aid.[43] The OECD DAC database provides disaggregated data for development aid by priority areas and aid committed for gender equality and women's empowerment as a proportion of total aid commitment in the six DMCs in 2019 (Figure 1.6). More than 60% of the aid coming from DAC members in Bhutan, Nepal, and Sri Lanka focused on achieving gender equality. Similar disaggregation, however, is not available for other excluded and vulnerable categories.

Figure 1.6: Distribution of Aid Commitment to Gender Equality and Women's Empowerment from Development Assistance Committee Members, 2019

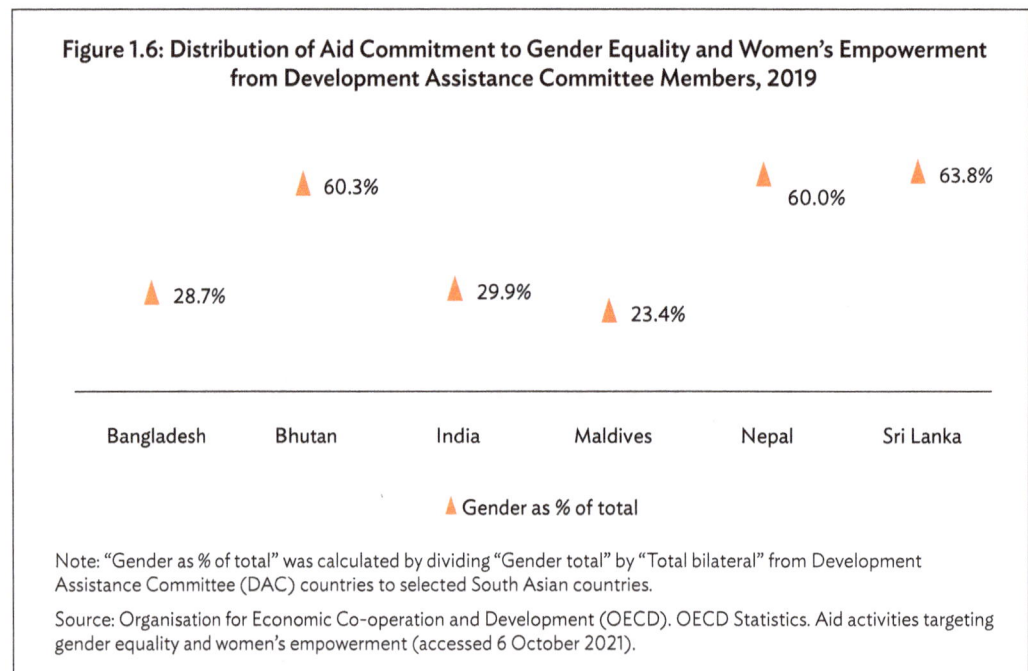

	60.3%			▲	▲ 63.8%
				60.0%	
▲ 28.7%		▲ 29.9%	▲ 23.4%		
Bangladesh	Bhutan	India	Maldives	Nepal	Sri Lanka

▲ Gender as % of total

Note: "Gender as % of total" was calculated by dividing "Gender total" by "Total bilateral" from Development Assistance Committee (DAC) countries to selected South Asian countries.

Source: Organisation for Economic Co-operation and Development (OECD). OECD Statistics. Aid activities targeting gender equality and women's empowerment (accessed 6 October 2021).

International Development Agencies

43.   ADB; the European Union; Foreign, Commonwealth and Development Office; Japan International Cooperation Agency; Swiss Agency for Development and Cooperation; United Nations (UN) agencies; United States Agency for International Development; and the World Bank are some of the key partners supporting the national governments across the six DMCs in achieving their GESI goals. Over decades of work, international development partners and donors have adopted, based

---

[42]   The aim of this section is not to present a comprehensive picture of the aid the SARD DMCs have received but to demonstrate that there have been responses to address the barriers of different disadvantaged groups.

[43]   OECD. 1999. DAC Guidelines for Gender Equality and Women's Empowerment in Development Cooperation. *Development Co-operation Guidelines Series*. Paris.

on good practices and lessons, different development approaches, supporting direct investments in activities for women and girls in specific sectors, and mainstreaming a gender perspective in all their policies and programs. Various donors and development partners have worked with excluded groups, such as older people, people with disabilities, and social identity groups (e.g., Adivasi Janajatis and Dalits in Nepal and other ethnic groups or tribes in Bangladesh and Sri Lanka, and scheduled castes, and scheduled tribes in India). International agencies have engaged with people with diverse SOGIESC in Bhutan, India, and Nepal and with the transgender community in Bangladesh and Sri Lanka. Since the nonbinary community is not recognized in Maldives, there has been no work done there for this group. Overall, aid interventions have contributed to positive results in improving education, health, and other essential capabilities of women and excluded groups.[44]

Civil Society Interventions

44.   Strategy 2030 affirms ADB's commitment to working with CSOs by tapping their unique strengths, such as local presence and specialized knowledge in social mobilization and community development, for supported projects with community development component.[45] OP1 (addressing remaining poverty and reducing inequalities), in particular, cites enhancing partnerships with stakeholders, including CSOs, to generate knowledge, share good practices, improve policy dialogue, and design policies that are participatory and socially inclusive.[46] ADB also sought CSOs' inputs for the development of the operational plans of the seven OPs of Strategy 2030. CSOs have also played an important role in designing and implementing the gender action plans (GAPs) of ADB's various sector projects. Moreover, CSOs have contributed to service delivery, providing resettlement and training support, generating awareness, aiding community participation, and conducting a needs assessment for various projects (footnote 46).

45.   Compared with ADB's other regional departments, SARD had the highest percentage (33%) of projects with planned CSO engagement in 2020.[47] Civil society has been very active in SARD member countries and plays an important role in creating awareness, mobilizing the communities, and advocating reforms. They have succeeded in influencing the discourse regarding achieving GESI of people with disabilities and older people in development processes. Addressing geographically hard-to-reach areas and income poverty has also received attention and investment. However, development partners, donors and CSOs acting on issues, such as gender and sexual identity, are still few. Issues of some religious minorities have also been challenging to address, depending on country-specific contexts.

[44]   L. Pickbourn and L. Ldikumana. 2016. The Impact of the Sectoral Allocation of Foreign Aid on Gender Inequality. *Journal of International Development*. Vol. 28. pp. 396–411.

[45]   CSOs are non-state actors whose aims are neither to generate profits nor to seek governing power. CSOs unite people to advance shared goals and interests. They have a presence in public life, expressing the interests and values of their members or others, and are based on ethical, cultural, scientific, religious, or philanthropic considerations. CSOs include NGOs, professional associations, foundations, independent research institutes, community-based organizations, faith-based organizations, people's organizations, social movements, and labor unions. ADB. 2009. *Civil Society Organization Sourcebook: A Staff Guide to Cooperation with Civil Society Organizations*. Manila.

[46]   ADB. 2020. *Highlights of ADB's Cooperation with Civil Society Organizations 2019*. Manila.

[47]   ADB. 2022. *Working Together for Development Results: Lessons from ADB and Civil Society Organization Engagement in South Asia*. Manila. The percentage of ADB projects with planned CSO engagement in 2020 was 24% in both the Central and West Asia Regional Department and Southeast Asia Regional Department, 15% in the East Asia Department, and 3% in the Pacific Department.

II. GENDER INEQUALITY IN SOUTH ASIA: ISSUES AND RESPONSES

A. Introduction: Definitions

46.   ADB defines gender as the "social facets of culture, religion, and class that condition the way in which masculine and feminine roles and status are constructed in each society. Gender relations are dynamic and changing over time in response to varying socioeconomic and ideological circumstances. They are neither static nor immutable. Rather they are changeable, subject to modification, renegotiation, and reinterpretation, unlike the universal and constant biological (sex) differences between males and females. As gender (the social differentiation between women and men) is socially and culturally constructed, gender roles and relations can be transformed by social changes."[48]

B. Status of Gender Equality Across the South Asia Department's Developing Member Countries

Gender Equality Indexes

47.   The Gender Development Index and Gender Inequality Index in Table 2. 1 show that women lagged behind men in many development indicators in 2021.[49] Specifically, the female Human Development Index (HDI) was lower than male HDI in all the six developing member countries (DMCs) indicating that women have lower socioeconomic well-being, education, health, and income. Sri Lanka had the best Gender Development Index, followed by Nepal, Maldives, Bhutan, Bangladesh, and India. Maldives and Sri Lanka did relatively better than the other DMCs in the Gender Inequality Index.

[48] ADB. 2003. *Policy on Gender and Development*. Manila. p. 27.
[49] The Gender Development Index is the ratio of the HDIs calculated separately for females and males, and the closer the value is to 1, the better is the state of gender equality. The Gender Inequality Index is the measure reflecting inequality in achievement between women and men in three dimensions: reproductive health, empowerment, and the labor market. A greater Gender Inequality Index indicates greater disparities.

Table 2.1: Gender Development and Inequality Indexes

DMC	HDI, 2021		Gender Development Index, 2021		Gender Inequality Index, 2021		Global Gender Gap Index, 2020	
	Female	Male	Value	Group[a]	Value	Rank	Value	Rank
Bangladesh	0.617	0.688	0.898	5	0.530	131	0.719	65
Bhutan	0.641	0.684	0.937	3	0.415	98	0.639	130
India	0.567	0.668	0.849	5	0.490	122	0.625	140
Maldives	0.709	0.766	0.925	3	0.348	83	0.642	128
Nepal	0.584	0.621	0.942	3	0.452	113	0.683	106
Sri Lanka	0.755	0.795	0.949	3	0.383	92	0.670	116

DMC = developing member country, HDI = Human Development Index.

Note: The HDI, Gender Development Index, and Gender Inequality Index ranks are based on a comparison of 191 countries, while the Global Gender Gap Index rank is based on a comparison of 156 countries.

[a] Group 1 comprises countries with high equality in HDI achievements between women and men (absolute deviation of less than 2.5%), group 2 comprises countries with medium to high equality in HDI achievements between women and men (absolute deviation of 2.5%–5%), group 3 comprises countries with medium equality in HDI achievements between women and men (absolute deviation of 5%–7.5%), group 4 comprises countries with medium to low equality in HDI achievements between women and men (absolute deviation of 7.5%–10%), and group 5 comprises countries with low equality in HDI achievements between women and men (absolute deviation from gender parity of more than 10%).

Sources: United Nations Development Programme. 2022. *Human Development Report 2021–22: Uncertain Times, Unsettled Lives: Shaping our Future in a Transforming World.* New York; and World Economic Forum. 2021. *Global Gender Gap Report 2021.* Geneva.

48.   The Global Gender Gap Index benchmarks the gender gaps in four dimensions (economic participation and opportunity, educational attainment, health and survival, and political empowerment) and tracks progress toward closing these gaps over time.[50] Countries with high Global Gender Gap Index scores and ranks (with 1 as the highest, indicating the closing of the gender gap) fare better in these dimensions. Overall, among the six DMCs, in 2020, Bangladesh performed the best because of its good performance in political empowerment (ranked 7 of 155 countries). However, Bangladesh performed lower than the other DMCs, except India, in economic participation and opportunity; lower than the other DMCs, except Nepal, in educational attainment; and lower than the other DMCs, except Maldives and India, in health and survival. Maldives was ranked 1 in educational attainment. India ranked 51 in political empowerment, better than Bhutan, Maldives, Nepal, and Sri Lanka.

Access to Social Resources and Services

49.   Table 2.2 presents sex-disaggregated data on three education indicators, giving some evidence of the gender gap indexes in Table 2.1. For instance, while the expected years of schooling are higher for females than males in all countries, the mean years of schooling for females are lower in all, except in Sri Lanka, with the widest gender differences existing in Nepal, followed by Bhutan and Bangladesh. Furthermore, except in Maldives, fewer females than males have completed at least a secondary level of education. This gap is most pronounced in Nepal, followed by India, Bhutan, and Bangladesh (Table 2.2).

---

[50]   World Economic Forum. 2021. *Global Gender Gap Report 2021.* Geneva.

Table 2.2: Education-Related Indicators by Sex, 2021

DMC	Expected Years of Schooling		Mean Years of Schooling		Population with at Least Secondary-Level Education (%)	
	Female	Male	Female	Male	Female	Male
Bangladesh	13.0	11.9	6.8	8.0	50.6	58.5
Bhutan	13.6	12.8	4.5	5.8	23.6	32.3
India	11.9	11.8	6.3	7.2	41.8	53.8
Maldives	14.2	11.9	7.1	7.5	46.4	41.5
Nepal	12.9	12.8	4.2	6.2	28.8	44.7
Sri Lanka	14.5	13.8	10.8	10.8	84.0	84.2

DMC = developing member country.

Source: United Nations Development Programme. 2022. *Human Development Report 2021–22: Uncertain Times, Unsettled Lives: Shaping our Future in a Transforming World.* New York.

50.   In the stakeholder consultations held for this assessment, the participants in Bangladesh pointed to gender norms (such as son preference), lack of women-friendly public spaces (such as in transportation), and incidents of sexual harassment in educational institutes as some of the key concerns limiting women's access to safe and inclusive education. This assessment is in line with a United Nations Entity for Gender Equality and the Empowerment of Women (UN Women) survey in 2013 in Bangladesh, which found that almost 76% of female students in higher education institutions had faced sexual harassment on post-secondary campuses.[51] The consultation participants also identified gender norms that place unpaid care burdens on girls, practices like child marriage, and restrictions on girls' mobility as barriers that can keep girls from returning to education after the pandemic. Moreover, adolescent girls faced a higher risk of not returning to school after the pandemic-induced lockdowns, especially in South Asia, where difficulties prevented them from accessing school and completing their education.[52] School closures can aggravate these difficulties, increasing the risks of early and forced marriage, sexual exploitation and abuse, early and unintended pregnancy, and female genital mutilation.[53] In India, for instance, about 10 million girls were at risk of dropping out of school because of the pandemic.[54]

51.   While women's life expectancy is higher than that of men in all DMCs, critical shortcomings exist in reproductive health care facilities. The maternal mortality ratios and adolescent birth rates are high in Bangladesh, Bhutan, and Nepal. Antenatal care coverage in Bangladesh, India, and Nepal is 75%–85%, lower than the 98.8% in Sri Lanka and 98.7% in Maldives (footnote 36). The consultation participants highlighted the inadequate health care infrastructure to address women's specific needs, such as contraception, menstrual management, pregnancy, and post-partum care, as key concerns. In addition, they mentioned inadequate sensitivity of health care professionals to these issues as an important gap in services.

---

[51]   H. Bhagani. 2015. *Addressing Sexual Harassment in Universities.* UN Women Asia and the Pacific.

[52]   United Nations Educational, Scientific and Cultural Organization. 2020. *UNESCO COVID-19 Education Response: How Many Students are at Risk of Not Returning to School?* Paris.

[53]   UNFPA. 2020. *Millions More Cases of Violence, Child Marriage, Female Genital Mutilation, Unintended Pregnancy Expected Due to the COVID-19 Pandemic.*

[54]   Right to Education Forum. 2021. *Policy Brief on Girls' Education.* New Delhi.

Access to Economic Resources and Services

52.   The main resource of any country is its labor force. However, the labor force participation rate, which is the proportion of the country's working-age population that engages actively in the labor market, is low in Bangladesh, Bhutan, India, and Sri Lanka with a rate of 70% or lower (Table 2.3). The gap between female and male labor participation rates is high, especially in Bangladesh, India, Maldives, and Sri Lanka. That means a significant proportion of women in the region either remain out of the labor force or are employed in the informal sector.

53.   The untapped female labor resource is more apparent in the unemployment rates in all DMCs, especially in Bangladesh and Sri Lanka in 2019 (Table 2.3). In that year, the female unemployment rate in the two countries was significantly higher than the male unemployment rate. Moreover, the pandemic worsened the unemployment rates in the six DMCs in 2021 and further widened the gender gap.

Table 2.3: Labor force Participation and Unemployment Rates in 2019 and 2021 by Sex

DMC	Labor Force Participation Rate, 2019[a]			Unemployment Rate, 2019[b]			Unemployment Rate, 2021[b]		
	Total	Female	Male	Total	Female	Male	Total	Female	Male
Bangladesh	61.5	38.5	84.2	4.4	6.8	3.4	5.2	7.9	4.1
Bhutan	70.0	62.3	76.7	2.5	3.3	2.0	4.3	5.6	3.5
India	52.1	22.3	79.6	5.3	4.9	5.4	6.0	4.5	6.3
Maldives	75.1	43.1	86.6	5.3	4.7	5.5	6.1	5.7	6.2
Nepal	85.7	85.3	86.1	3.1	2.9	3.3	5.1	4.9	5.2
Sri Lanka	57.5	37.6	79.1	4.3	6.9	3.0	5.4	8.4	3.9

DMC = developing member country.
[a] World Bank. Open Data. Labor force participation rate, total (% of total population ages 15–64 (modeled ILO estimate). (accessed 4 May 2022).
[b] World Bank. Open Data. Unemployment, total (% of total labor force) (modeled ILO Estimate) (accessed 4 May 2022).

54.   Even when women can secure employment, they remain concentrated in subsistence agriculture or informal sectors, where they experience low job security and low returns (Table 2.4). Almost 80% of employed women in India, Bangladesh, and Maldives are in agriculture-related sectors, yet they do not own a proportion of assets equal to men. For instance, according to the Agriculture Census of India, 2015–2016, women operated less than 14% of the total operational holdings, while the participation of female operational holders was concentrated in the marginal land category (72%).[55] Given the nature of women's employment, their gross national income per capita is significantly lower than that of men (Table 2.4). Moreover, with their concentration in informal and agriculture sectors, more women than men across the DMCs lost their jobs during the pandemic.[56] In Bangladesh, Bhutan, and Nepal, less than half of women have an account with a financial institution (Table 2.4).

---

[55]   Government of India; Ministry of Agriculture and Farmers Welfare; Department of Agriculture, Cooperation and Farmers Welfare. 2020. *All India Report on Agriculture Census 2015–16.* New Delhi.
[56]   G.Y. Gurol and G. Luchsinger. 2021. *Overview: In South Asia, COVID-19 Deepens Gender Disparities.* UN Women Asia and the Pacific.

Table 2.4: Employment and Income Indicators for Women

DMC	Women in Nonagricultural Employment, 2019 (% of total employment in agriculture)	Gross Nominal Income Per Capita, 2019 ($)		Women with Account at a Financial Institution or With Mobile Money Service Provider, 2017 (% of female population ages 15 and older)
		Female	Male	
Bangladesh	20.7	2,873	7,031	35.8
Bhutan	32.9	8,117	13,069	27.7
India	15.9	2,331	10,702	76.6
Maldives	21.7	7,908	22,931	...
Nepal	40.3	2,910	4,108	41.6
Sri Lanka	32.5	7,433	18,423	73.4

... = data not available, DMC = developing member country.

Source: United Nations Development Programme. 2020. *Human Development Report 2020—The Next Frontier: Human Development and the Anthropocene.* New York.

55.   During the consultations in each of the DMCs, the participants shared that even within the formal economy, women face barriers such as gender-based pay gaps, sexual harassment, discriminatory recruitment processes, or lack of an enabling environment (such as childcare facilities). There also exist multiple barriers for women entrepreneurs, such as access to markets, credit, and linkage or support services. For instance, the participants pointed to the lack of collateral-free loans in Bangladesh and Sri Lanka—in many instances, asset ownership lies with men. Lack of financial literacy further exacerbates women's economic dependence on men. In Bangladesh, participants assessed that since many women do not have individual bank accounts, their salaries go through their husband's accounts, curtailing their control over their earnings.

Social Practices, Participation, and Decision-Making

56.   Gender disparity is prevalent in South Asia and is linked to pervasive sociocultural gender biases in the region that weaken the participation of women in decision-making within relationships, families, and communities.[57] While women make up close to half of the population in each DMC, their representation in governments and leadership positions in workplaces remains low (Table 2.5). Nepal performs the best among the six DMCs, with one-third of its Parliament composed of women.[58] The low representation of women in Parliament has been linked with low prioritization of women's agenda and concerns in policies.[59] Similarly, even in workplaces, women occupy less than one-fourth of the seats in middle and senior management (Table 2.5).

---

[57]   United Nations Children's Fund (UNICEF) South Asia. Gender Equality in Primary and Secondary Education.
[58]   This information is based on UNDP data from 2019. However, a 2021 World Economic Forum report (Global Gender Gap Report) ranked Bangladesh seventh in closing the gender gap in political participation—the best performing among the six DMCs
[59]   ADB. 2016. *Sri Lanka: Gender Equality Diagnostic of Selected Sectors.* Manila.

**Table 2.5: Indicators Related to Women's Participation and Decision-Making
and Gender-Based Violence**
(%)

DMC	Women Married by Age 18	Seats in National Parliament	Seats in Local Government	Female Share of Employment in Middle and Senior Management	Intimate Partner Violence
Bangladesh	59	20.6	25.2	11.5	54
Bhutan	26	15.3	10.6	...	15
India	27	13.5	44.4	13.7	29
Maldives	2	4.6	6.1	19.5	16
Nepal	40	33.5	41	13.9	25
Sri Lanka	10	5.3	10.9	22.5	17

... = data not available, DMC = developing member country.

Source: United Nations Development Programme. 2020. *Human Development Report 2020—The Next Frontier: Human Development and the Anthropocene.* New York.

57.   Child marriages are still prevalent across the DMCs. For instance, more than half of women in Bangladesh and more than one-third in Nepal are married by the time they turn 18 (Table 2.5). Participants of the consultations in all DMCs also highlighted the prevalence of gender-based violence (GBV). For instance, more than half of the women in Bangladesh reported facing violence from an intimate partner at some point in their lives. Participants of the consultations also highlighted that violence against women increased during coronavirus disease (COVID-19) lockdowns. In India, domestic violence cases increased 230% from January to May 2020.[60] In Maldives, women aged 19–40 years were more than four times more likely to report as a survivor of GBV or domestic violence than their male counterparts.[61] In Sri Lanka, 47.5% of the women who participated in a study by the United Nations Population Fund (UNFPA) and the Department of Census and Statistics agreed with the statement that "a man should show he is the boss," and 46.5% agreed that "a good wife obeys her husband even if she disagrees."[62] The conventional perceptions of masculinity prevail in these areas and allow men to benefit from the privileges by exercising control of political, economic, and social affairs. The impact of this masculinity is not just restricted to benefits for men; adhering to this role of a "manly" man can also impact negatively on the mental and physical health of men (Box 2.1).

[60]   Impact and Policy Research Institute. 2020. Gender-Based Violence in the Context of the COVID-19 Pandemic and Lockdown. *Event report.* 29 December.
[61]   UNFPA Maldives Country Office. 2021. *Gender-Based Violence During COVID-19 Pandemic in The Maldives: An Analysis of Reported Cases.* Malé.
[62]   Government of Sri Lanka, Department of Census and Statistics. 2020. *Women's Wellbeing Survey 2019.* Battaramulla, Sri Lanka.

Box 2.1: The Gendered Impact of Masculinity

Structural barriers, negative gendered and societal norms, and socialization of girls and boys in the patriarchal societies of the South Asia Department's developing member countries have normalized violence and promoted masculine ideal behavior, such as dominance, self-reliance, and competition, and perpetuated gender stereotypes, which cause many women and girls to experience discrimination and violence in different spheres but also negatively impact men. Masculine ideal behavior can cause deep anxieties and strain the well-being and health of men leading at times to psychological problems. The cultural and social expectations that uphold men as "tough" and "in control" may also lead them to engage in risk-taking behaviors or suppress feelings.

Source: MenEngage Alliance. 2014. *Men, Masculinities, and Changing Power: A Discussion Paper on Engaging Men in Gender Equality from Beijing 1995 to 2015.* Washington, DC.

58.	An Asian Development Bank (ADB) study found that women spend almost 6 hours per day doing household chores, constraining them from being productively employed.[63] Given the disproportionate amount of time women spend on unpaid care work, they are often forced to compromise their health and leisure time for paid work. The pandemic has further exacerbated this disparity, with women across the region (and globally) reporting that they are spending an even higher amount of time on household chores.

Intersectionality

59.	Barriers to accessing social and economic resources and decision-making power for women in the six DMCs are compounded by overlapping vulnerabilities like geographic isolation, disability, old age, and disadvantaged social identities. For instance, participants of the stakeholder consultations assessed that women in rural areas face more barriers than women in urban areas. Because of the lack of service providers in rural areas, women lack access to basic health care facilities and other social services; the incidence of child marriage is also higher in rural areas.[64] Incidences of sexual exploitation of women with disability were highlighted in the consultations in the six DMCs. Women with disability are vulnerable to harassment and sexual abuse because of low awareness and the hassles they face in reporting these cases. A Maldivian study noted that women and girls with disability are subject to multiple forms of discrimination, but data on its impact is minimal.[65] Sexual abuse of people with disabilities remains unreported primarily because of their financial dependency on the perpetrator and lack of support from the community and state institutions. Skills development programs are not inclusive of the needs of women with disability, and they also face challenges in accessing education and health care because of a lack of disability-friendly infrastructure.

---

[63]	ADB. 2014. *Maldives: Gender Equality Diagnostic of Selected Sectors.* Manila.
[64]	UNICEF. 2014. *Ending Child Marriage: Progress and Prospects.* Geneva.
[65]	Child Advocacy Network of Disability Organizations. 2015. *Joint Submission to the Review of the Maldives by the Human Rights Council's Universal Periodic Review 2015.*

60.   Older women are likely to be more vulnerable than older men as they have a lower probability of having access to pensions and/or savings. For instance, the consultation participants remarked that the older war widows in Sri Lanka are disproportionately affected by the loss of livelihoods and homes as they lack resources for rehabilitation at their age. Social identities also exacerbate the degree of women's exclusion. For example, women from disadvantaged Adivasi Janajati (ethnic minorities) groups in Nepal suffer from lack of education, high incidence of poverty, child marriages, and societal discrimination. Dalit women have the lowest literacy rates in Nepal. According to a study, the prevalence of GBV in Nepal varied across caste and ethnic groups (44% of Madhesi Dalit and 38% of Muslim women experienced physical violence, while only 9% of hill Brahmin women did so).[66]

C.   Policy Analysis

61.   Each of the six South Asia Department (SARD) DMCs has specific acts and policies that address gender inequality and issues faced by women (Table 2.6). These include the National Gender Equality Policy of Bhutan, which aims to achieve gender equality in the economic, social, and political aspects with a specific focus on people with disabilities. Clause (3) of Article 243D of the Constitution of India ensures participation of women in Panchayati Raj Institutions by mandating one-third reservation for women out of the total number of seats to be filled by direct election and the number of offices of chairpersons of Panchayats.[67] Nepal has a separate fund for addressing GBV, and has livelihood generation programs and rehabilitation centers for GBV survivors. Sri Lanka, along with other countries, has a toll-free helpline and legal support services for survivors of GBV. The amended Decentralized Act 2019 of Maldives provides for increased political representation of women in the island councils, campaigns against GBV, the establishment of affordable daycare centers and shelters for survivors of domestic violence, and provisions for gender equality in sports. The Ministry of Gender, Family and Social Services in Maldives is working on addressing the challenges faced in implementing the country's Gender Equality Act, 2016. The ministry works toward mainstreaming gender policies across sectors, producing more gender-responsive budgets, identifying issues of vulnerable groups, and addressing them in a more holistic and consolidated way.

62.   Furthermore, SARD DMCs, except Maldives, have undertaken gender-responsive budgeting (GRB) for more than 5 years—more than 10 years in Bangladesh, India, and Nepal. Details are as follows:

  (i)   **Bangladesh.** Under the Medium-Term Budget Framework, "budget is prepared within a medium-term context and includes estimates and projections of revenues, financing and expenditures respectively for the next fiscal year and two subsequent years. Gender issues are embedded in the MTBF PROCESS. Under the MTBF approach, a strategic phase of budget planning is undertaken before the detailed annual budget estimate is prepared. At this phase, ministries are required to set out their plans for the next 3 years." [68] Poverty, gender, and climate issues are incorporated in Budget Circular-1 as specific items. However, not all ministries

---

[66]   World Bank Nepal. Reanalysis of NDHS data 2016 for the Country Level Gender Equality and Social Inclusion Assessment. Unpublished.

[67]   Government of India, Ministry of Panchayati Raj. 2020. *Representation in Panchayats*. Delhi.

[68]   Government of Bangladesh, Ministry of Finance, Finance Division. 2020. National Portal of Bangladesh. *Gender Budgeting Report 2017–2018. Chapter 1: Introduction*. Dhaka.

Table 2.6: Some Key Acts and Policies for Gender Equality of the Six Countries in South Asia

DMC	Key Acts and Policies
Bangladesh	Women and Children Repression Prevention Act, 2000
	Domestic Violence (Prevention and Protection) Act, 2010
	Dowry Prohibition Act, 2018
Bhutan	Domestic Violence Prevention Act of Bhutan, 2013
	National Gender Equality Policy, 2019
India	Sexual Harassment of Women at Workplace (Prevention, Prohibition and Redressal) Act, 2013
	Protection of Women from Domestic Violence Act, 2005
	Dowry Prohibition Act, 1961
	National Commission for Women Act, 1990
	The Constitution (73rd Amendment) Act, 1992
Maldives	Domestic Violence Prevention Act, 2012
	Gender Equality Act, 2016
Nepal	Gender Equality Act, 2006
	National Gender Equality Policy 2077 (2021)
	Domestic Violence (Offence and Punishment) Act 2066, 2009
Sri Lanka	Policy Framework and National Plan of Action to address Sexual and Gender-based Violence in Sri Lanka, 2016–2020
	Prevention of Domestic Violence Act, 2005
	Maternity Benefits Ordinance, 1985

DMC = developing member country.

Source: Extracted from the policy documents of the six countries.

applied the GRB tool—provided in the Medium-Term Budget Framework and the Recurrent, Capital, Gender, and Poverty (RCGP) model—because of its complexity and the uneven distribution of capacity development, especially in the use of the 14 indicators for assessing the impact of gender strategies, across ministries.[69] Similar to the Gender Budget Statement of India, the RCGP was assessed to have no clear contributions to planning and budgeting (footnote 69).

(ii)   **Bhutan.** In early 2014, the Government of Bhutan approved the Strategic Framework and Action Plan for Gender Mainstreaming and Gender Responsive Planning and Budgeting. In addition, an important inclusion in the Budget Call Circulars of 2 financial years (2013 and 2014) was the emphasis on the need for gender to be mainstreamed in sector activities.[70] However, although the Budget Call Notification of 2013–2014 and 2014–2015 instructed departments to ensure that their budget proposals are gender responsive, the officials could not appropriately act on the circulars in the absence of prior sensitization to the subject and in the absence of clear guidelines on how agencies need to report their progress.[71]

---

[69]   S. Kanwar. 2016. *Gender Responsive Budgeting in the Asia-Pacific Region: A Status Report.* New York: UN Women.

[70]   G. Thakur and B. Jhamb. 2016. *Gender Responsive Planning and Budgeting in Bhutan: From Analysis to Action.* UN Women. ADB supported this study.

[71]   Footnote 70, p. 86.

(iii) **India.** In 2005–2006, the Ministry of Finance issued the Gender Budget Statement, more known as Statement 20 of the Expenditure Budget Document Volume 1 by the Expenditure Division of the Ministry of Finance, which presents gender budget allocations in two parts: A and B (referred to in the Gender Budgeting Handbook 2015 as the gender budgetary allocations).[72] Part A reflects women-specific schemes, i.e. those that have 100% allocation for women, and part B reflects pro-women schemes, i.e. those where at least 30% of the allocation is for women (footnote 72). Statement 20 is a reporting mechanism that can be used by ministries and departments to review their programs through a gender lens and is an important tool for presenting information on the allocations for women. In 2007–2008, the government institutionalized gender budgeting by integrating gender into the outcome budget guidelines. The outcome budget is a progress card on how ministries have used the outlays or funds announced in the annual budget. Given these policies, a study commissioned by the International Monetary Fund in 2016 considered India to be a global best practice in GRB and an example in Asia, with the Ministry of Finance taking the lead in incorporating GRB in budget circulars, expenditure, budgets, and the outcome budget, and the GRB efforts extending from the national to subnational government levels.[73] However, a 2016 UN Women study found challenging areas, such as the lack of impact of the ex-post Gender Budget Statement on the planning and budgetary process, insufficient time and human resources of the gender budgeting cells, and weak centralized mechanisms for monitoring gender budgeting cells (footnote 69).

(iv) **Maldives.** According to a UN Women-commissioned study, "GRB work is at the inception stage in Maldives and many enabling factors and opportunities exist for initiating it." The study also noted that the "Ministry of Gender and Family and the [Ministry of Finance and Treasury] support GRB and have been responsive to UN Women's recent efforts to initiate dialogue on GRB."[74]

(v) **Nepal.** The Ministry of Finance formally introduced a GRB system in financial year 2007–2008. In compliance with this system, sector ministries are required to categorize their program budget according to the extent to which they support gender equality. The three prescribed categories are: directly gender responsive, indirectly gender responsive, and neutral.[75] The first indicates 50% of the allocation directly benefiting women, the second indicates 20%–50% benefiting women, and the third indicates less than 20% benefiting women. Nonetheless, according to the UN Women-commissioned study (footnote 69), the GRB system applied to small-scale (e.g., community-based infrastructure and irrigation) and not to large-scale projects (e.g., strategic roads, airport expansion, and hydro plants), which usually fall under the neutral category. Some of the criteria and sub-criteria of the GRB system were assessed to be difficult to quantify and could lead to arbitrary scoring (footnote 69).

---

[72] Government of India, Ministry of Women and Child Development,. 2015. *Gender Budgeting Handbook for Ministries/ Departments/State Governments/District Officials/Researchers/Practitioners.* New Delhi.

[73] L. Chakraborty. 2016. Asia: A Survey of Gender Budgeting Efforts. *International Monetary Fund Working Paper.* WP/16/150. pp. 7–8.

[74] Footnote 69, p. 133.

[75] Government of Nepal, Ministry of Finance, Budget and Programme Division. 2008. *Gender Responsive Budget.* Kathmandu.

(vi)   **Sri Lanka.** Though Sri Lanka was among the first countries to engage in GRB in 1997, the momentum seemed to slow down over the years. GRB took off again with the approval of the Cabinet Memorandum, 2016 on the allocation of at least 25% of project investment in rural economic development for women. Like in Bhutan and Maldives, GRB was considered at the inception phase in the UN Women study (2016).

63.   Of the six DMCs, India and Nepal appear to be advanced in instituting a gender audit. In India, the 11th Five Year Plan, 2007–2012 and the 12th Five Year Plan, 2012–2017 emphasized the commitment of the government to promote gender audit as an integral part of gender budgeting. The 12th Five Year Plan states, "Ministries/Departments will undertake gender audits of major programmes, schemes and policies. At the State level, mandatory gender audit of all Centrally Sponsored Schemes and Central Schemes would be undertaken. Building up the technical expertise to undertake gender audit would be integrated as part of the [gender budgeting] training programs. A quantum leap in this direction will be achieved by gender perspective being incorporated within the Expenditure and Performance audits conducted by [the Comptroller and Auditor General]."[76] According to a UN Women-commissioned study (footnote 69), the Government of India's Ministry of Women and Child Development developed gender audit guidelines and, as of February 2016, was in a dialogue with the Comptroller and Auditor General for the formalization of the guidelines. In Nepal, the government issued in 2008 the Local Body Gender Budget Audit Guidelines, which were revised into the Gender-Responsive and Social Inclusive Budget Formulation and Audit Guidelines in 2012. However, according to the UN Women study, as of 2016, the analysis focused on internal organizational operations rather than on beneficiary-focused programs.

D.   Gender Equality Features of South Asia Department Projects

64.   This section presents the results of the assessment of the gender features of 19 SARD projects in three sectors (energy, transport, and urban development) categorized gender equity theme (GEN), effective gender mainstreaming (EGM), and some gender elements (SGE) (footnote 21). These projects were selected based on the criteria listed in Chapter 1, paras. 17, 18 and 19 of this report; Appendix 1 contains the list of projects. SGE projects were included if a DMC had no GEN or EGM project under the three stated sectors.

65.   The assessment (i) identified the projects' gender features that are in line with the leave no one behind (LNOB) framework's three pillars: understand for action, empower for change, and include for opportunity (explained in Chapter 1, paras. 9 and 11; and Table 1.1); and (ii) checked if they have the key gender mainstreaming elements in four areas: (a) policies that seek to understand and address gender inequality, (b) institutional arrangements that locate responsibilities for ensuring the achievement of the projects' gender equality targets,

---

[76]   Government of India, Planning Commission. 2013. *Twelfth Five Year Plan (2012–2017) Social Sectors Volume III*. New Delhi. p. 179.

(c) programming and budgeting directed at supporting gender equality targets, and (d) a monitoring and reporting system that captures gender equality results.

66.   As SARD's actions for gender equality and social inclusion (GESI) intertwine in many projects, many project features mentioned in the following sections also apply to the social inclusion of some disadvantaged groups.

Overview of the Gender Equality Features of Reviewed Projects

67.   Based on the project administration manuals and other documents, the following are the key gender equality features of the 19 reviewed projects, grouped according to the LNOB framework pillars:

(i)   **Understand for action.** Eighteen projects included mapping and assessment-related activities to understand the situation of women.[77] ADB processes have several steps to understand the situation of women during the project design stage. The initial poverty and social analysis (IPSA) analyzes gender issues and identifies how the project can contribute to gender and development. The reviewed project documents indicate that women's empowerment and gender equality aspects were assessed.[78] Collection of sex-disaggregated data was included in the project performance monitoring system.

(ii)   **Empower for change.** All projects aimed to facilitate women's participation in training and project-generated employment and livelihood and their representation in decision-making committees. The Third Small Towns Water Supply and Sanitation Sector Project[79] in Nepal included an output indicator for the leadership training of women executives in the local bodies. All 19 projects reported activities relating to including women (as project beneficiaries) in selected activities, such as training and public awareness campaigns).

(iii)   **Include for opportunity.** Fifteen projects provisioned for gender training of contractors and project staff and included the gender-related provisions of the core labor standards in the bidding documents.

68.   The assessment of the GESI mainstreaming elements of the 19 projects also shows the following:

(i)   **Policies.** Some projects (a) collected sex-disaggregated data and evidence on the causes of the exclusion that women face and existing responses, such as the Power Transmission and Distribution Efficiency Enhancement Project in Nepal[80] and the

---

[77]   The Kulhudhuffushi Harbor Expansion Project (2016–2020) did not include any surveys or studies to identify women passenger trips as it was categorized SGE.

[78]   For example, the IPSA of the Third Small Towns Water Supply and Sanitation Sector Project in Nepal recognizes the lack of women in decision-making. The IPSA of the Strategic Road Improvement Project in Nepal discusses the increase in women's employment during road construction and their access to markets and services. The IPSA of SGE projects like Sri Lanka's Supporting Electricity Supply Reliability Improvement Project expectedly (given their gender categorization) have limited discussion of gender issues.

[79]   ADB. Nepal: Third Small Towns Water Supply and Sanitation Sector Project.

[80]   ADB. Nepal: Power Transmission and Distribution Efficiency Enhancement Project.

South Asia Subregional Economic Cooperation Dhaka-Northwest Corridor Road Project in Bangladesh;[81] and (b) have policy provisions addressing the barriers to gender equality and women's empowerment, such as the Supporting Electricity Supply Reliability Improvement Project in Sri Lanka,[82] whose gender action plan (GAP) provisioned for an assessment of the livelihood development needs of women to improve and expand their existing operations and the collection and analysis of gender and social data to monitor the change in the life of beneficiaries. Similarly, under the Third Small Towns Water Supply and Sanitation Sector Project in Nepal (footnote 79), a socioeconomic survey sought to cover a representative sample of 10% of the service area to generate a sex-disaggregated socioeconomic profile.

(ii)   **Institutional arrangements.** Some projects have consultant teams with international and national gender experts responsible for implementing the GAP or GESI action plan of projects categorized GEN and EGM. In projects categorized SGE, the social safeguard officer handles gender-related tasks. The project management team has overall gender or GESI monitoring and reporting responsibilities).

(iii) **Programming and budgeting.** Some projects have (a) human resource or personnel policies for gender-specific responsibilities (e.g., childcare, breastfeeding, flexible work time); and (b) activities to establish an enabling environment for gender equality and women's empowerment, such as the Bangladesh Power System Enhancement and Efficiency Improvement Project[83] and the Second City Region Development Project in Bangladesh,[84] where the GAP included the construction of a composting plant with gender-inclusive facilities like sex-segregated wash blocks and women's breastfeeding and resting rooms. However, the intersecting discrimination experienced by women of disadvantaged groups was not acknowledged or addressed in any of the projects).

(iv)   **Monitoring and evaluation.** Collection of sex-disaggregated data was included in some projects' project performance monitoring systems.

Gender Features of the South Asia Department's Energy Projects

69.   All five reviewed energy sector projects were categorized EGM. The main gender equality features of these projects were (i) increasing energy access in rural areas, including for women; (ii) enhancing women's participation in training programs and employment; (iii) collecting sex-disaggregated data and evidence about the causes of women's exclusion and existing responses; (iv) including policy provisions addressing the barriers to gender equality that women face; and (v) including gender indicators in the projects' monitoring and evaluation systems and reporting templates.

---

[81]   ADB. Bangladesh: South Asia Subregional Economic Cooperation Dhaka-Northwest Corridor Road Project.
[82]   ADB. Sri Lanka: Supporting Electricity Supply Reliability Improvement Project.
[83]   ADB. Bangladesh: Bangladesh Power System Enhancement and Efficiency Improvement Project.
[84]   ADB. Bangladesh: Second City Region Development Project.

70.   Other gender mainstreaming elements and gap of the reviewed energy projects were the following:

(i)   **Policy.** The Nepal Power Transmission and Distribution Efficiency Enhancement Project (footnote 80) classified households of ethnic minorities, households headed by senior citizens, households headed by single women, households including people with disabilities, and households below the poverty level as "vulnerable households." The Bangladesh Power System Enhancement and Efficiency Improvement Project (footnote 83) and Madhya Pradesh Energy Efficiency Improvement Investment Program—Tranche 1[85] address issues of women in rural areas.

(ii) **Institutional arrangements.** As the reviewed projects were categorized EGM, specific consultants were recruited for the implementation of the gender or GESI action plan. Training of different team members was included. An exemplary project was the Madhya Pradesh Energy Efficiency Improvement Investment Program in India (footnote 85), which engaged a national service delivery nongovernment organization (NGO) for GAP implementation, and each project implementation unit had a focal person responsible for the social aspect of the project.

(iii) **Programming and budgeting.** Some projects had facilities for gender responsibilities (e.g., childcare, breastfeeding, flexible work time) and institutional capacity strengthening in gender mainstreaming. A project worth noting is the Bangladesh Power System Enhancement and Efficiency Improvement Project (footnote 83), which established a women-friendly working environment by providing childcare facilities. However, no project aimed to work with men to change toxic masculinity.

Gender Features of the South Asia Department's Transport Projects

71.   Of the six reviewed projects in the transport sector, four were categorized EGM and two SGE. The performance indicators were primarily related to increased access to rural areas, enhanced women's participation in training programs and employment, safer and more efficient access to livelihood, and strengthened institutional capacity of the implementing agencies. Some transport projects addressed intersectional issues by having road design features friendly to older people, women, children, and the disabled.

72.   The other gender mainstreaming elements and gaps were the following:

(i)   **Policy.** All four EGM projects collected sex-disaggregated data and evidence on the causes of women's exclusion and responses and policy provisions addressing barriers to gender equality. The SGE-categorized Thimphu Road Improvement Project[86] conducted consultation workshops with institutions, where safety measures for women and children were discussed.

---

[85] ADB. India: Madhya Pradesh Energy Efficiency Improvement Investment Program - Tranche 1.
[86] ADB. Bhutan: Thimphu Road Improvement Project.

(ii) **Institutional arrangements.** Some projects had clear institutional arrangements (within the executing agency or implementing agency project team) for GAP or GESI action plan implementation and supervision and included GESI responsibilities in the functions of the executing agency and implementing agency project team (aside from the gender or GESI team or gender consultant). For example, the project implementation consultancy services of the South Asia Subregional Economic Cooperation Dhaka—Northwest Corridor Road Project, Phase 2 (Tranche 2) (footnote 81) had responsibilities for facilitating social and gender-related activities and conducting gender mainstreaming activities and employment of poor people and affected people, particularly women, in civil works.

(iii) **Programming and budgeting.** Some projects provided training in gender mainstreaming to staff and contractors. No project had (a) facilities for gender-specific responsibilities (e.g., childcare, breastfeeding, flexible time); and (b) activities to reduce toxic masculinity.

(iv) **Monitoring and evaluation.** ADB has a template for the gender or GESI action plan progress implementation report. The project administration manual directs the regularity of the submission of these reports to ADB, which the implementing agencies follow. All four EGM transport projects integrated gender indicators in their monitoring and evaluation systems and reporting templates. The two SGE projects, the Thimphu Road Improvement Project (footnote 86) and the Kulhudhuffushi Harbor Expansion Project,[87] expectedly had no explicit gender indicators in their monitoring and evaluation systems; however, the monitoring of gender issues and gender-related activities were incorporated in the two projects' progress reports.

Gender Features of the South Asia Department's Water and Other Urban Infrastructure and Services Projects

73.	Of the eight reviewed projects in the water and other urban infrastructure and services sector, two were categorized GEN, four EGM, and two SGE. Two projects had a GESI action plan (while four had GAPs), which ensured that gender and social activities were implemented and monitored at regular intervals. The projects' performance indicators were primarily on increased access to water supply and sanitation facilities, enhanced women's participation in training and employment, improved women's participation in water users' groups, and provision of menstrual hygiene management facilities. The projects also focused on addressing intersecting disadvantaged experienced by women from poor-income communities and other disadvantaged women. All eight projects collected sex-disaggregated data, which started at baseline. The projects had clear institutional arrangements (within the executing agency or implementing agency project team) for GAP or GESI action plan implementation and supervision. GESI responsibilities were integrated into the functions of the executing agency or implementing agency project team (apart from the gender or GESI team or gender consultant), and gender performance indicators were integrated into the projects' monitoring and evaluation systems and reporting templates.

[87] ADB. Maldives: Kulhudhuffushi Harbor Expansion Project.

74.   Other gender mainstreaming elements and gaps were as follows:

(i)   **Policy.** Seven of the eight projects collected sex-disaggregated data and evidence on the causes of women's exclusion and existing responses and policy provisions addressing barriers to gender equality. The SGE-categorized Phuentsholing Township Development Project[88] did not collect sex-disaggregated data.

(ii)   **Programming and budgeting.** Some projects had activities to create an enabling environment for gender equality. Under the Second City Region Development Project (footnote 84) in Bangladesh, a GAP indicator included the construction of a composting plant with gender-inclusive associated facilities, like sex-segregated wash blocks and women's breastfeeding and resting rooms. No project had facilities for gender-specific responsibilities (e.g., childcare, breastfeeding, flexible time) and activities that aimed to reduce toxic masculinity and transform discriminatory gender and social norms impacting women.

E.   Good Practices and Lessons Learned

75.   This section provides an overview of good practices in GESI mainstreaming drawn from the documents of 15 selected SARD projects (Appendix 1 contains the list of ADB projects reviewed for good practices) and consultations with selected ADB project staff, civil society organizations (CSOs), international development agencies, and government agencies. Each good practice, as presented in para. 75 (i) to (iii), is grouped under the LNOB framework's three pillars (understand for action, empower for change, and include for opportunity).

(i)   **Understand for action**
(a)   In the **Emergency Assistance Project** in Bangladesh,[89] which enhanced gender-inclusive infrastructures with a focus on women's safety, the project team validated the infrastructure design through inclusive public consultations with women beneficiaries by understanding if their needs were met adequately or if modifications were required.
(b)   In the **Madhya Pradesh Urban Services Improvement Project,**[90] the project team conducted a detailed safety audit to identify safety barriers faced by women while accessing public infrastructure.
(c)   In the **Delhi-Meerut Regional Rapid Transit System Investment,**[91] inclusive consultations were conducted with stakeholders along the industrial corridor to better understand the constraints faced by the project-affected people and integrate actions addressing these constraints into the GESI action plan.

---

[88]   ADB. Bhutan: Phuentsholing Township Development Project.
[89]   ADB. Bangladesh: Emergency Assistance Project.
[90]   ADB. India: Madhya Pradesh Urban Services Improvement Project.
[91]   ADB. India: Delhi-Meerut Regional Rapid Transit System Investment Project.

(d)   The project teams of the Second Chittagong Hill Tracts (CHT) Rural Development Project in Bangladesh, the Madhya Pradesh Urban Services Improvement Project, the Rajasthan Urban Sector Development Program, and the Delhi-Meerut Regional Rapid Transit System Investment in India attributed the success of project interventions to the needs assessment conducted with target beneficiaries, including women.

(ii)   **Empower for change**

(a)   The project team of **Supporting Kerala's Additional Skill Acquisition Program in Post-Basic Education** in India[92] followed a public–private partnership model in the construction of gender-sensitive facilities (e.g., sex-segregated toilets and sanitary napkin dispensers and disposers) in the community skills park and skills development center. In the public–private partnership model, private employers set up gender-sensitive training centers and conducted training activities with particular attention to women, which proved to be very effective.

(b)   **Supporting Kerala's Additional Skill Acquisition Program in Post-Basic Education** (footnote 92) also conducted counseling sessions to orient the women beneficiaries on the training sessions and their employment opportunities in male-dominated programs, and trained them in nontraditional skills, such as construction and repair work.

(c)   In Bhutan, the **Skills Training and Education Pathway Upgradation Project**[93] reserved 32% of residential facilities to be constructed as technical training institutes for female students. Also, while the project supported the participation of women in courses that are traditionally associated with them (e.g., tourism and hospitality, tailoring and/or dressmaking, food packaging), it also encouraged women to take up male-dominated courses, such as automotive and construction.

(d)   In India, the **Rajasthan Urban Sector Development Program**[94] leveraged family support to ensure women's participation in project training and activities.

(e)   The **Inclusive Micro, Small, and Medium-Sized Enterprise Development Project**[95] in Maldives designed a special loan window for women(called the Women Entrepreneurs Loan) to encourage women entrepreneurs to start or expand their businesses and avail themselves of the business development services of the business centers established or strengthened under the project.

---

[92]   ADB. India: Supporting Kerala's Additional Skill Acquisition Program in Post-Basic Education.
[93]   ADB. Bhutan: Skills Training and Education Pathways Upgradation Project.
[94]   ADB. India: Rajasthan Urban Sector Development Program.
[95]   ADB. Maldives: Inclusive Micro, Small, and Medium-Sized Enterprise Development Project.

(f) As part of the **Bangladesh Emergency Assistance Project** (footnote 89), concrete bathing facilities safer for women's use were constructed for displaced people from Myanmar in Cox's Bazar District. Streetlights were also installed, which led to improved safety, as women can now fetch water and use restrooms at night.

(g) In the **Bhutan Health Sector Development Program,**[96] all infrastructure-related investments have gender-friendly designs, including separate toilets for women and breastfeeding rooms.

(iii) **Include for opportunity**

(a) In the **Skills Sector Enhancement Program in Sri Lanka,**[97] an advisory committee composed of women beneficiaries was formed to guide the ministries and project teams in creating a conducive GESI environment based on their experiences.

(b) To enable women to enter men-dominated work, the **Madhya Pradesh Urban Services Improvement Project** (footnote 90) engaged the contractors and, with their support, encouraged the participation of women workers in the construction of infrastructure. This approach facilitated the employers' acceptance of the women workers and changed their attitudes toward women.

(c) Part of the **Delhi-Meerut Regional Rapid Transit System Investment Project** (footnote 91) was the conduct behavioral change training for service providers, such as bus drivers and conductors, to make them more receptive to the idea of women drivers.

(d) The **Skills Sector Enhancement Program** in Sri Lanka (footnote 97) was viewed positively by the Ministry of Youth Affairs and Skills Development because the program's GESI action plan was aligned with its GESI agenda. The ministry was willing to allocate financial and human resources for the project. Institutionalization of gender mainstreaming activities was also sustained after project completion because of the ministry's commitment to GESI.

(e) The collaboration of ADB and Bengaluru Metro Rail Corporation Limited from the project planning phase was a crucial success factor in the **Bengaluru Metro Rail Project.**[98] The strong support of the rail company facilitated the effective implementation of the project plans, including the GESI-related measures.

---

[96] ADB. Bhutan: Health Sector Development Program.
[97] ADB. Sri Lanka: Skills Sector Enhancement Program.
[98] ADB. India: Bengaluru Metro Rail Project.

(f)   The **Madhya Pradesh Urban Services Improvement Project** (footnote 90) successfully created a sense of ownership among the beneficiaries (communities in small and medium-sized towns, especially women and poor people) through community volunteer-based initiatives. Similarly, in the **Inclusive MSME Development Project** in Maldives (footnote 95), the involvement of the executing and implementing agencies in preparing the GAP instilled in them a sense of ownership of the plan and ensured the sustainability of project outcomes.

(g)   In the **Bengaluru Metro Rail Project** (footnote 98), GESI was institutionalized through a gender-sensitive operation manual. In addition, there was dedicated technical assistance (TA) project to ensure that key elements of GESI were implemented.

76.   Good practices were also drawn from the programs and initiatives of CSOs, which participated in the stakeholder consultations. Some of these programs and initiatives are as follows (this list is not exhaustive and does not cover all initiatives of many CSOs in the six DMCs):

(i)   **Understand for action.** Various CSOs in India that work with migrants have directed their efforts at conducting surveys, including collecting gender- and age-disaggregated data on the migrants' conditions and challenges, and profiling them to understand their gender- and age-differentiated needs and improve their access to social security schemes accordingly.

(ii) **Empower for change**

(a)   Many CSOs across the six DMCs provide vocational training and skills-building activities to increase the level of competency of women. Some have partnered with private firms to create more employment opportunities for youth, especially young women.

(b)   Various CSOs bring the training activities to where women live and congregate to promote their wider participation. Further, the CSOs arrange on-site childcare facilities.

(c)   Various nonprofit organizations have been working across the DMCs to develop the entrepreneurship capacities (and improve the resilience) of women; people with disabilities; people with diverse sexual orientation, gender identity and expression, and sex characteristics (SOGIESC); the rural population; and youth.

(d)   Various NGOs in India, such as PRADAN, support the formation of self-help groups of women to create awareness of various social issues, increase women's confidence in their economic abilities, and drive them to take a greater role in household decision-making.

(e) Various NGOs, such as Grameen Evam Samajik Vikas Sanstha in India, promote activities that lead to women's economic growth, education, and awareness of their rights. To address gender inequality in pay, Grameen Evam Samajik Vikas Sanstha encouraged the unionization of women workers and supported the diversification of available job opportunities.

(f) CSOs in India are involved in strengthening the capacities of elected women representatives in local governments and ensuring that women, especially single and widowed women, enjoy their inheritance land property rights and be recognized as women farmers to access resources of the government for women farmers.

(iii) **Include for opportunity**

(a) Naripokkho, a CSO working for women in Bangladesh, conducts advocacy work to improve the accountability and quality of services of state service providers, such as police stations, courts, and government health care facilities.

(b) The Azad Kishori in India connects adolescent girls to science, technology, engineering, and mathematics education opportunities. In another intervention, the Azad Kishori trained women to become skilled drivers, a field that is traditionally reserved for men. To allay the fears and apprehensions of participants' families and change their perspectives toward women's involvement in nontraditional careers and jobs, the NGO conducted regular sessions with participants' family members, including men.

(c) CSOs in India work with different departments, including health and police, for the effective implementation of GBV response centers at the referral hospital level.

F.   Conclusions and Way Forward

Summary of Findings

77.   The assessment of the gender equality context in all six DMCs of ADB in South Asia shows that gender inequality persists and that the gender gap in different dimensions (economic, political, health, and education) has worsened because of the COVID-19 pandemic. Some of the key highlights of the assessment are as follows:

(i) Discriminatory practices, entrenched in social norms, have constrained women, especially those from excluded and vulnerable groups, from accessing resources and opportunities that government and development partners provide.

(ii) The multiple intersections of gender, old age, disability, social identity, diverse SOGIESC, geographic location, income poverty, young age (disadvantaged youth), and migrant status have created overlapping dimensions of exclusion for many women.

(iii)   The six countries have favorable laws and policy frameworks for gender equality and women's empowerment, with functional ministries and institutional arrangements to implement these laws and policies. However, effective policy implementation has been a challenge across all DMCs. Also, many of these laws and policies do not explicitly address the overlapping disadvantages women and girls of excluded and vulnerable groups face.

(iv)   The government and CSOs in the six DMCs and ADB's SARD, with their long years of work in gender and development, have exemplary practices in GESI mainstreaming.

Way Forward for ADB's South Asia Department

78.   This section and similar sections in the next chapters on other disadvantaged groups present the views of the participants of the stakeholder consultations on SARD's possible next actions in the DMCs. In this chapter, these recommendations are grouped into DMCs, as some of them are country specific.

(i)   Bangladesh

(a)   **Empower for change.** Support the engagement of women agencies and organizations in interventions for disaster and climate change management.

(b)   **Include for opportunity.** Facilitate the coordination and complementarity of development partners' support for GESI policy dialogues, with the representation of women's organizations and networks; support programs to address the water crisis in the CHT, where the primary sufferers are women; adopt adaptive management in implementing GESI programs or projects so that they can be more open to target corrections based on the actual situation in local communities; and invest in making public infrastructures and services gender inclusive, including by changing harmful social and gender norms.

(ii)   Bhutan

(a)   **Understand for action.** Create awareness of GBV.

(b)   **Include for opportunity.** Support programs that tackle women's health issues; invest in promoting female labor force participation by mobilizing private sector support.

(iii)   India

(a)   **Understand for action.** Support a study on the issues of single women and widows in different sectors and projects.

(b)   **Empower for change.** Promote the recognition of single women and widows as vulnerable persons and engage and prioritize them for livelihood skills or enterprise development; facilitate the recognition of women as farmers and provide them opportunities to access resources allocated to farmers; and include women and involve elected women representatives in project-created institutional mechanisms.

(c) **Include for opportunity.** Promote the engagement of men and other patriarchal social institutions, such as jati panch (caste leadership), religious leaders, and local government institutions, in women's empowerment by including men in training and meetings that aim to change traditional perspectives on women; identify and address bottlenecks in women's education (particularly in science, technology, engineering, and mathematics) and women's employment, especially in the formal sector; employ a holistic approach to women's empowerment by taking their heterogeneity into consideration, addressing stereotypes, and sensitizing men so they will engage in household work too and contribute to women's economic independence; support the conversion of informal work to formal work to enhance the benefits for women and other vulnerable groups engaged in such work, facilitate the collection of data on their numbers and profiles, and promote laws and programs aimed at protecting workers; and in advancing gender equality, look beyond binaries and include issues that women, girls, and nonbinary people experience because of their disadvantaged intersecting identities, and support forums tackling these issues.

(iv) Maldives

(a) **Understand for action.** Support the collection and sharing of women's stories regarding their involvement in ADB projects to encourage other women to be involved.

(b) **Empower for change.** In community development projects, emphasize the importance of consulting women during the planning phase, such as in identifying appropriate waste management sites (because women are primarily responsible for disposing household waste).

(c) **Include for opportunity.** Support advocacy for improving the legal system for addressing GBV. Engage men in these initiatives; and develop programs to create awareness and change the mindsets of people, including women, on the types of employment that women can do.

(v) Nepal. **Include for opportunity.** Raise the gender awareness of men in leadership positions and involve them in gender mainstreaming; assist programs that aim to address the social and economic impacts of the COVID-19 pandemic; and promote the convergence of GESI initiatives of the government, development partners (like ADB), and CSOs.

(vi) Sri Lanka

(a) **Understand for action.** Identify and address the barriers and challenges that women entrepreneurs face.

(b) **Empower for change.** Encourage women's participation in vocational training in nontraditional sectors.

(c) **Include for opportunity.** Assist the government in creating a common
platform to discuss gender issues and the need to respond to them in a
holistic manner (including at the policy level); assist programs that address
sexual harassment in public transport; and support the strengthening of the
Ministry of Women and Child Affairs.

III. OLD AGE IN SOUTH ASIA: ISSUES AND RESPONSES

A. Introduction: Definition

79.   The definition of older people varies in the six developing member countries (DMCs) and is linked with the retirement age.[99] The governments of Bangladesh, India, Nepal, and Sri Lanka define those age 60 and above as older people, while Bhutan and Maldives define them as age 65 and above.

B. Status of Older People in South Asia Department Developing Member Countries

Key Indicators

Population

80.   In the six DMCs, because of an improved quality of life, decreased mortality, lower fertility, and increased life expectancy, the number of people older than 60 years is increasing rapidly (Table 3. 1).

81.   As per 2020 estimates of the World Bank Group, Sri Lanka has the largest population of older people (ages 65 and above) in South Asia at 11%, while Maldives has the smallest at 4% (Table 3. 1). There are more older women than older men in India, Nepal, and Sri Lanka.[100] Older women comprise 52% of older people in the six DMCs. Older people are likely to increase significantly in the coming years. The projection is that in 2050 almost 23% of the population in Sri Lanka; almost 21% in Maldives; and almost 16% in Bangladesh, Bhutan, and India will be older than 60. This is likely to have far-reaching economic and sociological consequences for these countries.[101]

[99]   Though the United Nations (UN) uses the term "older people," the terminology is not standardized across the South Asia Department (SARD) DMCs. Nepal has a Ministry for Women, Children, and Senior Citizens but the other countries have government policies or documents using the term "elderly." In Bhutan, the king established the Royal Society for Senior Citizens, but the government ministries use "elderly" in their documents. This report primarily uses the term "older people" interchangeably with "elderly," people of "old age," and "senior citizens."
[100] World Bank. Open Data. Population ages 65 and above (% of total population) (accessed 9 May 2022). The computation of percentages of women and men is based on the data on the population of female older people (65 and above) and male older people versus the total population of older people.
[101] United Nations Department of Economic and Social Affairs, Population Division. 2015. *World Population Ageing 2015*. New York.

Table 3.1: Key Indicators Related to Older People
(%)

DMC	Estimated Population of Older People				Women/Men Older People 2020	
	2019[a]	2020[c]	2030[b]	2050[a]	Women	Men
Bangladesh	5.2	5.2	11.5	15.8	49.6	50.4
Bhutan	6.1	6.2	11.6	15.8	45.2	54.8
India	6.4	6.6	12.5	13.8	51.7	48.3
Maldives	3.6	3.6	11.7	20.9	48.8	51.2
Nepal	5.8	5.8	10.8	12.8	54.6	45.4
Sri Lanka	11.2	11.2	21	22.6	57.7	42.3

DMC = developing member country.

[a]   United Nations Department of Economic and Social Affairs, Population Division. 2020. *World Population Ageing 2019*. New York.
[b]   United Nations Department of Economic and Social Affairs, Population Division. 2015. *World Population Ageing 2015*. New York.
[c]   World Bank. Open Data. Population ages 65 and above (% of total population) (accessed 9 May 2022).

Source: Asian Development Bank (South Asia Department).

82.   By 2050, the old age dependency ratio is estimated to increase in all countries, with the highest dependencies in Maldives and Sri Lanka.102 The higher percentage of older women than older men living alone could indicate the independence of a larger number of older women or more older women needing assistance (Table 3. 3).

Table 3.2: Old Age Dependency Ratio, 2019 and 2050
(%)

DMC	2019	2050
Bangladesh	08.9	25.8
Bhutan	10.3	24.8
India	11.0	22.5
Maldives	05.1	34.4
Nepal	10.8	19.8
Sri Lanka	18.9	42.5

DMC = developing member country.

Note: The old age dependency ratio is defined as the population aged 65 and older per 100 people of working age (20–64 years).

Source: United Nations Department of Economics and Social Affairs, Population Division. 2020. *World Population Ageing 2019*. New York.

Access to Social Resources and Services

83.   With the increased population of older people, requirements for care services have increased but are currently inadequate in all six DMCs. Old age care infrastructure is either almost absent or deficient in meeting the needs of older people. In Sri Lanka, eldercare homes can accommodate about 7,100 elders, accounting for 0.2% of the population aged more than

102 Old age dependency ratio is defined as the number of people aged 65 or older per 100 people of working age 20–64. OECD. Old-age dependency ratio.

Table 3.3: Percentage of People Age 65 and Older, Living Arrangements
(%)

DMC (Data Source)	Living Alone Women	Living Alone Men	Living with Spouse Only Women	Living with Spouse Only Men	Living with Child(ren) Women	Living with Child(ren) Men	Living with Grandchild(ren) Women	Living with Grandchild(ren) Men
Bangladesh (2011 PUMSa)	7.2	1.1	5.4	14.6	7.5	22.6	...	...
India (2009 PUMSa)	7.3	2.5	9.1	19.9	4.4	9.6	1.4	1.7
Nepal (2011 PUMSa)	6.4	2.5	7.5	12.7	3.8	9.1	3.1	2.9

... = data not available, DMC = developing member country, PUMS = Public Use Microdata Samples.

Note: No data for Bhutan, Maldives, and Sri Lanka.

Source: United Nations Department of Economic and Social Affairs, Population Division. 2020. *World Population Ageing 2020 Highlights: Living Arrangements of Older People.* New York. p. 34.

60 years. Further, most eldercare homes are not designed or intended to provide long-term care, as they lack the necessary staff or financial resources to take care of elders who need 24-hour nursing and assistance in activities of daily living.[103] Aged care in the DMCs is generally left with families, usually with children looking after older parents. There are no state- or private-owned elderly care facilities in some countries, such as Maldives.[104] In India, a study evaluating old age homes and daycare centers funded by the Ministry of Social Justice and Empowerment revealed that most old age homes do not have ambulances or readily available medical facilities for older people.[105]

84.   The participants of the stakeholder consultations in all six DMCs highlighted the lack of sufficient medical facilities and specialized health care for older people. In particular, the lack of gerontologists, geriatric wards in hospitals, and specific services like physiotherapy and psychotherapy was raised. A survey of more than 10,000 respondents across northern, southern, western, eastern, and central India in May–June 2018 showed that 62.1% of the older people did not get any palliative care.[106]

85.   Maldives does not have specific facilities for geriatric care, and old-age-related minor illnesses are treated at multipurpose hospitals. There are very few nongovernment organizations (NGOs) in Malé that aim to develop an awareness of aging or prevent and delay age-related illnesses.[107] Nepal has only three registered geriatricians (one geriatrician for every 100,000 older people). Among the various health institutions, only eight have started geriatric services. Moreover, despite the government's policy to establish geriatric wards in every hospital with more than 100-bed capacities, the lack of skilled doctors and paramedics has been a constraint.[108]

[103] ADB. 2019. *Growing Old Before Becoming Rich: Challenges of an Aging Population in Sri Lanka.* Manila.
[104] *Maldives Financial Review.* 2021. Ageing Ungracefully. 24 June.
[105] Research and Development Initiative Pvt. Ltd. 2018. *Evaluation Study on Functioning of Old Age Homes/Day Care Centre's and Integrated Rehabilitation Centers for Drug Addicts.* New Delhi. The introduction section mentions a scheme whose recent revision was enforced on 1 January 2015, indicating that the study was done in or after 2015.
[106] Agewell Foundation. 2019. *Annual Report, 2018–19.* New Delhi.
[107] A. Nazra. 2018. Perceptions of Ageing Among Older Adults Living in Male', Maldives and Implications for Provision of Support. *International Journal of Social Research and Innovation.* 2 (1). pp. 37–60.
[108] R. Kandel. 2018. Ageing and the elderly. *The Kathmandu Post.* 6 December.

Access to Economic Resources and Services

86.   As the capacity to work gradually diminishes with aging, older people become more and more financially dependent. Table 3.4 presents the social security allowances, old age allowance, and/or pension schemes in the six DMCs with varying eligibility criteria and benefits.

Table 3.4: Social Security Allowances and/or Pension Schemes for Older People			
Bangladesh	Bangladesh provides about $6 per month to its older people.[a]	**Bhutan**	Bhutan has a national pension scheme, which covers public sector employees, and a traditional kidu (welfare) system, which provides living allowances for disadvantaged senior citizens.[b]
India	In India a monthly cash allowance of $3 is provided to citizens aged 60 to 79 years and $7 to those aged 80 years and older who are below the poverty line.[c]	**Maldives**	Maldives provides about $325 per month to all citizens who are 65 and older and has a mandatory contributory retirement pension scheme for all public and formal sector workers.[d]
Nepal	Nepal provides social security allowance for Dalit and single women senior citizens older than 60 years, and other senior citizens older than 70 years.[e]	**Sri Lanka**	Sri Lanka pays a senior citizens allowance of $11 per month to enrolled beneficiaries aged 71–99 and about $30 to elders aged 100 years and older.[f]

[a] Government of Bangladesh, Department of Social Services. Old Age Allowance (in Bengali).
[b] Yonten Phuntsho. A Perspective on Older Persons In Bhutan. Thimpu.; and National Pension and Provident Fund. *Annual Report 2020–2021*. Thimphu.
[c] Government of India, Pensioners' Portal. 2019. *Schemes and Programmes Being run by the Various Ministries/Departments of Government of India, for Welfare of Senior Citizens.* India.
[d] Government of Maldives, Pension Office. Basic Pension; and Government of Maldives, Pension Office. Senior Citizens Allowance.
[e] Government of Nepal, Nepal Law Commission. 2018. *The Social Security Act, 2075 (2018).* Kathmandu.
[f] Government of Sri Lanka; Ministry of Women, Child Affairs and Social Empowerment; National Secretariat for Elders. Our Services: Senior Citizens' Allowance Over 70 Years and Giving "Centenary" Allowance Over 100 Years.

Source: Asian Development Bank (South Asia Department).

87.   The stakeholder consultation participants in Bangladesh, Nepal, India, and Sri Lanka assessed that current allocations and benefits need to increase for the growing population of older people. Bangladesh, for instance, has pension policies to ensure social security in old age for retired government employees only.[109] In India, the Ministry of Social Justice and Empowerment at the central level and social welfare departments at the state-level agencies have financial assistance schemes for older people. In addition, income insecurity was identified as one of the major causes of vulnerability in old age; older people depended greatly on their earnings to support themselves and their families, especially since the social security amounts were insufficient.[110]

[109] HelpAge International, East Asia and the Pacific Regional Office. Ageing population in Bangladesh.
[110] UNFPA. 2012. *Report on Status of Elderly in Select States of India, 2022.* New Delhi.

88.   There are few economic opportunities for older people even if they are willing and able to work. In some cases, the lack of contemporary skills and education prevents older people from exploring post-retirement income-generating opportunities even when they are physically and mentally capable. In India, the quality of life for elderly index, which highlights the overall situation and well-being of older people, showed low performance of 21 states across the educational attainment and employment pillar for older people and stated that there is scope for improvement in these areas.[111] In Maldives, most older people have no income-earning opportunities and are dependent on government pension schemes. Their labor force participation rate was a mere 16%, and labor underutilization was 34%.[112] In Nepal, a high proportion of older people (about 66%) continue working after the age of 60, but employment is most often concentrated in the informal sector and agriculture, typically associated with high levels of vulnerability and low wages.[113] In Sri Lanka poverty among older people is higher than among the rest of the population, indicating their limited income and independent income sources. Income from work in the formal sector decreases after 60, which is the retirement age.

Social Practices, Participation, and Decision-Making

89.   Across the six DMCs, families are traditionally expected to look after older people. However, this informal social support system has declined with increasing urbanization, changing family structures, rural–urban migration, and growing labor force mobility. In addition, the traditional living arrangements of older people are changing as families are becoming smaller and more dispersed, thereby eroding the ability of extended family systems to function as social safety nets. Older people initially live with their spouse, or their spouse and children, and after the demise of their spouse, when they can no longer support themselves independently, they co-reside with their adult children. The difficulties experienced by older people across the countries depend on their life circumstances, financial capacities, and health status (with differences between and within countries based on gender, caste, ethnicity, location, income, and age group).

90.   According to the consultation participants, key concerns across the DMCs are abandonment, neglect, verbal abuse and disrespect by family members, physical hardship (because of health concerns), emotional ill-being and isolation (reduced social interactions leading to loneliness and feelings of helplessness), social discrimination, and difficulty in accessing different care services. Table 3.5 provides available data on the abuse of older people in the DMCs.

---

[111]   Government of India, Press Information Bureau. 2021. Quality of Life for Elderly Index assesses well-being of India's ageing population. News release. 11 August.
[112]   Government of Maldives, National Bureau of Statistics. 2018. *Household Income and Expenditure Survey 2016: Analytical Report III: Employment.* Malé.
[113]   R. Holmes, S. Bhandary, and C. Jha. 2019. *Gender Equality and Social Inclusion Analysis of the Social Protection System in Nepal: Final Report.* Oxford, United Kingdom: High-Quality Technical Assistance for Results (HEART).

Table 3.5: Statistics on Abuse of Older People

Bangladesh	While no official national estimates exist, a study conducted in the Chitmahal area found that most older people (71.5%) were neglected or abused. This included those who were abused psychologically (50.4%), abused financially (60.4%), experienced treatment-related neglect (40.0%), and abused physically (1.5%).[a]	Bhutan	A study by the National Statistics Bureau found 17.8% of the respondents had suffered verbal abuse and 16.7% economic abuse. Neglect was suffered by 12.5% of the respondents, 12.4% suffered emotional abuse, and 5.4% suffered physical abuse.[b]
India	In India, 5% of the elderly have reportedly experienced ill treatment, of whom half have experienced it occasionally (i.e., once in 2 months), one-third only a few times (i.e., at least once in a year), and about 14% frequently (at least once in a fortnight). Older women experienced more ill treatment than older men.[c]	Maldives	In 2019, 83 cases of older person abuse were reported to the Ministry of Gender, Family, and Social Services. Among the cases reported in 2019, 62.7% of the victims were males, and 37.3% were females.[d]
Nepal	In Nepal, 1,311 cases of older person abuse were recorded in 2012–2018. The abuse was mainly physical, financial, neglect, psychological, and sexual, wherein most of the cases were neglect. The death of older people because of neglect and abuse was 1,013 during this period.[e]	Sri Lanka	A cross-sectional descriptive study, published in 2014, reported that out of 530 elders studied at a hospital, the total overall rate of abuse was 38.5%, while the rate of physical abuse was reported to be 5.6%.[f]

[a] Md. R. Awal, U.K. Majumder, and Md. M. Haque. 2020. Factors Associated with Abuse and Neglect of the Elderly Peoples of Chitmahal Areas in Bangladesh. *Asian Journal of Education and Social Studies.* 8 (1). pp. 34–50.

[b] Business Bhutan. 2017. Elderly Citizens Face Various Forms of Abuse. 19 September.

[c] Government of India, Ministry of Health and Family Welfare, National Programme for Health Care of Elderly and International Institute for Population Sciences. 2020. *Longitudinal Ageing Study in India, Wave-1: An Investigation of Health, Economic, and Social Well-being of India's Growing Elderly Population.* Mumbai.

[d] Corporate Maldives. 2020. Gender Ministry Statistics Show Decline in Elder Abuse Cases. 16 June.

[e] Ageing Nepal. Ageing Nepal home page.

[f] A. Edirisinghe et al. 2014. Elder abuse among outpatient department attendees in a tertiary care hospital in Sri Lanka. *Ceylon Medical Journal.* 59 (3). pp. 84–89.

Source: Asian Development Bank (South Asia Department).

Intersecting Inequalities Faced by Older People of Disadvantaged Groups

91.   The vulnerabilities that older people face are further compounded by their intersecting disadvantaged identities like gender; disability; sexual orientation, gender identity and expression, and sex characteristics (SOGIESC); geographic isolation; and income status. Older women, particularly widows, face additional challenges concerning health care, mobility, and financial independence. In Bhutan, older women experience a higher unemployment rate (3%) than older men (2%).[114] The defined contribution pension schemes for retirees disadvantage older women given the gender income and wage disparity in Maldives. As women of prime working ages are less likely to be in higher-paying jobs because they have to forfeit certain jobs because of conflicts with their roles in the

---

[114] L. Dorji et al. 2017. *Understanding the Situation of Elderly Citizens in Bhutan.* Thimphu: National Statistics Bureau. p. 9.

household, they benefit less from such a pension system than men.[115] In 2020, 20.2% of all retirement pension scheme beneficiaries were women, while men accounted for the remaining 79.7%.[116] The World Health Organization reported that women have slightly better life expectancy and healthy life expectancy at birth than men in Nepal.[117] The policies on aged care in Nepal have focused mainly on providing allowances and pensions; but majority of the population have to depend on familial support and personal savings or daily wages. For women, the exposure to gender-related inequalities and discrimination across the life course, including lower levels of education, wage differentials, income opportunities, mobility constraints, and a lack of voice and agency, result in lower incomes and fewer assets to help them maintain an adequate standard of living in old age.[118]

92.   Older people with disabilities form a large group because of aging-related functional limitations, such as speech disability; hearing disability; visual disability; and agility (locomotion, walking, climbing of stairs, body movement, and dexterity). For instance, about 70% of older people in Sri Lanka experience disability, with about 22% having vision problems and 20% having hearing difficulties. The prevalence of all difficulties is, in general, higher among women (footnote 103).

93.   Geographic isolation makes access to basic health care services or facilities even more challenging for older people living in rural areas of hilly Bhutan, remote atolls of Maldives, and rural Nepal (footnote 118). Opportunities to contribute to society are also impacted by intersectional inequalities.

C.   Policy Analysis

94.   The constitution of each country has provisioned for the care of older people. All the South Asia Department (SARD) DMCs except Bhutan have acts and policies for older people, some of which are in Table 3.6.

Table 3.6: Key Acts and Policies for Older People

DMC	Policies
Bangladesh	National Policy on Older People, 2013
	Maintenance of Parents Act, 2013
Bhutan	National Policy for Senior Citizens (under preparation) 2022
India	Maintenance and Welfare of Parents and Senior Citizens Act, 2007
	National Policy on Older People, 1999
Maldives	Maldives Pensions Act, 2009
Nepal	National Action Plan for Senior Citizens, 2005, Senior Citizens Act, 2006, Social Security Act, 2018
Sri Lanka	Protection of the Rights of Elders Act, 2006

DMC = developing member country.

Source: Extracted from the six countries' policy documents.

[115] J. El-Horr and R.P. Pande. 2016. *Understanding Gender in Maldives: Toward Inclusive Development*. Washington, DC: World Bank Group. p. 29.

[116] Government of Maldives, National Bureau of Statistics. *Statistical Yearbook of Maldives 2021: Pension and Social Protection*. Malé.

[117] World Health Organization, Regional Office for South-East Asia. 2021. *Nepal: Gender and Health*. World Health Organization. Regional Office for South-East Asia.

[118] S. Shrestha et al. 2021. Elderly care in Nepal: Are existing health and community support systems enough. *SAGE Open Medicine*. 9 (2).

95.   Additional government interventions addressing the issues of older people were highlighted during the consultations with civil society organizations (CSOs) and government officials. In India, the latest government policy for older people is the Maintenance and Welfare of Parents and Senior Citizens Act, 2007.

96.   In Maldives, according to the consultation participants, the government has introduced various schemes and interventions, e.g., introducing universal health coverage for all (including older people), and building a database by conducting a nationwide assessment on the status of the elderly and a draft national law on the elderly. Similarly, in Nepal, the government engages in various activities to ensure the rights of senior citizens as per the Senior Citizen Act, 2006.[119] The major activities include social security allowances; old age homes for single older women; and efforts to preserve Ayurvedic knowledge in selected fields, such as herbal medicine, music, and history. According to the consultation participants in Nepal, a good practice by the government is that it mandates any hospital with more than 50 beds to have a geriatric ward, and there are also provisions for geriatric training of physicians and nurses, and free ambulance services for older people.

97.   Sri Lanka has almost 2.5 million older people constituting about 11.2% of the population. To protect the rights of older people and to improve their well-being, two institutions, the National Secretariat for Elders and the National Council, have been established. Some interventions or programs by the secretariat include (i) cash allowances; (ii) elder committees to conduct education awareness programs, health programs, and programs to make them self-sustainable; (iii) minimum facility projects, under which they provide facilities, such as small bathrooms, tiling, and electric connections, depending on requirements; (iv) self-employment grants; and (v) old age homes with provisions for special support for vulnerable groups, such as people with disabilities. In addition, the secretariat has provisions for daycare centers, providing older people with assistive devices, and a board to address and investigate the complaints filed by older people. According to the participants of the consultation in Sri Lanka, some areas for potential improvement include providing (i) telemedicine services; (ii) training and retraining of caregivers, primary health care workers, and social workers; and (iii) economic opportunities and market linkages to older people. Moreover, the participants said that it was difficult to educate older people population about the pandemic because of their limited communication with the outside world, which prevented them from knowing the severity of the situation. They identified isolation as one of the biggest problems faced by the older population and the major barrier to awareness about the pandemic.

D.   South Asia Department Projects Aiming to Benefit Older People

98.   This section presents an assessment of the integration of actions to understand and address the issues of older people in 19 selected projects of SARD. These projects were selected based on the criteria listed in Chapter 1, paras. 17, 18 and 19. The assessment was on whether

---

[119]   Government of Nepal, Nepal Law Commission. 2006. *Senior Citizens Act, 2063 (2006)*. Kathmandu.

they have the key mainstreaming elements in four areas: (i) policies that seek to understand and address the issues of older people, (i) institutional arrangements that locate responsibilities for ensuring the achievement of GESI targets focused on older people, (iii) programming and budgeting directed at supporting older people, and (iv) a monitoring and evaluation system that captures and reports project GESI results experienced by older people. It can be assumed that the issues and initiatives covered in the chapter on disability (Chapter 4) also apply to some extent to older people.

99.   Overall, the assessment shows that the integration of concerns of older people in SARD operations is in its inception phase. Of the 19 projects reviewed for this assessment, six partially integrated actions aiming to benefit older people. In the reviewed energy projects, the only mainstreaming element (from the list in paras. 9 and 98) are the policy provisions addressing the barriers that older people, especially women and those from disadvantaged groups face, which are found in one of the energy projects, the Power Transmission and Distribution Efficiency Enhancement Project in Nepal (2017–2022) (footnote 80). This project classified households headed by senior citizens (along with single women-headed households, households with a member with disability, and below poverty level households) as vulnerable households, with additional assistance provisioned for them.

100.   Compared to the energy sector projects, some of the reviewed transport projects have more actions for older people, such as the following:

(i)   Disaggregation of data by age and other relevant social variables and collection of evidence about the causes of exclusion of older people and existing responses.

(ii)   Policy provisions that address the barriers faced by older people in the transport sector. Examples of projects with these provisions are the (a) **Integrated Road Investment Program** (tranches 1–4) in Sri Lanka,[120] which had policy directives to mention the program's impact on many different groups, including older people (particularly in the road design features); and (b) **Kulhudhuffushi Harbor Expansion Project** in Maldives, (footnote 87) which included provisions for integrating features friendly to older people, women, children, and the disabled in the designs (such as slope ramps) of the harbor.

(iii)   The **Second Rural Connectivity Investment Program** in India[121] provides inclusive road design features by taking into consideration the specific needs of vulnerable groups, including older people, through participatory consultations during the design phase.

101.   Some projects in the water and other urban infrastructure and services sector have features addressing the concerns of older people, such as the following:

(i)   Disaggregation of data by age, sex, and other relevant social variables and collection of evidence about the causes of exclusion of older people and existing responses.

---

[120]   ADB. Sri Lanka: Integrated Road Investment Program (Tranche 4).
[121]   ADB. India: Second Rural Connectivity Investment Program – Tranche 1.

Under the Dhaka Environmentally Sustainable Water Supply Project in Bangladesh,[122] older people (older than 65) were identified as one of the vulnerable groups in the socioeconomic surveys. Under the Local Government Enhancement Sector Project in Sri Lanka,[123] the social monitoring report included data disaggregated by age, which the project used for deciding on the provision of facilities like ramps and handrails for their ease of use, including of people with disabilities.

(ii)   Policy provisions that address the barriers to GESI faced by older people, especially women and those from disadvantaged groups. Examples were the inclusion of consultations with older people and other excluded and vulnerable groups in the project consultation and participation plan, and the provision of public sanitation facilities friendly to older persons under the **Local Government Enhancement Sector Project** in Sri Lanka (footnote 123). The GAP of the **Second City Region Development Project** in Bangladesh (footnote 84) had activities that ensured the benefits of excluded and vulnerable groups, including older people.

(iii)   The **Second City Region Development Project** (footnote 84) includes road design features that are friendly to older people.

E.   Good Practices in Responding to the Issues of Older People

102.   Another set of 15 ADB projects in South Asia was selected to identify SARD's good practices in responding to the issues of women and excluded and vulnerable groups, including older people. Three of these projects have features for older people that are in line with the "Leave-No-One-Behind" (LNOB) framework pillars (i) empower for change, and (ii) include for opportunity (Chapter 1, paras. 9 and 11 and Table 1.1 provide definitions of the three pillars):

(i)   **Empower for change.** The COVID-19 Active Response and Expenditure Support Program in Maldives[124] provided cash assistance for 3 months during the pandemic to 4,000 vulnerable poor and vulnerable households headed by single, widowed, divorced, or disabled women; this group is assumed to include older women.

(ii)   **Include for opportunity**
   (a)   The **Delhi-Meerut Regional Rapid Transit System Investment Project** in India (footnote 91) explicitly mentioned the inclusion of older people among the project's considerations in designing the transport infrastructure and aimed to ensure that their transportation needs and concerns were met. GESI features included commissioning dedicated coaches and four seats in each coach for women, with additional seats reserved for pregnant women, older people, and people with disabilities. Seats for women, older people, and people with disabilities were reserved in all feeder buses operated by the National Capital Region Transport Corporation.[125]

---

[122]   ADB. Bangladesh: Dhaka Environmentally Sustainable Water Supply Project.
[123]   ADB. Sri Lanka: Local Government Enhancement Sector Project.
[124]   ADB. Maldives: COVID-19 Active Response and Expenditure Support Program.
[125]   ADB. 2020. *Report and Recommendation of the President to the Board of Directors: Proposed Multitranche Financing Facility to India for the Delhi–Meerut Regional Rapid Transit System Investment Project.* Gender Equality and Social Inclusion Action Plan (accessible from the list of linked documents in Appendix 2). Manila.

(b) The **Bengaluru Metro Rail Project** in India (footnote 98) included in its objectives the provision of an efficient, safe, and inclusive transport system for all commuters that caters to the needs of older people.

103.   Good practices in responding to the issues of older people, relevant to the three pillars of the LNOB framework (understand for action, empower for change, and include for opportunity), can be drawn from the initiatives of stakeholder organizations that participated in the consultations. Examples include the following:

(i)   **Understand for action.** In Bangladesh, the Sir William Beveridge Foundation gathered data on the skills and resources of older people in poor and flood-prone areas to identify income-generating activities that older people can do.

(ii)   **Empower for change**

(a)   The programs of the Sir William Beveridge Foundation aim to address the impact of old age, disability, and lack of knowledge about certain diseases; train older people on how to prevent and deal with these diseases; and arrange for income-generating activities that they can handle based on their physical ability.

(b)   In India, the Agewell Foundation and Dignity Foundation are among the various CSOs working for the welfare and empowerment of older people. Key initiatives of the Agewell Foundation include (1) job placement—since 2002, they have helped 90,000 older people get jobs such as managing directors, peons, and tutors; and (2) distribution of adult diapers to those in need. The initiatives of Dignity Foundation aim to enable older people to lead active lives through easy access to trusted information, opportunities for productive aging, and social support services.

(c)   Aged Care Maldives engaged in outreach programs in remote islands to provide health care services for older people.

(d)   In Sri Lanka, the National Secretariat for Elders, a government agency, has been (1) providing cash allowances of SLRs5,000 ($13.5) to people older than 60 years and with a minimum income of SLRs6,000 ($16.2) since 2012 (however, they have not been able to provide this allowance to all older people; hence, there is a waiting list of 238,000 older people for this service); (2) assisting elder committees by holding awareness programs and health programs; (3) providing some minimum facilities, such as small bathrooms; (4) providing self-employment grants; and (5) running elderly homes.

(iii)   **Include for opportunity**

(a)   Among the objectives of Dignity Foundation in India is to change people's mindset about aging.

(b)   Aging Nepal works with educational institutions to spread knowledge about gerontology and develop a curriculum to change people's attitudes toward older people.

F.   Conclusions and Way Forward

Summary of Findings

104.   The assessment of the situation of older people in the six DMCs shows the increasing need of older people, especially older women and those from disadvantaged groups, for assistance. The assessment's highlights are as follows:

(i)   In the six DMCs, the proportion of older people is increasing and, by 2050, is expected to be 23% in Sri Lanka; 21% in Maldives; 16% in Bangladesh, Bhutan, and India; and 11% in Nepal. Overall, in South Asia, there are more older women (at 52%) than older men.

(ii)   The increased percentage of older people implies the need for more care services, which are inadequate in all six DMCs.

(iii)   While all six DMCs have social security allowances or old age pension schemes, the allocations and coverage of benefits are not sufficient. Moreover, income insecurity is one of the major causes of vulnerability in old age. There are few economic opportunities for older people even if they are willing and able to work.

(iv)   The traditional family support system has weakened because of increasing urbanization, changing family structures, rural–urban migration, and increasing labor force mobility. The higher percentage of older women than older men living alone could indicate more older women capable of living independently or needing more assistance. Key concerns are abandonment; neglect; verbal abuse by family members; health problems; emotional ill-being; and isolation leading to loneliness and feelings of helplessness, social discrimination, and difficulty in accessing care services.

(v)   These vulnerabilities and hardships are further compounded by intersecting disadvantages because of gender, disability, belonging to the diverse SOGIESC community, geographic isolation, and income status or poverty.

(vi)   All six DMCs have laws and policies promoting the welfare of older people.

(vii)   ADB has initiatives to assist older people in South Asia, but these initiatives are limited.

(viii)   Stakeholder organizations that participated in the consultation workshops have good practices in responding to the issues of older people, relevant to the three pillars of the LNOB framework (understand for action, empower for change, and include for opportunity).

Way Forward for the South Asia Department

105.   The increasing proportion of older people in the six DMCs, especially in Maldives and Sri Lanka, suggests the need to prioritize interventions to understand, empower, and include them. To respond to this need, according to the participants of the stakeholder consultation workshops, SARD may consider the following actions (classified under the three LNOB framework pillars):

(i)   **Understand for action**

    (a)   Examine (1) the distinct needs of older people based on their gender, abilities and disabilities, living arrangements, geographic locations, and income status; (2) the available resources, infrastructure, and facilities allocated for their development; and (3) the presence or absence of policies that facilitate the transformation of their situation along the three LNOB pillars.

    (b)   Assess the capabilities and attitudes (toward older people) of those who care for them and the factors that drive these capabilities and attitudes.

(iii)   **Empower for change**

    (a)   Empower older people by attending to their holistic needs—e.g., physical care; social interactions; economic development; health and well-being (mental, emotional, psychological); social protection; and participation in decision-making. Specific approaches can be drawn from the good practices of consulted stakeholder organizations in the six DMCs, and the suggestions of the consultations' participants (mostly from CSOs).

    (b)   **General.** Encourage the youth to take care of and help older people develop technological knowledge for better access to services (e.g., internship programs).

    (c)   **Health.** Increase telehealth services and improve the accessibility of quality care services for older people.

    (d)   **Economic.** Support postretirement jobs and income-generation schemes, train older people for employment (jobs or self-employment) based on their physical and mental abilities, and ensure easy access to social protection schemes for those who are no longer capable of paid work.

    (e)   **Political.** Involve older people in governance structures and programs that concern them (e.g., the national-level committee for older people in Maldives).

(iii)   **Include for opportunity**

    (a)   Transform attitudes toward older people through investment in the education sector (curriculum on aging and how to manage older people).

    (b)   Promote mobility and accessibility: make buildings and transport infrastructure and facilities friendly to older people (e.g., provision of ramps, toilets, railings).

    (c)   Support legal and policy dialogues to refine policies for older people's social protection.

    (d)   Provide dedicated public spaces (e.g., recreation places) in urban areas for older people, where they can interact with each other.

    (e)   Develop or strengthen community care services for older people.

IV. DISABILITY IN SOUTH ASIA: ISSUES AND RESPONSES

A.   Introduction: Definitions

106.   The Convention on the Rights of Persons with Disabilities (2006) states that "disability is an evolving concept and that disability results from the interaction between people with impairments and attitudinal and environmental barriers that hinder their full and effective participation in society on an equal basis with others."[126] All developing member countries (DMCs) have accepted the World Health Organization framework on the International Classification of Functioning, Disability, and Health.[127] Appendix 3 provides an overview of definitions of disability in each DMC.

B.   Status of People with Disabilities in the Six South Asia Department Developing Member Countries

Key Development Indicators

Population

107.   The disability prevalence rates in the six DMCs vary, with the highest in Maldives (9.2%) and the lowest in Bangladesh (1.6%) (Table 4.1). The disability prevalence rate is higher among females in Bhutan, Maldives, and Sri Lanka. In the six DMCs, the average disability prevalence rate among females (average of 4.6%) is higher than that among males (average of 4.0%). That means, overall, there are more females with disability in the region.

Access to Social Resources and Services

108.   According to the participants of the stakeholder consultations, access to education for people with disabilities in all DMCs is constrained by a lack of disabled-friendly infrastructure, assistive technology, special educators, caregivers, nonadaptive school curricula and examinations, and the prevalence of stigma and discrimination. School enrollment rates, literacy rates, and

---

[126] United Nations (UN). 2008. *Convention on the Rights of Persons with Disabilities and Optional Protocol.* New York. p 1.
[127] World Health Organization. International Classification of Functioning, Disability and Health.

Table 4.1: Disability Prevalence Rates
(%)

DMC	Total	Female	Male
Bangladesh[a]	1.6	1.2	1.9
Bhutan[b]	2.1	2.3	2.0
India[c]	2.2	2.0	2.4
Maldives[d]	9.2	10.5	7.8
Nepal[e]	2.2	2.0	2.5
Sri Lanka[f]	8.7	9.6	7.7

DMC = developing member country.

[a] The Bangladesh total disability prevalence rate presented in this table is based on the gender-disaggregated number of people with disabilities according to the updated report of the Department of Social Services' Disability Information System, Government of Bangladesh, Department of Social Services. Department of Social Services, home page. The total population of 2,551,385 people with disabilities is divided by the total population in 2020 reported in World Bank. Open Data. Population, total (accessed 06 May 2022); the female disability prevalence rate is their number (982,536) divided by the female population (per the World Bank data), and the male disability prevalence rate is their number (1,566,130) divided by the male population in 2020 (per the World Bank data). The Disability Information System also reports 2,719 transgender individuals with disability.

[b] Government of Bhutan, National Statistics Bureau of Bhutan. 2018. *2017 Population & Housing Census of Bhutan: National Report*. Thimphu. p. 40.

[c] Government of India, Ministry of Statistics and Programme Implementation, Social Statistics Division. 2016. *Disabled People in India: A Statistical Profile 2016*. New Delhi.

[d] Government of Maldives; Ministry of National Planning, Housing and Infrastructure; National Bureau of Statistics. 2020. *Demographic Characteristics by Disability: Household Income and Expenditure Survey 2019*. Malé.

[e] Government of Nepal, National Statistics Office. 2023. National Population and Housing Census 2021, Population Size and Distribution (accessed 20 April 2023).

[f] Government of Sri Lanka, Department of Census and Statistics. 2014. *Census of Population and Housing 2012: Key Findings*. Battaramulla, Sri Lanka. p. 58; and *Census of Population and Housing 2012: Population Tables*. p.2 . Disability prevalence rate was based on the percentage of population ages 5 and above (total of 18,615,577) who reported difficulty in at least one domain (total of 1,617,924). Female and male disability prevalence rates were computed from data provided—43% of those who reported having difficulty in at least one domain were males and 57% were females—versus male population ages 5 and above (8,977,411) and female population ages 5 and above (9,638,166).

Source: Asian Development Bank (South Asia Department).

performance of children with disability in school remain low across the countries. Table 4.2 provides statistics on the educational attainment of people with disabilities in the South Asia Department (SARD) DMCs.

109.   Similarly, access to adequate health care for people with disabilities is impacted by the shortage of disability-friendly infrastructure in health centers; untrained service providers; challenges pertaining to the delivery of health services like early diagnosis, referral, and intervention services; and limited access to psychotropic medications and assistive devices, which aggravates people with disabilities' health-related vulnerability. Bangladesh, for instance, is believed to lack a proper official distribution system and financing to support the delivery of assistive devices.[128] According to the consultation participants, lack of affordability is a significant reason for not possessing assistive technology in Bangladesh. Moreover, distance and stigma also limit access (footnote 128). Assistive service providers like interpreters are also scarce in the region.

Access to Economic Resources and Services

110.   Of the total working-age population (15–64 years), 32.9% have disability in Maldives and 5.2% in Sri Lanka (Table 4. 3). Of the working-age population with disability in Maldives, a

[128] Institute of Development Studies. 2020. *Bangladesh Situational Analysis*. Brighton, United Kingdom.

Table 4.2: Statistics on Educational Attainment of People with Disabilities

Bangladesh	The primary school enrollment rate in Bangladesh is 97% overall, while only 11% of children with disability receive any form of education. For children with disability who do go to school, literacy rates are lower and performance poorer than the rest of the children.[a]	**Bhutan**	Bhutan's literacy rate for people with disabilities is 26.6% and 71.4% for those without disability.[c] In Bhutan, school-related factors, such as "insufficiency of appropriate facilities and equipment" and "capacity of teachers," are ranked high as obstacles to implementing quality learning in schools for children with disability.[c]
India	Among people with disabilities aged 7 years and older in India, 52.2% were literate (the total adult literacy rate is 74.0%). Among those aged 15 years and older, 19.3% had a secondary educational level or above,[e] which is below the national figure of 37.6%.	**Maldives**	There is only one school dedicated to children with disability in Maldives. In 2018, almost all 15- to 17-year-olds without disability completed primary education (98%), whereas only four out of five adolescents in the same cohort with disability (79%) completed primary education.[b]
Nepal	In Nepal, the literacy rate of people with disabilities (40%) was lower than that of those without disability (61%). About 35% of children (5 to 10 years old) with disability were out of school compared to the 5% without disability.[d]	**Sri Lanka**	Of children aged 5–14 with disability in Sri Lanka, 23.5% are excluded from mainstream education (98.2% children are reported to be attending school) and among those who do attend mainstream schools, participation in educational activity decreases with age.[f]

[a] Institute of Development Studies. 2020. *Bangladesh Situational Analysis*. Brighton, United Kingdom.
[b] U. Drukpa. 2021. Despite inclusive schools in the country, the enrollment of children with disabilities is still low. *The Bhutanese*. 12 April; and R. Sakurai. 2017. Challenges for implementing Inclusive Education in Bhutan. *Journal of International Cooperation in Education*. 19 (2). pp. 71–81.
[c] Government of India, Ministry of Statistics and Programme Implementation. 2019. NSS Report No. 583: People with Disabilities in India NSS 76th Round (July–December 2018). News release. 23 November.
[d] United Nations Department of Economic and Social Affairs. 2019. *Disability and Development Report: Realizing the Sustainable Development Goals by, for and with Person with Disabilities 2018*. New York.
[e] United Nations Children's Fund (UNICEF) Nepal. 2018. *Disability in Nepal: Taking Stock and Forging a Way Forward*.
[f] UNICEF Sri Lanka. *Every Mind: Equal rights to education for children with Learning Disabilities in Sri Lanka*.

Source: Asian Development Bank (South Asia Department).

large majority (60.2%) are women; in Sri Lanka, a slightly higher percentage (51.8%) are men.[129] However, in both DMCs, the labor force participation rate and the employment-to-population ratio of women with disability are significantly lower than those of men. These data indicate the intersecting disadvantages that women with disability in the two DMCs experience. The same situation is assumed to be true for the other four DMCs.

111.   Consultation participants indicated that the high school dropout rates among people with disabilities could be caused by the discriminatory attitudes of peers and educators and the lack of disability-friendly infrastructure in the school, leaving them with little scope to enroll in

[129] UN Economic and Social Commission for Asia and the Pacific. 2021. *Disability at a Glance 2021: The Shaping of Disability-Inclusive Employment in Asia and the Pacific*. Bangkok. pp. 74, 77, 78. The UN commission has no data for Bangladesh, Bhutan, India, and Nepal.

**Table 4.3: Economic Indicators for People with Disabilities in
Selected Developing Member Countries**
(%)

DMC	Working Age			Labor Force Participation Rate			Employment to Population Ratio		
	Total	Women	Men	Total	Women	Men	Total	Women	Men
Maldives	32.9	60.2	39.8	48.79	37.0	66.6	45.76	34.63	62.56
Sri Lanka	5.2	48.2	51.8	15.07	8.77	22.34	14.72	8.53	21.89

DMC = developing member country.

Notes:
1. Percentage of people with disabilities (of total working-age population), percentage of females with disability (of total people with disabilities of working-age population), and percentage of males with disability (of total people with disabilities of working-age population) are computed from Table 1.1 (Working-age population thousands) in United Nations Economic and Social Commission for Asia and the Pacific. 2021. *Disability at a Glance 2021: The Shaping of Disability-Inclusive Employment in Asia and the Pacific.* Bangkok. p. 74.
2. The United Nations Economic and Social Commission for Asia and the Pacific has no data for the other DMCs.

Source: United Nations Economic and Social Commission for Asia and the Pacific. 2021. *Disability at a Glance 2021: The Shaping of Disability-Inclusive Employment in Asia and the Pacific.* Bangkok. pp. 74, 77, 78.

higher education, which may hinder their ability to compete in the job market. Further, according to the consultation participants, compulsory requirements of educational certificates restrict their entry into certain jobs, especially in the formal sector. In India, for example, 36% of the people with disabilities were working in 2016.[130] Among those who were workers, 31% were agricultural laborers. The employment situation of people with disabilities was worse in the private sector, where only a minimal number were employed, despite incentives provided by the government. The consultation participants highlighted the need for more programs related to skills training that support disability employment. These training programs require special disability-friendly logistical arrangements and facilities (like inclusive infrastructures and interpreters), but such needs are not pre-identified or addressed, resulting in a lack of participation. The participants also said that there are serious concerns regarding vocational training systems for people with disabilities because of a mismatch between job demands and skills development.

112.   In the labor market, attitudinal barriers prevent people with disabilities from accessing employment opportunities and credit. According to the consultation participants, even when at work, they may not be aware of their rights in the workplace, often leading to discrimination and harassment. In India, among people with disabilities aged 15 years and older, the labor force participation rate in 2018 was 23.8%.[131] A study in Sri Lanka noted that employment in the private sector is available only to a small percentage of individuals with disability. This is a consequence of the negative attitudes and lack of sensitivity of employers.[132] The consultation participants suggested that the work environment should be made more conducive for people with disabilities (Box 4.1). Further, there is a need to monitor indicators like their retention and labor force participation, on-the-job training, and sensitization workshops in the workplace.

[130] Government of India, Ministry of Statistics and Programme Implementation, National Statistical Office, Social Statistics Division. 2021. *People with Disabilities (Divyangjan) in India—A Statistical Profile: 2021.* New Delhi.
[131] Government of India, Ministry of Statistics and Programme Implementation. 2019. NSS Report No. 583: People with Disabilities in India NSS 76th Round (July–December 2018). News release. 23 November.
[132] K. Satanarachchi. 2018. *Unlocking the Potential of Youth with Disabilities by Strengthening Labour Market Participation.* UNDP. 24 August.

> **Box 4.1: Making Work Environment More Conducive for People with Disabilities**
>
> During a consultation with a representative from the Government of Nepal as part of this assessment, the representative noted the following: "Efforts should be made to see how the work environment can be made more compatible with the needs of people with disabilities. For example, the equipment and office space should be disability friendly. The recruitment processes and interviewers should be sensitized. A mix of affirmative action and accommodative strategies could be employed. This could include provision of additional time in tests as the visually impaired may need more time if they need to use braille or deaf applicants may need the additional time to communicate with the sign language interpreter. Similarly, the medium of any examination or interview should make accommodations for disability (for instance, using devices they are familiar with, or having the option of an oral or digital format)."
>
> Source: Consultation with a government representative from Nepal for this assessment.

113.   These challenges lead to limited prospects, higher unemployment, and higher poverty and deprivation for people with disabilities. For example, in Bangladesh, the unemployment rate for adults with disability is higher (1.9%) compared to people without disability (1.5%), and workers with disability are likely to be paid less than others for doing the same work, especially in manual jobs (footnote 128). In Nepal, a study found that 60.5% of people with disabilities were likely to have a lower income per month as compared to only 44.2% of those with no disability, and households with at least one member with a disability also scored lower on most indicators of quality of living than households without disabled members.[133] In Sri Lanka, based on the National Census of 2012, only 29.0% of people of working age with disability were economically active, and 70.9% did not have opportunities for economic participation in the country's development.[134]

Social Practices, Participation, and Decision-Making

114.   The participants of the stakeholder consultations in the six DMCs shared that people often perceive disability as a curse and hold superstitions that result in the social ostracization of people with disabilities. Families hide members with disability, which results in the neglect of those individuals. Often, parents think spending money on educating children with disability is not worthwhile. Communities and employers also regard disability as a burden and assume that people with disabilities are incapable of becoming productive members of society. As a result, according to the consultation participants, the representation of people with disabilities remains low in workplaces and political institutions.

115.   In India, a study noted that attitudes of families, service providers, people with disabilities themselves, and the community at large constrain people with disabilities from realizing their full social and economic potential. Communities believe people with disabilities have lower capacities, and the internalization of negative attitudes reinforces social marginalization.[135] In Sri Lanka, negative social attitudes are commonplace, such as believing that people with disabilities are helpless and

[133] B. Rohwerder. 2020. *Disability Inclusive Development: Nepal Situational Analysis, June 2020 Update.* Brighton, United Kingdom: Institute of Development Studies.

[134] P. Mendis and B. Perera. 2019. *Disability Policy Brief for Law Makers, Administrators and Other Decision Makers.* Colombo: International Centre for Ethnic Studies. p. 5

[135] R.K. Panda. 2016. *Social Exclusion and Inequality: Opportunities in Agenda 2030—A Position Paper on State of Socially Excluded Groups (SEGs) and Framework of Action.* Wada Na Todo Abhiyan, Socially Excluded Task Force/NACDAOR, Center for Equity Studies, World Vision and Welthungerhilfe, and Global Call to Action against Poverty. p. 15.

will always be dependent on others. In addition, there is a general unwillingness to make simple changes, such as in a workplace to accommodate a jobseeker with a disability (footnote 135).

116.   People with disabilities are vulnerable to physical and sexual abuse because of their limited communication ability, mobility constraints, and lack of status in society. According to the consultation participants, the ability of people with disabilities to report offenses against them and raise their voices is curtailed, as it is difficult for them to show proof of social injustice. In Maldives, a study found people with disabilities more than four times more likely to have experienced violence compared to people without disability and that almost half of the people with mental health conditions reported experiencing violence, which was significantly higher than people with other impairments.[136] Lack of awareness about rights among people with disabilities, their family members, the community, and service providers is a major issue in the DMCs.

Intersectionality

117.   The intersection of disability with gender, caste, ethnicity, location, and income results in deeper exclusion. Women and girls with disability are more vulnerable to violence (physical, sexual, and emotional abuse), and in some cases, become disabled because of the violence inflicted upon them. A report highlighted instances of women and girls with intellectual and developmental disability in Nepal being subject to forced sterilization and use of contraceptives.[137] Women with disability are also the most vulnerable group in postwar and post-conflict situations in Sri Lanka, experiencing the highest levels of gender-based violence (GBV), abject poverty, stigmatization, and exclusion. Access to resources like education, employment, and treatment and health care facilities for girls and women with disability is also challenging because of the patriarchal norms in the DMCs. In Maldives, the unemployment rate of women with disability is more than twice as high (10%) as that of men with disability (4%).[138] In Bangladesh, 79% of women with disability completely lost their income during the COVID-19 shutdown period, compared to 69% of men with disability.[139] In India, there are several hurdles to girls with disability accessing and remaining in education.[140] First, when deciding to invest in the education of a girl with a disability, families tend to prioritize the education of male siblings. Second, disability-friendly transport and commute options to reach school are scant. Third, barriers, like the absence of special educators and of accessible toilets and other basic infrastructural facilities restrict the education of girls with disability.

118.   Social identities are also linked to disability prevalence. For example, in India, among different social groups, the scheduled castes had the highest disability rate of 2% (3% men and 2% women) (footnote 130). In Nepal, rates and risks of disability among indigenous peoples are reportedly high for various reasons, including greater level of poverty, poor quality of prevention, lack of suitable

[136] L.M. Banks et al. 2020. No One Left Behind? Comparing Poverty and Deprivation between People with and without Disabilities in the Maldives. *Sustainability*. 12 (2066).

[137] Autism Care Nepal Society et al. 2018. *Shadow Report submitted to the Committee on the Rights of People with Disabilities in its 19th session for the Country Review of the Federal Democratic Republic of Nepal*. United Nations Committee on the Rights of People with Disabilities.

[138] Government of Maldives; Ministry of National Planning, Housing and Infrastructure; National Bureau of Statistics. 2020. *Disability in Maldives: Household Income and Expenditure Survey 2019*. Malé.

[139] Innovision. 2021. *COVID 19 Impact on Vulnerable Groups—Digest 5: People with Disabilities*. Dhaka.

[140] UNICEF Regional Office for South Asia. 2021. *Disability-Inclusive Education Practices in India*. Kathmandu.

rehabilitation services, increased exposure to environmental degradation, climate change impacts, natural and other disasters, conflict, and a higher rate of being victims of violence (footnote 133).

119.   Geographic exclusion exacerbates disability issues as most services are centralized in capital cities (like specialized health care services for certain types of disability). Therefore, people in the remote atolls of Maldives and the rural and hilly regions of Bhutan and Nepal experience added difficulties. In Nepal, experiences of stigma and discrimination differ depending on where people live. In rural areas, children with disability and their caregivers reported more stigma or discrimination toward disability (footnote 133). In Bhutan, more people with multiple disabilities lived in rural (4,487) than in urban (901) areas.[141] In India, 69% of the population with disability resides in rural areas (footnote 130).

C.   Policy Analysis

120.   All DMCs have dedicated acts and policies for uplifting and empowering people with disabilities and for addressing the barriers they experience. The six DMCs also have provisions for protecting and promoting the rights of those with intersecting disadvantaged identities (e.g., poor women with disability belonging to minority ethnic groups). However, not all policies address issues related to intersecting inequalities. Table 4.4 provides a list of policies for people with disabilities in the SARD DMCs.

121.   **Bangladesh.** Until the mid-1990s, the government barely recognized the barriers faced by people with disabilities in Bangladesh. This has changed, and Bangladesh has come a long way in recognizing and prioritizing disability issues. This change started when the Government of Bangladesh first passed the Disabled Welfare Act in 2001. While this is merely a welfare act and

Table 4.4: Key Acts and Policies for People with Disabilities

DMC	Policies
Bangladesh	Disability Welfare Act, 2001
	Rights and Protection of People with Disabilities Act, 2013
Bhutan	National Policy for People with Disabilities, 2019
India	The Rights of People with Disabilities Act, 2016
	The National Trust for the Welfare of People with Autism, Cerebral Palsy, Mental Retardation and Multiple Disabilities Act, 1999
	National Policy for People with Disabilities, 2006
Maldives	Disability Act, 2010
Nepal	Rights of People with Disabilities Act, 2017
	Rights of People with Disabilities Regulation, 2020
Sri Lanka	The National Disability Act, 1996
	National Policy on Disability, 2003

DMC = developing member country.
Source: Extracted from the six DMCs' policy documents.

[141] *Kuensel*. 2018. Disability Prevalence Higher in Rural Bhutan. 28 June.

does not guarantee disability rights, it has generated momentum for formulating appropriate and rights-based laws or policies for people with disabilities in the country. The People with Disabilities Rights and Protection Act, 2013 further changed the inclusion of people with disabilities in the political structure. Being a rights-based act, it opened the door for the organizations and activists working for people with disabilities to be more visible, and it enabled these organizations to influence the concerned authorities to be more active in addressing the needs of people with disabilities. However, the consultation participants from CSOs working in the disability space in Bangladesh assessed that despite existing disability policies in the country's five-year plan, there have been some implementation gaps. The consultation participants said that there is a need for greater coordination between the National Coordination Council, the National Executive Council, and the 1,200 committees formed to attend to disability issues to actively address the difficulties faced by people with disabilities.

122.   **Bhutan.** Constitutional provisions, acts (such as the penal code), and other legislation in Bhutan give special consideration to disability concerns. The government looks at addressing the economic well-being of people with disabilities, as well as their access to opportunities, employment, education, and other basic needs. In 2019, the Gross National Happiness Commission (GNHC), the government's central planning agency, approved the National Policy for People with Disabilities along with an action plan on its implementation. Some initiatives by the GNHC are making landmark infrastructures accessible, developing schools for deaf people including special technologies and equipment, conducting needs assessments to assess the disability situation and needs, exploring the possibility of issuing drivers' licenses to persons with disability, conducting workshops to make disaster management and contingency plans that are inclusive to people with disabilities, developing certifications for people with disabilities to help identify the kind of support they need, and incorporating disability needs in all relevant projects. However, participants from the GNHC indicated a lack of resources, which makes it difficult to effectively implement these plans.

123.   **India.** In India, the Department of Empowerment of People with Disabilities was formed under the Ministry of Social Justice and Empowerment to promote the rights and welfare of people with disabilities. One of the department's major focus areas is the education and economic empowerment of people with disabilities. Some of the department's other initiatives include providing disability rehabilitation, encouraging the private sector to employ people with disabilities, and providing shelter homes or grants. The department also has some provisions specifically for women in the area of skills training and credit provision policies.[142] India has a pension plan for people with disabilities in the range of $4–$7 per month.

124.   **Maldives.** According to the consultation participants in Maldives, the well-designed Disability Act, 2010 has not been effectively implemented. They further said that legislation within the act, such as a registry of people with disabilities to enable the provision of social protection schemes, has not been implemented because of a structural problem. Particularly, the Disability Council of Maldives at the Ministry of Gender, Family, and Social Services is responsible for the implementation of the Disability Act, but its authority to influence and its capacities are limited. Moreover, the policies and programs in the country are disability neutral, which means

---

[142]   ADB. Regional: Supporting the Operational Priority 1 Agenda: Strengthening Poverty and Social Analysis.

that people with disabilities are not looked upon as a special group that needs assistance but are provided services and opportunities as any able-bodied person. According to the consultation participants, another major barrier is the lack of awareness about the laws and policies for people with disabilities among the citizens and CSOs.

125.   **Nepal.** In Nepal, amendments were made to legislations—e.g., Rights of People with Disabilities Act, 2017; Rights of People with Disabilities Act (First Amendment), 2018; and Rights of People with Disabilities Regulation, 2020—to reflect the Convention on the Rights of People with Disabilities provisions after the Government of Nepal adopted it in 2009. However, the continuing stigmatization of people with disabilities was identified by stakeholders during the consultations, as one of the possible barriers to achieving the objectives of the key acts and policies.

126.   **Sri Lanka.** In Sri Lanka, the biggest challenge faced by people with disabilities is the lack of education, which results in their lack of employment. According to the consultation participants, although there is a quota of 3% to ensure job opportunities for people with disabilities, it does not necessarily account for the different types of disabilities and is not implemented widely.

D.   South Asia Department Projects Aiming to Benefit People with Disabilities

127.   This section presents an assessment of the extent to which actions addressing the issues of people with disabilities are integrated into the 19 projects selected for this GESI assessment (Chapter 1, paras. 17, 18 and 19 includes the criteria for the selection and Appendix 1 provides the list of these projects). Similar to the assessment of SARD project actions for older people in Chapter 3, this assessment identified project disability-related actions in four areas: (i) policies that seek to understand and address the issues of people with disabilities, (ii) institutional arrangements that locate responsibilities for ensuring the achievement of GESI targets focused on disability, (iii) programming and budgeting directed at supporting people with disabilities, and (iv) a monitoring and evaluation system that captures and reports project disability-related GESI results.

128.   The assessment shows that some projects (under the transport and water and other urban infrastructure and services sectors; none in the energy sector) incorporated actions related to the following:

(i)   **Policies.** This encompassed the collection of data disaggregated by disability and evidence on the causes of the exclusion of people with disabilities and policy provisions, such as disability-friendly facilities (including accessible transport facilities and separate toilets), addressing the barriers to GESI experienced by people with disabilities, (e.g. the Local Government Enhancement Sector Project— Additional Financing in Sri Lanka143 and the Second City Region Development Project in Bangladesh (footnote 84).

---

143   ADB. 2016. *Report and Recommendation of the President to the Board of Directors: Proposed Loan for Additional Financing to the Democratic Socialist Republic of Sri Lanka for the Local Government Enhancement Sector Project.* Manila.

(ii) **Programming and budgeting.** This was achieved through the inclusion of project activities or features benefiting people with disabilities, such as disability-friendly footpaths in the Thimphu Road Improvement Project (footnote 86) and disability-friendly features in the designs of the harbor in the Kulhuduffushi Harbor Expansion Project (footnote 87). There were no projects with disability-related actions under the two areas (i.e., institutional arrangements and monitoring and evaluation system) in any of the three sectors.

E.   Good Practices in Responding to Disability Issues

129.   In addition to the assessed 19 projects, 15 more SARD projects were reviewed to identify good practices in responding to disability. The following projects explicitly mentioned people with disabilities as among their targeted beneficiaries:

(i) **Supporting Kerala's Additional Skill Acquisition Program in Post-Basic Education** (footnote 92). This program included the construction of classrooms, community skills parks, and skills development centers with disability-friendly infrastructural design (e.g., handrails, hand bars, ramps, tactile flooring, braille boards, signage, and lifts).

(i) **Bengaluru Metro Rail Project** (footnote 98). A transect walk was organized in a metro station involving people with disabilities and transgender individuals to identify difficulties they experienced in accessing and moving within the train station and during their train commute; the project adapted disability-friendly rail transport infrastructure design.

(i) **Delhi–Meerut Regional Rapid Transit System Investment Project** (footnote 91). This adopted GESI-sensitive infrastructure. The project's GESI action plan requires consulting people with disabilities on the design features of the regional rapid transit system; dedicating seats for them in each train coach and all National Capital Regional Transport Corporation-operated feeder buses; providing separate toilets in all stations and at least one step-free access route and one step-free emergency route for a person in a wheelchair to travel from the road to each station, concourse, platform, and train; reserving at least 4% of National Capital Regional Transport Corporation and operation and maintenance personnel in the regional rapid transit system for people with disabilities, as per the Rights of Persons with Disabilities Act, 2016; and giving hearing, visual, and physical mobility assistive aids to 1,000 people with disabilities as a pilot test of socially inclusive mobility measures.

(ii) **COVID-19 Active Response and Expenditure Support Program** (footnote 124). This program in Maldives included households headed by women with disability among the beneficiaries of its 3-month cash assistance during the pandemic.

130.   The participants of the stakeholder consultations shared the following good practices (grouped into the three pillars of the LNOB framework) of their respective organizations in responding to disability concerns.

(i)   **Understand for action**

    (a)   The Centre for Disability in Development in Bangladesh assessed the age and disability inclusiveness of the response to the humanitarian crisis in the country's Cox's Bazar area in 2017. The assessment showed that the response had (1) limited awareness and practice in identifying people with disability, (2) very few disability-friendly services or camp terrains, (3) limited or no participation or consultation with people with disability in the community and camp activities, and (4) no demonstration of recognition of their skills and capacities

    (b)   The Maldives Association of Persons with Disabilities collected disability data in three atolls through a door-to-door survey.

(ii) **Empower for change**

    (a)   In India, the Samarthanam Trust for the Disabled is among the CSOs that work for the socioeconomic empowerment of people with disabilities. It provides, among others, quality education (with 600 students with disability enrolled), accommodation (hostels for women with disability), nutritious food (midday meal programs for schools with children with disability), vocational training (livelihood resource centers providing skills training to people with disabilities), and placement-based rehabilitation. It assists about 50,000 to 100,000 people with disabilities.

    (b)   The Care Society in Maldives initiated disability-inclusive community-based rehabilitation programs with the involvement of island communities in geographically excluded areas.

    (c)   The National Federation of the Disabled-Nepal provides several services for the empowerment of people with disabilities, such as a help desk and construction of disability and rehabilitation homes. It also contributed to the development of a provincial policy on disability and the establishment of the province-level coordination committee for people with disabilities.

(iii) **Include for opportunities.** The Disability Organisations Joint Front in Sri Lanka works as a pressure group to promote and protect the rights of people with disabilities. For instance, it lobbies for the enactment of a sign language act and the issuance of driving licenses to deaf people, and raises awareness on the 2017 UN Guidelines on achieving Sign Language Rights for All.

F.   Conclusions and Way Forward

Summary of Findings

131.   The disability statistical data in the six DMCs show that, on average, there are more females with disability in the region. This overall picture is because of the high proportion of females with disability in Bhutan, Maldives, and Sri Lanka. Moreover, in Maldives, a large proportion of the working-age population (15–64 years) have disability (32.9%), and among the working-age population with disability, the large majority (60.2%) are women. Against this backdrop, this assessment highlights the following:

(i)   **Situation**
(a)   While there are more women than men with disability in the region, particularly in the working-age population, the data show more women out of the labor force, unemployed, and with less access to economic resources.
(b)   Sociocultural beliefs and barriers affect the ability of people with disabilities to access development opportunities. In all six countries, they are perceived negatively, and their capacities are undervalued.
(c)   Their access to opportunities and services is further constrained by the lack of disability-friendly infrastructure, facilities, technology, and human resources with competencies in disability management. Hence, a large proportion of people with disabilities have not received any form of education (many are school dropouts) and have no access to quality care services.
(d)   Even when they obtain a job, they are not aware of their rights in the workplace, and many employers and co-employees or coworkers lack sensitivity to their needs and are not aware of their rights, often leading to discrimination and harassment.
(e)   All DMCs have dedicated acts and policies for the empowerment of people with disabilities. However, there are policy implementation gaps because of, among others, inadequate resources and limited participation of people with disabilities.

(ii)   **Responses**
(a)   In SARD's portfolio, as shown in the assessment of the 19 projects, only a few projects incorporate actions addressing disability issues, including those of women with disability. In projects that aim to benefit people with disabilities, the institutional arrangements and monitoring and evaluation systems that could ensure these benefits are lacking.
(b)   There are local resources in the form of disability-focused government programs and CSOs working on disability issues. However, the assessment found that they are encountering challenges in the implementation of laws, policies, and programs.

Way Forward for the South Asia Department

132.   ADB considers disability inclusion as essential for the effective implementation of Strategy 2030 and, hence, includes the percentage of disability-inclusive operations as one of the 27 tracking indicators of its four-level Corporate Results Framework, 2019–2024. It has a road map for strengthening disability-inclusive development (2021–2025) with five core priority components.[144] The road map aims to develop a more systematic approach to implementing disability-inclusive development in ADB. To monitor and measure ADB's progress in strengthening its disability-inclusive interventions, particularly the extent to which its projects incorporate disability inclusion elements, it has developed a disability inclusion marker system with a four-level scale: the lowest is 0, which means no disability inclusion or no enabling conditions for disability inclusion, and the highest is 3, which means that it is principally or significantly disability inclusive (Table 4.5). In 2021, to pilot the use of this marker, ADB assessed 34 projects of SARD. The results are consistent with the findings of this assessment. The Delhi–Meerut Regional Rapid Transit System Investment Project (Tranche 1) (footnote 91), which was among the 15 projects assessed for good practices in this GESI assessment, was given the highest rating of 3.

Table 4.5: Assessment of 34 South Asia Department Projects using ADB's Disability Inclusion Marker System, 2021

Rating	Rating Description
3	Principally or significantly disability inclusive
2	Some disability inclusion elements
1	Enabling conditions for disability inclusion, no explicit disability inclusion elements
0	No disability inclusion, no enabling conditions for disability inclusion

ADB = Asian Development Bank.
Source: ADB.

---

[144] The five core components of ADB's road map on disability inclusive development are as follows: (i) coordinate actions on disability inclusion across different departments and sectors of ADB and develop capacity within the organization; (ii) establish partnerships to leverage advocacy impact; (iii) establish a culture of data disaggregation and publishing disability sensitive analysis; (iv) develop sector guidelines and gradually expand the portfolio of disability-inclusive development interventions; and (v) strengthen disability inclusion standards in ADB workplaces, policies, and practices. ADB. 2022. *Strengthening Disability-Inclusive Development: 2021–2025 Road Map.* Manila.

133.   In the same year, after the piloting of the marker, ADB assessed the disability-inclusive features of 27 more projects of SARD. This assessment found 18 of the 27 projects with different levels of disability-inclusive features, with two COVID-19 response projects getting the highest rating of 3. These were the Responsive COVID-19 Vaccines for Recovery Project under the Asia Pacific Vaccine Access Facility in Sri Lanka and Nepal. The project in Sri Lanka included people with disabilities among excluded and vulnerable groups to be assisted. The project in Nepal collected disaggregated data on the targeted beneficiaries by different social categories, including disability, and aimed to ensure that they benefit from its services.

134.   ADB's recognition of the importance of integrating disability-inclusive elements in its operations and the call for assistance from the DMCs serve as a strong incentive for SARD to prioritize its responses to disability issues in its DMCs. This push is further strengthened by the strong evidence of the intersection of disability and gender inequality, which is an equally important concern of ADB, in that more women with disability experience discrimination and disadvantages in the DMCs. In line with this assessment, the following are actions that SARD may consider (classified under the three LNOB framework pillars), according to the participants of stakeholder consultations in the six DMCs:

    (i)   **Understand for action**
        (a)   Provide assistance to partner government agencies and CSOs in establishing or strengthening their disability database or management information systems, including collecting data disaggregated by disability, sex or gender, age, social identity, income status, and geographic location.
        (b)   Collect data or evidence on the barriers to gender equality and social inclusion that people with disabilities, especially women with disability, experience, and their current resources to eliminate these barriers.
        (c)   Assess different initiatives for disability-inclusive development of the government, CSOs, and private sector along the three pillars of the LNOB framework.

    (ii)   **Empower for change**
        (a)   Support projects and programs that target to holistically benefit and empower people with disabilities who are in the margins, especially those experiencing intersecting discrimination because of gender, age, social identity, income status, and geographic location, among others.
        (b)   Assist in forming a resource pool of disability experts and networks of organizations of people with disabilities and support groups in each DMC that can move forward the disability agenda.

    (ii)   **Include for opportunity**
        (a)   Support the review of laws, policies, and programs that are critical to disability-inclusive development.
        (b)   Assist in the review and transformation of the educational system toward aligning with the principles and elements of disability-inclusive development.
        (c)   Invest in programs and projects in key sectors (transport, energy, water and other urban infrastructure and services, finance, education, and health)

to create an enabling physical, social, and legal environment for disability-inclusive development.

(d) Promote the creation of mechanisms for continuous exchanges among organizations of people with disabilities and support groups (from the government, CSOs, and private sector) on local, national, and regional initiatives for disability-inclusive development.

V. SOCIAL IDENTITY IN SOUTH ASIA: ISSUES AND RESPONSES

A.   Introduction: Definitions

135.   In four of the six developing member countries (DMCs) of the Asian Development Bank (ADB) in South Asia, [145] several groups experience exclusion based on their caste and ethnic and religious identities. For this gender equality and social inclusion (GESI) assessment, these identities are called "social identities." In Bangladesh, these groups include ethnic and tribal communities and religious minorities. India formally recognizes and defines these groups, such as scheduled castes (the official term for Dalits according to the Constitution of India), scheduled tribes (indigenous people officially regarded as socially disadvantaged), other backward classes, nomadic tribes, denotified tribes, particularly vulnerable tribal groups, pastoral communities, and religious minority groups. In Nepal, these groups include the Dalits, [146] Adivasi Janajatis (indigenous nationalities), Muslims, and Madhesis (plains people from the Terai region). In Sri Lanka, they include the Tamils, Muslims, and Wanniyala-Aetto (an indigenous tribe known as forest dwellers). Appendix 4 presents the different social identities and their populations in the four countries.

B.   Status of People with Disadvantaged Social Identities

Access to Social Resources and Services

Bangladesh

136.   The various ethnic minority groups of Bangladesh are largely concentrated in the geographically inaccessible and/or rural areas and experience different forms of social, political, and economic exclusion. As a consequence of their social identity and geographic exclusion, the overall socioeconomic situation of ethnic minority groups is below the national average. In the

---

[145] Maldives has no caste, ethnic, and/or religious diversity, and Bhutan approaches its diversity through a geographical dimension.

[146] Dalits in Nepal are defined as "those communities who, by virtue of atrocities of caste-based discrimination and untouchability, are most backward in social, economic, educational, political and religious fields, and are deprived of human dignity and social justice." National Dalit Commission. Nepal/Dalits.

districts of the Chittagong Hill Tracts (CHT), where most Bangladeshi ethnic minority groups live, health services, such as antenatal care visits and assistance during delivery and postnatal care by medically trained personnel, were reportedly lower than national figures in 2018. For example, Khagrachhari district in CHT recorded rates of 30% antenatal care visits (compared to 48% nationally) and 7% postnatal care visits (compared to 16% nationally).[147]

137.   Similarly, the immunization coverage in CHT is recorded to be considerably lower than the national average, with full immunization coverage by the age of 12 months at 51% compared to 71% overall in Bangladesh (footnote 147). Although the government has sought to improve the access and use of health services among the ethnic minority groups through targeted health sector policies and programs, those living in remote and rural areas remain underserved.

India

138.   Though the Government of India formally recognizes the disadvantages faced by certain groups because of their social identity, and though various targeted social policies exist for their betterment, these groups continue to face access limitations as historical exclusion and discriminatory social norms remain embedded in the social fabric. This is reflected in the disaggregated health and education data published by the government (Table 5.1).

139.   For the majority of scheduled tribes who live in geographically excluded hamlets, remote regions and districts, and hilly and forested areas,[148] access issues are compounded by rough terrain, high disaster risk and the conflict-prone nature of the geographical areas with high settlements of indigenous peoples. There are 75 tribal groups that have been categorized particularly vulnerable tribal groups by the government, and there are about 25 scheduled tribe groups whose literacy rates range from 0% (Jarawas and Sentinelese scheduled tribe groups in Andaman and Nicobar Islands) to 30% (Gandia, Omanatya, Amanatya in Odisha).[149] The consultation participants said that one of the key barriers to accessing education or a difficulty faced by scheduled tribes in school has been the use of the state's official language (rather than the children's tribal language or mother tongue) as the medium of instruction.

140.   Both scheduled castes and scheduled tribes have many subgroups, and some lag further behind. Some tribal groups, for instance, have specific features, such as dependency on hunting for food, pre-agriculture level of technology, zero or negative growth of population, and extremely low level of literacy. Multiple challenges, such as poverty, illiteracy, unsafe drinking water, poor sanitary, difficult terrain, malnutrition, poor maternal and child health services, unavailable health and nutritional services, and superstition have affected their health status negatively. Diseases like anemia, upper respiratory problems, malaria, acute diarrhea, and micronutrient deficiency are common among them. The status of education is equally bad, with average literacy rates estimated to be about 10% to 44% (footnote 148).

[147] United Nations, Department of Economic and Social Affairs. 2018. *State of the World's Indigenous Peoples: Indigenous Peoples' Access to Health Services.* New York.
[148] T. Benedikter. 2013. *Minority Languages in India: An Appraisal of the Linguistic Rights of Minorities in India.* Bozen/Bolzano: EURASIA-Net.
[149] Government of India, Vikaspedia. Particularly Vulnerable Tribal Groups.

Table 5.1: Health and Education Data of India, Disaggregated by Social Identity Groups
(%)

Indicator	Scheduled Caste	Scheduled Tribe	Total Population
Literacy rate (2011)[a]	66.07 Females: 27.47 Males: 38.60	58.9 Females: 24.6 Males: 34.3	72.9
Pass rate in high school examinations[b]	69.0	62.0	75.0
Dropout rate (primary school, Class One –Five)[c]	1.46	2.83	1.45
Dropout rate (Upper primary school, Class Six to Eight)[c]	3.56	6.03	3.02
Stunting (low height for age) rates among children[d]	42.8	43.8	38.4
Proportion of underweight (low weight for age) children[d]	39.1	45.3	35.8
Wasting (low weight for height) levels in children[d]	21.2	27.4	21.0

[a] Literacy rates were computed from Office of the Registrar General & Census Commissioner, India. 2021. *Census Tables for 2011. C-08 (ST): Educational level by age and sex for population age 7 and above (scheduled tribes); C-08 (SC): Educational level by age and sex for population age 7 and above (scheduled castes)* (accessed 2 March 2023).
[b] For Pass rate in high school examinations: Ministry of Human Resource Development. Bureau of Planning, Monitoring & Statistics. 2012. *Results of High School and Higher Secondary Examinations.* New Delhi. (Accessed 1st May 2023)
[c] For Dropout rate: Ministry of Education. Department of School Education and Literacy. 2021-22. *Dropout Rate by Gender, Level of School Education and Social Category.* (Accessed 1st May 2023)
[d] For health statistics: International Institute for Population Sciences and ICF. 2017. *National Family Health Survey (NFHS-4), 2015–16: India.* Mumbai: International Institute for Population Sciences.

Source: Asian Development Bank (South Asia Department).

141.   The nomadic tribes of India were formally known and notified as "Criminal Tribes of India" by the colonial British rulers as per the Criminal Tribe Act of 1871. In 1952, the Government of India "denotified" them as "criminal tribes." The nomadic and denotified tribes are nomadic and have no permanent settlement in most cases. They lack basic identity proof and, hence, are unable to access government social protection schemes and other social assistance programs. The particularly vulnerable tribal groups are the most vulnerable tribal groups as they still live their primitive lifestyle and are mostly forest dependent.

142.   The pastoral communities are caste groups with unique ethnic cultures, traditions, and specific occupations around livestock rearing. They live in some of the difficult geographic locations like the desert of Rajasthan, kutch (shallow wetland during the rainy season and dry areas during other seasons) in Gujarat, and the Himalayan ranges of Himachal Pradesh. Some pastoral communities belong to other backward classes, and others are nomadic tribes.

143.   The Muslim community had the lowest enrollment rate in higher education in India, accounting for just 4.5% of students in 2015. This increased to 5.2% in 2018–2019.[150] The poor advancement of Muslims is also reflected in health indicators.[151]

[150] Government of India, Ministry of Human Resource Development, Department of Higher Education. 2019. *All India Survey on Higher Education 2018–19.* New Delhi. p. ii.
[151] A. Singh. 2017. *Mounting Discrimination Declining Hope: Dilemma of an Indian Muslim.*

Nepal

144.   In Nepal, health, education, and other socioeconomic outcomes vary greatly based on social identities. As per the latest available disaggregated HDI values in Nepal, among the four major caste and ethnic or religious clusters, the Brahmins and Chhetris had the highest HDI value, followed by the Janajatis, Dalits, and Muslims.[152] The Nepal Social Inclusion Survey has developed a composite index covering 16 indicators. This includes indexes of education, health, access to media, and social security.[153] Dalits, Muslims, Madhesi other backward classes, Madhesi Brahmin and Chhetri, and Tarai Janajati fell far below the national average, and Hill Brahmin, Hill Chhetri, and Newar were much higher than the average. Dalits (both Madhesi and Hill), Muslims, Madhesi other backward classes, and Tarai Janajati were the groups with the lowest indicators across sectors. These groups cover 51 subcaste groups and are close to 40% of Nepal's population.

145.   The reanalyzed data of the Nepal demographic and health survey 2016 showed that Hill Brahmins had the highest literacy rate (76%) followed by Newars (72%). Madhesi Dalits had the lowest literacy rate at 28%, with only 11% of women being literate. The consultation participants assessed that while the government has ensured universal education under the Education for All Program, discriminatory attitudes from peers and faculty at school have limited the impact of this intervention. Of Tarai women, 40% were illiterate or had no formal education, compared to 20% of women in the hills and 36% in the mountains.[154] Non-Nepali mother languages have impacted the Madhesi groups and the mountain, hill and Tarai Janajati groups in their access to education and thus their access to occupation opportunities, especially in the formal sector. Language barriers have also hampered their access to government services and their ability to participate actively in local and national governance. While language barriers impact both Janajati and Madhesi groups, the different subgroups of Janajatis face a deeper disadvantage because of the smaller size of their populations.[155] The consultation participants observed the lack of formal recognition of the education of Muslim children in madrassas (an Islamic place of instruction); hence Muslim children who go to madrassas remain far behind other children in recognized level of educational attainment.

---

[152] Government of Nepal, National Planning Commission and UNDP. 2014. *Nepal Human Development Report 2014: Beyond Geography, Unlocking Human Potential*. Kathmandu. The caste and/or ethnicity disaggregated HDI values are available only as of 2014.

[153] The 16 indicators included in the composite index are as follows: (i) graphic composite index, (ii) Index of education, (iii) Index of health, (iv) index of media, (v) Index of social security, (vi) social composite index, (vii) Index of food and shelter, (viii) Index of access to market, (ix) index of well-being, (x) economic composite index, (xi) governance composite index, (xii) index of linguistic advantage, (xiii) index of nondiscrimination, (xiv) index of sociocultural capital, (xv) gender norms and values composite index, and (xvi) composite social inclusion index. Tribhuvan University, Central Department of Anthropology. 2020. *State of Social Inclusion in Nepal: Caste, Ethnic and Gender: Evidence from Nepal Social Inclusion Survey 2018*. Kathmandu.

[154] Lawyers' Association for Human Rights of Nepalese Indigenous Peoples and the International Work Group for Indigenous Affairs. 2014. *A Study on the Socioeconomic Status of Indigenous Peoples in Nepal*. Kathmandu.

[155] Government of Nepal, National Planning Commission Secretariat, Central Bureau of Statistics. 2014. *Population Monograph of Nepal: Volume III (Economic Demography)*. Kathmandu.

Sri Lanka

146.   In Sri Lanka, access to education of Muslim, Tamil, and Sinhalese children is constrained by the lack of Tamil-speaking teachers and the limited number of Sinhala- and English-speaking teachers, especially in the north and east of the country. After the implementation of the Assisted Schools Act 1960, where the government took over religion-based schools, the emphasis on maintaining a balanced ratio of minority groups in schools has reduced. The consultation participants said that there are also no systems for reserving seats for these groups in schools even though quotas in universities exist.

147.   The plantation economy also broadly conforms to the caste system, and some caste groups have the lowest educational levels, life expectancy, and mortality rates. Alcoholism, domestic violence, poor housing, lack of support in old age, and widespread poverty have added to their social marginalization.[156] The health care system in the estates (plantation) region is poorer than in other regions. According to the survey conducted by a nongovernment organization (NGO) working in these areas, children in estates have low birth weight and remain stunted and underweight compared to those in other regions in the country.[157]

Access to Economic Resources and Services

Bangladesh

148.   The average income of ethnic minority groups is less than the national average (26% less in CHT, 41% less in the plains). People in these areas rely overwhelmingly on the agriculture sector (80% in the plains, 72% in CHT). For certain groups, this reliance is higher (for Santals, Mahato, and Pahan, the reliance on agriculture is as high as 93%). On average, two-thirds of the tribal peoples in the plains are landless.

149.   As a result, the poverty rate for these groups is higher than the national average of 30% (65% in CHT and above 80% in the plains).[158] According to the consultation participants, insecurity over land ownership persists even though the government has put in place policies to safeguard their rights and address land-grabbing problems. Notwithstanding the 1997 Chittagong Hill Tracts Agreement between the ethnic minorities and the government, these groups still experience challenges, such as limited power and functions given to the CHT institutions and difficulty in the preservation of the characteristics of the tribal area in the region and the demilitarization and rehabilitation of the internally displaced. The complexities negatively impacting the land rights of minorities are high, and 70% of claims submitted by minorities remain unsolved. The results have been large-scale land-grabbing by the advantaged people. This has resulted in displacement and migration, loss of livelihood, and threats to the culture of the ethnic minority groups. Forest-dwellers in the plains suffer criminalization of their livelihoods and deprivation of their use of forest commons.[159] Coronavirus disease (COVID-19) has severely

---

[156]   K.T. Silva, P.P. Sivapragasam, and P. Thanges. 2009. Caste Discrimination and Social Justice in Sri Lanka: An Overview. *Indian Institute of Dalit Studies Working Paper Series*. III (6).

[157]   International Movement Against All Forms of Discrimination and Racism. 2016. *Racial Discrimination in Sri Lanka: Submission to 90th Session of the Committee on the Elimination of Racial Discrimination*.

[158]   Government of Bangladesh, Ministry of Health and Family Welfare. 2017. *Framework for Tribal Peoples Plan*. Dhaka.

[159]   A. Hussain. 2019. Ethnic Minorities in Bangladesh and Their Human Rights. *Daily Sun*. 9 April.

impacted the lives and livelihoods of these people. A study of ethnic minorities in the plains showed that about 92% of community members experienced a sharp loss of income because of the pandemic. As a result, the number of ethnic minorities living in extreme poverty cause of deforestation and forest degradation in 2020.[160]

India

150.   A large number of scheduled castes and scheduled tribes reside in the rural areas and are heavily dependent on the agriculture sector (including livestock and forest products), making them vulnerable to economic shocks. They are mainly landless families who work for wages in the fields of landlords. Census 2011 data showed that about 80% of scheduled tribes work in the agriculture sector. Their dependence on shifting cultivation and its ban (as the practice was considered largely harmful for forests) left the scheduled tribes vulnerable to poverty, unemployment, and misery. With their traditional occupations sometimes declared illegal (e.g., hunting and living on forest products), some subgroups of scheduled tribes live on the margins of society in dire poverty, surviving by doing simple income-generating activities. In 2011-12, below-poverty-line scheduled tribes were 45% in rural and 24% in urban areas.[161] The Forest Rights Act, 2006 provides ownership and land-use rights to the scheduled tribes over forests, but the state has the right to define the forest areas as a village or reserved forest.[162]

151.   Scheduled castes also face occupation-based discrimination and have been associated with certain jobs, such as cleaning washrooms, sewer cleaning, and skinning dead cattle, because of caste-based norms. According to data by the Ministry of Social Justice and Empowerment, the government has caste-related data of 43,797 identified manual scavengers, and more than 42,500 of them are members of scheduled castes.[163] Also, caste untouchability restricts and makes the entry of scheduled castes into some occupations difficult, e.g., grocery stores, government food security centers, or *aganwadi* (rural child care center).

152.   Moreover, many tribal communities practice seasonal migration for 6 to 8 months, with a high rate of distress migration, particularly in unorganized or informal sectors (e.g., as laborers in the agriculture and construction industries) given the very poor working and living conditions.

153.   Also in India, communities categorized as nomadic and denotified tribes, though formally denotified as "criminal tribes" by the Government of India in 1952, continue to experience stigma, harassment, severe marginalization, and loss of traditional occupations because of their historical identity as criminal castes. As described in the 2017 report of the National Commission for Denotified, Nomadic, and Semi-Nomadic Tribes, "the De-notified Nomadic and Semi-Nomadic Tribes are the most neglected, marginalized, and economically and socially deprived communities. These communities differ greatly on the scale of deprivation.

[160] S. Drong. *Indigenous Workers Face Unemployment and Destitution in the Wake of the Pandemic.* Minority Rights.
[161] Press Information Bureau. Government of India, Ministry of Tribal Affairs. 2021. *There have been considerable improvements in quality of life of Scheduled Tribes over the years.* Delhi.
[162] S. Kumar. 2020. Forest Rights Act Enables State Control of Land and Denies Most Adivasis and Forest Dwellers Land Rights. *EPW Engage.* 55 (6).
[163] S. Sengar. 2021. Over 42,500 Are SC Out Of 43,797 Identified Manual Scavengers: Govt Data on Banned Practice. *Indiatimes.* 2 December.

Most of them have been living a life of destitution for generations and still continue to do so with uncertain and gloomy future... Haunted by all — from common mosses to law enforcers—they lead a precarious existence, bereft of the rights that are bestowed upon the legitimate citizens of the nation."[164]

Nepal

154.   In Nepali society, the caste hierarchy, as a sociocultural construction, broadly corresponds to the economic positions or class locations of various caste groups. People belonging to the Dalit caste tend to be poor because of their relatively low access to land, opportunities, and resources as compared to those belonging to other caste groups.[165]

155.   Traditional occupations of Dalits are considered low status, and they are deprived of proper remuneration or wages. In the assessment of the consultation participants, the monthly social security allowances allocated for the Dalits in Nepal are nominal. Dalits continue to experience discrimination, with any seeming attempts at upward social mobility violently shut down.[166] A significant number of Dalit families continue to live below the poverty line, indicating that they continue to face barriers in accessing public resources. Reanalyzed data from the 2011 Nepal living standards survey and the 2016 Nepal demographic and health survey showed that the highest per capita income of NRs63,234 ($492.98) was for Hill Brahmins, while the lowest per capita income of NRs24,241 ($188.98) was for Madhesi Dalits and NRs25,404 ($198.05) for Hill Dalits.[167] Within the Tharu community (Tharu people are an ethnic group, a subgroup of Adivasi Janajati, living in the Tarai of South Nepal), the primary economic activity is agriculture. Poor levels of education because of language barriers have prevented the majority of the community from engaging in other economic opportunities.[168]

Sri Lanka

156.   In Sri Lanka, certain caste groups face social pressure to pursue hereditary caste-based occupations (such as sanitation work). Despite marginal improvements, these groups continue to experience low educational achievements, extreme poverty, overcrowding, and poor asset ownership (footnote 157).

157.   Settlements in Sri Lanka can be found in three major sectors: urban, rural and estate. The estate sector covers the areas around tea and coffee plantations that are largely inhabited by Tamil descendants of workers brought from southern India during the 19th century. Although

[164] Government of India, Ministry of Social Justice and Empowerment. 2017. *National Commission for Denotified, Nomadic, and Semi-Nomadic Tribes: December 2017 Report*. New Delhi. p. 3.
[165] International Labour Organization in Nepal. 2005. *Dalits and Labour in Nepal: Discrimination and Forced Labour*. Kathmandu.
[166] *UN News*. 2020. More "Can and Must be Done" to Eradicate Caste-based Discrimination in Nepal. 29 May.
[167] World Bank Group Nepal. Reanalysis of Nepal Living Standards Survey 2011 Data for Country Level Gender Equality and Social Inclusion Assessment. Unpublished.
[168] C. Castillejo. 2017. *Ethnic and Indigenous Groups in Nepal's Peacebuilding Processes*. Oslo: Norwegian Centre for Conflict Resolution.

the estate sector houses only 4.4% of the population nationally, this percentage goes as high as 18.9% in Central Province and 12.8% in Uva Province.[169] The socioeconomic status of people in the estate sector is considerably lower than that in the urban or rural sectors because of low levels of education, poor decision-making skills, and poor infrastructure.[170]Asset ownership rates in the estate sector, for example, remain well below the national average. Furthermore, more than 60% of the estate population falls in the bottom 40% of the national per capita consumption distribution, making a large portion of the Estate sector vulnerable to poverty.[171] The right to housing is a serious problem faced by the plantation community. According to the household income and expenditure survey conducted in 2009–2010, 56% of the plantation workers lived in dilapidated "line rooms" (housing with space needs of one person).[172] According to the Center for Poverty Analysis, this figure was 57% in 2015 (footnote 157).

158.   The consultation participants described the minority religious groups as mostly belonging to poor communities, indicating the need for support with respect to employment and livelihood opportunities. Ethnic minorities remain underrepresented in public sector employment in comparison to their proportion in the population, including national schools and divisional secretariats, and administrative subunits. Up-Country Tamils constitute 0.31%, Muslims constitute 3.29%, and North-Eastern Tamils constitute 5.26% of state sector employees (employees of the national government (and its agencies), and their representation in the provincial public sector (in provincial governments (and their agencies) is only slightly better, where Up-Country Tamils constitute almost 2%, Muslims 6%, while North-Eastern Tamils 14% (footnote 157).

Social Practices, Participation, and Decision-Making

Bangladesh

159.   There exists a low administrative representation of ethnic minority groups in Bangladesh, and the Constitution does not acknowledge any special political arrangements for them. As a result, small ethnic minority communities, particularly those who are from the plains, have limited political participation. In the union *parishad* (rural council) elections of 2016, no chairperson from the plain communities was elected.[173] The consultation participants highlighted the need for the government and donors and development partners to deeply engage the ethnic minority groups in decision-making processes about policies and programs affecting them. They also highlighted that implementation gaps and lack of disaggregated data and geographical mapping had been the primary obstacles in ensuring proportionate budgetary allocations for the different ethnic minority groups.

---

[169] ADB. 2016. *Sri Lanka: Gender Equality Diagnostic of Selected Sectors.* Manila.
[170] S. Dharmadasa and P.W.T.P. Polkotuwa. 2016. Income Diversification of Estate Sector in Sri Lanka. *Journal of Business Studies.* 3 (2). pp. 27–39.
[171] D.L. Newhouse, P.S. Becerra, and D. Doan. 2016. *Sri Lanka. Poverty and Welfare: Recent Progress and Remaining Challenges.* Washington, DC: World Bank. p. 18
[172] Government of Sri Lanka, Department of Census and Statistics. 2010. *Household Income and Expenditure Survey: 2009/10 Preliminary Report.* Battaramulla, Sri Lanka. p. 40.
[173] Kapaeeng Foundation. 2017. *Joint Submission to the United Nations Human Rights Committee.* Dhaka.

160.   Religious minorities have experienced discrimination and segregation, despite the constitution emphasizing the equality of all faiths and the secularity of the state. The main discriminatory patterns identified are criticism of rituals and practices, verbal harassment, poor services, exploitation of labor and money, verbal threats, physical attack, obstruction of festival celebrations, and land dispossession.[174]

India

161.   Although the attitudes toward the scheduled castes and scheduled tribes are changing, discriminations persist through identity-based occupations (e.g., cleaning, sweeping, sanitation work, removal of animal carcasses, agricultural labor); social practices (e.g., low acceptance for intercaste relationships and marriage); and use of public facilities (e.g., educational institutes). For scheduled tribes, the traditional patterns of tribal life with their beliefs and customs are, at times, not accepted by the dominant population groups, resulting in a gradual erosion of their tribal identity.[175]

162.   The 73rd amendment of the Indian Constitution stipulates the reservation of seats for women in general, including those from scheduled castes, scheduled tribes, and other backward class communities, in the *panchayat raj* (local self-government body in India) proportionate to their population.

163.   International principles and standards on social identity groups, such as nondiscrimination and equality, and the right of minorities to enjoy their own culture, practice their religion, use their language, and exercise each of their economic, social, and cultural rights without prejudice, are yet to be fully internalized, according to some agencies devoted to the issues of social identity groups.[176] Related to this concern, the consultation participants highlighted the need to enhance understanding, knowledge, and sensitivity to caste-related issues by including courses on caste sensitivity in educational institutions.

Nepal

164.   Caste-based Discrimination and Untouchability (Offense and Punishment) Act 2068 (2011) and subsequent amendments have been implemented in Nepal to address the caste-based discrimination and "untouchability" practices within Nepali society. However, in the assessment of the consultation participants, such practices persist as mindsets that are difficult to change.

165.   Caste-based discrimination results in Dalits, who comprise 13.8% of Nepal's population, experiencing restrictions on the use of public amenities, deprivation of economic opportunities, and general neglect by the state and society. They are deprived of human dignity and discriminated against in religious and cultural spheres (footnote 168). They lack access to meaningful representation in leadership, ownership, and decision-making positions, with mere

[174] Minority Rights Group International. World Directory of Minorities and Indigenous Peoples—Bangladesh: Hindus.
[175] V. R. Lobo. 2015. *Koragas' Status and Development – A Study*. Chennai. Chapter 1.
[176] Evangelical Fellowship of India. 2017. *Religious Minorities in India: Targeted Hate and Violence by Non State Actors, and Issues of Impunity.*

8% representation in the Parliament.[177] The consultation participants assessed that the lack of awareness within the Dalit community regarding their rights prevents them from accessing the various economic and social uplifting-related opportunities provided by the government. They further said that while there has been some progress in recent years, major challenges remain, especially in combating impunity, building national institutions, and delivering justice in a timely manner in line with international standards.

166.   The consultation participants highlighted the need to enhance the understanding of non-Madhesi people about the concerns of the Madhesi community. Additionally, they said that while most development projects focus on physical infrastructure and access, it is the development of the language, culture, lifestyle, traditions, skills, and knowledge in herbal medicine within the Adivasi Janajati community that is also crucial for their inclusion.

Sri Lanka

167.   Religion plays a significant role in daily life in Sri Lanka and strongly correlates with ethnicity—most Sinhalese are Buddhist, and most Tamils are Hindu. The Constitution of Sri Lanka grants Buddhism a "foremost place" and obligates the state to "protect and foster" Buddhism. The Christian community (covering various denominations) encompasses both Sinhalese and Tamil ethnic groups.

168.   Evangelical Christians have been regarded with suspicion and a threat to Buddhism and Sinhala culture. Harassment, threats, intimidation, and discrimination against Evangelical Christians have persisted for decades, with restrictions on Christian places of worship as illegal or unauthorized.[178]

169.   Incidents of violence in 2018, which involved intimidation, including physical and verbal threats against pastors and their congregations, disruption of worship services, and demands for the closure of churches, reflected the underlying tensions in the society. Christians and Muslims have been the target of hate campaigns and violence. Christian churches and Muslim religious places have been attacked since the beginning of the civil war in 1983.[179] The Wanniyala-Aetto ("forest dwellers" or indigenous people living in the tropical forest) continue to face discrimination and harassment, forced relocation, and marginalization. As the Wanniyala-Aetto people have lost connections to their ancestral lands and links with their cultural and spiritual traditions, they have experienced high rates of alcoholism and mental illness.[180]

177   B. Paswan. 2018. Dalits and Women the Most Under-Represented in Parliament. *The Record.* 3 March.
178   Minority Rights Group International. World Directory of Minorities and Indigenous Peoples: Sri Lankan Christians.
179   M.A. Yusoff and A. Sarjoon. 2019. Post-War Religious Violence, Counter-State Response and Religious Harmony in Sri Lanka. *Journal of Educational and Social Research.* 9 (3). pp. 211–223.
180   Minority Rights Groups International. World Directory of Minorities and Indigenous Peoples: Sri Lanka Wanniyala-Aetto (Veddhas).

Intersectionality

170.   Women from disadvantaged social identity groups represent one of the most vulnerable groups facing the highest forms of exclusion and discrimination in most of the six DMCs. For example, women from ethnic minority communities in Bangladesh are highly susceptible to violence. Moreover, malnutrition, anemia, and malaria are the common diseases in the hills where ethnic minority groups live. In almost every sphere of political and public life of the country, these women are excluded from important decision-making roles and positions. For example, in the *upazila parishad* (subdistrict council) elections in 2014 and *pourashava* (municipality) elections held in 2015, the performance of women from ethnic groups was remarkably poor.[181]

171.   In India, scheduled caste women and girls experience intersecting discriminations based on caste, class, and gender. Common forms of violence against the majority of scheduled caste women are verbal abuse (62% of total women), physical assault (55%), sexual harassment and assault (47%), domestic violence (43%), and rape (23%).[182] In the labor market, inequalities based on social identities are compounded further by gender. According to the National Sample Survey 2011–2012, rural women comprised 35% of casual laborers, of whom scheduled caste women constituted 51%, and scheduled tribe women 39%.[183] The average wages per day of scheduled caste women was ₹90 ($1.11) per day, while women of the category called "other" earned on an average around ₹251 ($3.01) per day.[184] Like other women, a majority of scheduled caste women were not eligible for paid leave because of the contractual nature of their employment.[185]

172.   In Nepal, women, especially of disadvantaged groups like the Madhesi, experience problems in land ownership, citizenship, and a lack of independence in going out to participate in the job market. The consultation participants said that Dalit women are forced into demeaning jobs; are extremely vulnerable to sexual exploitation; and are often victims of trafficking, gender-based violence (GBV), and forced sexual labor. The national index of empowerment and inclusion suggests Dalit women are the most marginalized—worse off than Dalit men. Within the Dalit communities, the women of the Badi group in Karnali province face a greater degree of exclusion and are largely looked down upon as sex workers.[186] Madhesi Dalit women endure additional forms of exclusion based on lingual, identity, and regional disparities. Caste-based discrimination also affects Dalit women's access to education, health care, and other services for overcoming poverty.[187] Women from several communities, especially Muslim communities, require the permission or approval of male members to participate in different programs such as savings and credit programs, training in different events. There are 40% women representatives at the local level as part of the affirmative action in the Constitution of Nepal, but the affirmative action does not include Janajati or Muslim women or Madhesi women. The consultation participants added that women Dalit leaders who have been elected are at times seen as token representatives and are unable to make meaningful contributions to uplift the community.

[181]   International Work Group for Indigenous Affairs. Indigenous peoples in Bangladesh.
[182]   A. Irudayam s.j., J.P. Mangubhai, and J.G. Lee. 2006. *Dalit Women Speak Out: Violence Against Dalit Women in India.* New Delhi: National Campaign on Dalit Human Rights.
[183]   Oxfam India. 2019. *Mind The Gap: The State of Employment in India.* New Delhi.
[184]   All India Dalit Mahila Adhikar Manch–National Campaign on Dalit Human Rights. 2018. *Voices Against Caste Impunity; Narratives of Dalit Women in India.* New Delhi.
[185]   S. Menon, D. Tomy, and A. Kumar. *Female Work and Labour Force Participation in India: A Meta-Study.* New Delhi: Sattva Consulting and UNDP.
[186]   International Dalit Solidarity Network. Dalit Women in Nepal.
[187]   Feminist Dalit Organization and International Dalit Solidarity Network. 2018. *Report of Dalit Women of Nepal on CEDAW Convention: Review of Nepal—71st Session.* Kathmandu, London, Geneva.

173.   In Sri Lanka, women of different communities experience multiple levels of exclusion from their own and other communities. Muslim women are the least educated among the women of Sri Lanka and the most reluctant to enter the workforce, as religious and cultural prejudices constrain them from participating in the public domain. Customary laws, such as Kandyan law for the Kingdom of Kandy, Thesavalma, and Muslim law are followed by different groups of Sri Lankans for issues such as marriage, adoption, transfer of property, and inheritance. These laws usually impact women negatively as they include ethnic, caste, class, and gender discriminatory aspects, such as the regulations under the Muslim Marriages and Divorce Act (1975), and property laws within the Hindu community, which have led to women from these communities facing added barriers. There have also been underreported instances of violence against women belonging to religious minority groups. Further, minority religious groups mostly belong to poor communities and, since after the civil war, various incidents of violence against them have been reported.[188]

C.   Policy Analysis

174.   The four SARD DMCs covered in this section have various acts and policies to promote and protect the rights and welfare of their various ethnic, tribal, and caste minorities (Table 5.2). However, while most countries have acts and policies to promote and protect the rights of these groups, no country has yet completely or to a large extent addressed the intersectional barriers they face.

Table 5.2: Acts and Policies for Social Identity Groups

DMC	Policies
Bangladesh	Small Ethnic Communities Cultural Institutions Act, 2010
	Christian Religious Welfare Trust (Amendment) Act, 2018
	Framework for Tribal Peoples Plan, 2015
India	The Protection of Civil Rights Act, 1955
	National Commission for Backward Classes Act, 1993 National Commission for Schedule Caste, 2004 National Commission for Schedule Tribe, 2004 National Commission for Minority, 1993
	The Scheduled Castes and the Scheduled Tribes (Prevention of Atrocities) Act, 1989
Nepal	Caste Based Discrimination and Untouchability (Offence and Punishment) Act, 2011
	Tribal Peoples' Commission Act, 2017
Sri Lanka	Prevention of Social Disabilities Act, 1957

DMC = developing member country.
Source: Extracted from the six DMCs' policy documents.

175.   In India, the constitutional provision for scheduled castes and scheduled tribes requires the allocation of proportional budget across ministries. Hence, there are various commissions and statutory bodies under the Ministry of Social Justice and Empowerment and the Ministry

---

[188]   UN Human Rights Treaty Bodies. 2016. Critical Issues and Questions to be Raised with the Sri Lankan Government at CEDAW Constructive Dialogue, Joint Submission by the Women's Action Network and its Member Organisations.

of Tribal Affairs that support scheduled castes, scheduled tribes, and other backward classes or minorities. The Ministry of Tribal Affairs administers the scheme for the Development of Vulnerable Tribal Groups for their comprehensive socioeconomic development. The scheme covers 75 identified particularly vulnerable tribal groups in 18 states and the union territory of Andaman and Nicobar Islands.[189] The government also implements the Pradhan Mantri Awas Yojana (PMAY), which aims to provide housing for all by 2024. The PMAY has two components: (i) PMAY Gramin, or (ii) PMAY rural and PMAY urban. Among the targeted beneficiaries of PMAY Gramin are scheduled castes, scheduled tribes, minorities, and tribals who cannot afford a housing unit.[190] The National Backward Classes Finance and Development Corporation provides a wide range of income-generating activities, and the National Scheduled Tribes Finance and Development Corporation plays a leading role in the economic development of scheduled tribes by providing financial assistance at concessional rates of interest. This corporation also has an exclusive scheme for the economic development of scheduled tribe women. The Ministry of Minority Affairs works to ensure a more focused approach toward religious minorities in India and have addressed intersectionality in policies. Most of the policies are targeted at economically weak sections, and provisions have been made for women as well. Some of these schemes are Pradhan Mantri Jan Vikas Karyakram (Prime Minister's Peoples' Development Program); the Pre-matric, Post-Matric and Merit-cum-Means Based Scholarship Schemes; the Credit Enhancement Guarantee Scheme for Scheduled Castes and Scheduled Tribes; housing schemes; and other poverty reduction programs.[191]

176.   The consultation participants highlighted some barriers and implementation issues in Bangladesh, Nepal, and Sri Lanka. In Bangladesh, a major concern was the limited policies at the national level for the ethnic minority groups in the plains. In Nepal, there are acts in the Constitution of Nepal citing caste-based discrimination and untouchability as a crime. Although a Dalit commission has been formed, discrimination against these groups continues. In Sri Lanka, to address the issues faced by the community, the Department of Muslim Religious and Cultural Affairs focuses on getting different segments of the community to work together and eliminate internal conflicts and construct a mechanism for the preservation, promotion, and development upliftment of Muslims. Interventions include conducting situational analysis; identifying strengths, weaknesses, opportunities, and threats experienced by the community; and creating an understanding among communities through interfaith leadership programs. According to the consultation participants, despite these efforts, Muslims, especially women, experience discriminatory practices, GBV, and sexual assault.

---

[189] Government of India, Ministry of Tribal Affairs, Press Information Bureau. 2019. Welfare of Particularly Vulnerable Tribal Groups. News release. 4 July.

[190] Government of India. Pradhan Mantri Awas Yojana - Gramin (PMAY-G).

[191] Pradhan Mantri Jan Vikas Karyakram is designed to address the development deficits of the identified Minority Concentration Areas by supporting the states and/or union territories in creating infrastructure to improve the quality of life of the people and reduce societal imbalances. Government of India. National Portal of India. Pradhan Mantri Jan Vikas Karyakram. The Merit-cum-Means Scholarship Scheme provides financial assistance to poor and meritorious students belonging to minority communities to enable them to pursue professional and technical courses. Press Information Bureau, Ministry of Minority Affairs. Scholarship Scheme for Minority Communities. The Credit Enhancement Guarantee Scheme for Scheduled Castes aims to encourage and promote entrepreneurship among the scheduled castes who are oriented toward innovations and growth technologies by supporting banks in the form of a credit enhancement guarantee (minimum ₹1,500,000 and maximum ₹50,000,000) against products such as working capital loans. Government of India, Ministry of Social Justice and Empowerment. Credit Enhancement Guarantee Scheme for Scheduled Castes.

D.   South Asia Department Projects Aiming to Benefit Disadvantaged Social Identity Groups

177.   This section presents an assessment of the extent to which 13 selected projects in four DMCs (Bangladesh, India, Nepal, and Sri Lanka) integrated actions that respond to the social inclusion needs and issues of disadvantaged social identity groups. Similar to the previous chapters, the assessment looked at actions in four areas: (i) policies that seek to understand and address the issues of disadvantaged social identity groups, (i) institutional arrangements that locate responsibilities for ensuring the achievement of GESI targets focused on them, (iii) programming and budgeting directed at supporting these groups, and (iv) a monitoring and evaluation system that captures and reports project GESI results experienced by disadvantaged social identity groups.

178.   Overall, the assessment results in four areas are as follows:

    (i)   **Policies**
        (a)   Six (one each from Bangladesh, India, and Sri Lanka, and three from Nepal) of 13 projects (in all three covered sectors—energy, transport, and water and other urban infrastructure and services) collected disaggregated data on the social identity groups and evidence on the causes of their exclusion and stakeholders' responses.
        (b)   Some projects (in all three covered sectors) had policy provisions addressing the barriers to GESI experienced by disadvantaged social identity groups. Examples of these policy provisions are identifying women-headed and other vulnerable households; providing them with water supply connections; and promoting the participation of women and those from poor and excluded groups in training, awareness building, and bioengineering-related activities, among others. The **Bangladesh Power System Enhancement and Efficiency Improvement Project** (footnote 83) included the preparation of a socioeconomic profile by gender and ethnic minority and proposed specific actions to benefit vulnerable indigenous peoples and minorities.

    (ii)   **Institutional arrangements**
        (a)   Some projects (in the energy and water and other urban infrastructure and services sectors) had institutional arrangements to ensure the implementation and achievement of targets addressing the issues of social identity groups.
        (b)   Some projects (in the energy and water and other urban infrastructure and services sectors) included responsibilities for implementing and supervising actions targeting social identity groups in the functions and terms of reference of the executing agency and implementing agency project team.

    (iii)   **Programming and budgeting**
        (a)   Some projects (in the three covered sectors) included activities specifically intended for disadvantaged social identity groups and aimed at establishing an enabling environment for GESI. Examples of these activities are orientation and sensitization of all project stakeholders on undertaking

environmental management; promoting inclusive and gender-sensitive community awareness; enjoining contractors to employ poor women, vulnerable groups, affected people, and indigenous peoples; ensuring equal pay for work of equal value; and promoting occupational health and safety, and proper water supply and sanitation facilities.

(b) However, no projects had human resource or personnel policies[192] to ensure the provision of facilities supporting the inclusion of social identity groups and activities to transform discriminatory social and gender norms impacting the members of disadvantaged social identity groups.

(iv) **Monitoring and evaluation.** Some projects (in the water and other urban infrastructure and services sector) had monitoring and evaluation systems and reporting templates that captured and reported project GESI results that benefited the disadvantaged social identity groups.

E.   Good Practices in Responding to Disadvantaged Social Identity Issues

179.   The assessment of the second set of 15 projects of SARD (the same projects referred to in Chapter 3 on older people and Chapter 4 on disability) identified the following good practices in responding to the GESI issues of disadvantaged social identity groups.

(i) The **Second Chittagong Hill Tracts Rural Development Project** in Bangladesh[193] involved ethnic groups, including women, in the identification of the best location of the small feeder roads or paths that would improve people's access to basic services, markets, and educational and religious institutions, and would create opportunities for communication with other villages. They were also involved in the identification of community structures, such as a small footbridge, irrigation drainage, and stairs, to be constructed under the project. The project also held gender awareness training for the indigenous village heads.

(ii) The **Third Small Towns Water Supply and Sanitation Sector Project** in Nepal (footnote 79) collected data disaggregated by indigenous group and gender. The project aimed to provide the socially excluded groups with access to proper sanitation and safe drinking water.

180.   During the stakeholder consultations, the participants shared their respective organizations' initiatives related to the disadvantaged social identity groups in their countries. Examples of these initiatives—grouped into the three pillars of the "Leave-No-One-Behind" (LNOB) framework—are as follows (definitions of these three pillars are in Chapter 1, paras. 9 and 11 and Table 1. 1):

---

[192] Human resource or personnel policies refer to policies that provide facilities for gender-specific responsibilities and support for specific interest groups (e.g., childcare; breastfeeding facilities; flexible timings; and facilities for people with disabilities, older people, and social identity groups).

[193] ADB. Bangladesh: Second Chittagong Hill Tracts Rural Development Project.

(i) **Understand for action.** The India Institute of Dalit Studies conducts studies on the socioeconomic status of Dalits and scheduled caste communities; discrimination and social exclusion in India; and impacts of government policies on the scheduled castes, scheduled tribes, and others. In these studies, they include gender as an indicator.

(ii) **Empower for change**

    (a) The Bangladesh Indigenous People's Forum and Kapaeeng Foundation in Bangladesh assist indigenous communities by developing their capacity to promote and protect their rights.

    (b) The Asia Foundation supported the formation and operations of 36 Dalit youth committees in Bangladesh. These committees helped people in their communities to register for the COVID-19 vaccination program.

    (c) Darbar Sahitya Sansad in India formed Dalit women into self-help groups to start making small savings, link them with local banks, and develop them as community leaders.

    (d) Action for Social Advancement in India works for the welfare of poor tribal groups (scheduled castes and scheduled tribes) and other marginal communities. They provided shallow bore wells and dug wells, which increased farmers' income, and gave trainings on organic farming, water management, fishery, and livestock management to enhance their livelihoods.

    (e) The Feminist Dalit Organization in Nepal organizes and empowers Dalit women to fight for their rights, access different schemes, strengthen their voice, and reduce discrimination.

    (f) The Dalit NGO Federation provides a common forum for raising the collective voice of the Dalit community and ensuring their rights, dignity, and opportunity through policy influencing, networking, and alliance building.

(iii) **Include for opportunity.** The National Christian Evangelical Alliance of Sri Lanka uses technology to change mindsets (e.g., a virtual museum to trace events that have impacted religious freedom in the country, and an e-learning platform) and educate people about religious extremism.

F.　Conclusions and Way Forward

Summary of Findings

181.　The most disadvantaged people in the six member countries of ADB in South Asia can be found among the excluded and vulnerable caste, ethnic, and religious groups. Not only are they largely concentrated in geographically inaccessible areas, but they also experience different forms of social, political, and economic exclusion. As a result, they have the least access to resources and services and are least regarded in society because of discriminatory social norms and stereotypes. Among the members of these groups, the most disadvantaged are women and children.

182.　However, there are positive initiatives being undertaken in local communities to address their social exclusion issues. The four countries covered in this assessment (Bangladesh, India, Nepal, and Sri Lanka) have laws and policies that promote and protect the rights of social identity groups.

183.   While SARD has only a few projects addressing the social exclusion of disadvantaged social identity groups, these projects can be sources of lessons. In addition, the government and civil society organizations (CSOs) that work on the issues of disadvantaged social identity groups, including those who participated in the consultations and willingly shared their initiatives, are GESI champions from whom SARD can draw further lessons, particularly in relation to the three pillars of the LNOB framework.

Way Forward for the South Asia Department

184.   During the stakeholder consultations, the participants articulated the following possible courses of action for SARD:

(i)   **Understand for action**
   (a)   Support the collection of statistical data on excluded and vulnerable caste and ethnic groups in the DMCs, with the active participation of their organizations.
   (b)   Conduct a deep dive analysis of policies, programs, and practices of the government, CSOs, and private sector related to the disadvantaged social identity groups; seek to understand and support the aspirations of the social identity groups.

(iii)   **Empower for change**
   (a)   In the construction and rehabilitation of infrastructure and technologies, involve the social identity groups as local workers; during project design and implementation, ensure the inclusiveness of these infrastructures and technologies.
   (b)   Support the strengthening of the capability of CSOs, including social identity-based organizations, to complement the government's efforts to promote GESI. Invest in programs for the improvement of community capital and cohesion of disadvantaged social identity groups.
   (c)   Assist initiatives that aim to enable the disadvantaged social identity groups to have meaningful political representation and participation in all levels of government.
   (d)   Ensure that assisted programs and projects are results oriented, and disadvantaged social identity groups are beneficiaries and active players.
   (e)   Support programs for their social and economic development; provide assistance to those with entrepreneurial interests and potential.

(iii)   **Include for opportunity**
   (a)   Support the development of a school curriculum that aims to build a positive image of Dalits and other minority groups and to raise awareness about their rights and dignity.
   (b)   Support collaborative approaches (involving ADB, governments, CSOs, and private or business organizations) to address the GESI issues of disadvantaged social identity groups.

VI. DIVERSE SEXUAL ORIENTATION, GENDER IDENTITY AND EXPRESSION, AND SEX CHARACTERISTICS IN SOUTH ASIA: ISSUES AND RESPONSES

A.   Introduction: Definitions

185.   People with diverse sexual orientation, gender identity and expression, and sex characteristics (SOGIESC) include those attracted to people of the same sex (homosexual) or both (bisexual) or who fall outside the male-female biological binary (intersex individuals) and whose gender identity and expression differ from the sex designated at birth or who exhibit nonbinary gender expressions (transgender men and women).[194]

186.   The South Asia Department (SARD) developing member countries (DMCs) have varying definitions of these sexual and gender identities. The term "gender and sexual minorities" is used in the Constitution of Nepal. The Supreme Court of Nepal has mandated the addition

---

[194]   SOGIESC is a set of general categorizations applicable to all people as all people have a sexual orientation, gender identity, gender expression, and sex characteristics. Sexual orientation refers to a person's physical, romantic, and/ or emotional attraction toward other people. Gay men and lesbians are attracted to individuals of the same (as their own) sex. Heterosexual people are attracted to individuals of different (from their own) sex. Bisexual people may be attracted to individuals of the same or different sex. Gender identity reflects a deeply felt and experienced sense of one's own gender. A person's gender identity can be aligned with the sex assigned to them at birth or not. Transgender is an umbrella term for people whose gender identity and/or expression is different from cultural expectations based on the sex they were assigned at birth. Trans women identify as women but were classified as males when they were born; trans men identify as men but were classified as females when they were born; and other transgender people do not identify with the binary gender identities at all. Intersex people are born with physical or biological sex characteristics (e.g., sexual anatomy, reproductive organs, hormonal patterns, and/ or chromosomal patterns) of both males and females. Gender expression is one's demonstration (e.g., behavior, dress, and social interaction) of gender identity (one's view of self as woman, man, or queer), either as dominantly masculine or dominantly feminine or a combination of masculine and feminine traits. A person's gender expression is not always linked to the person's biological sex, gender identity, or sexual orientation. Adapted from UN Free and Equal. Definitions; and M.V.L. Badgett and R. Sel. 2018. *A Set of Proposed Indicators for the LGBTI Inclusion Index.* New York: UNDP.

of the category *anya* (other) representing non-cisgender or transgender identities[195] in all official documents, and for Nepalese identifying as such to be given citizenship documents reflecting their SOGIESC.[196] In Bangladesh, in 2013, the Cabinet made a landmark decision to reflect the presence of *hijras* (transgender persons) in national identification documents and censuses, which was the first step to the legal recognition of *hijras*.[197] On 26 January 2014, the Government of Bangladesh announced the recognition of the "third gender" by publishing the following statement: "The Government of Bangladesh has recognized the hijra of Bangladesh as a Hijra sex."[198] However, despite the progressive policy action, the lack of clear guidelines on the qualifying characteristics of the third gender has resulted in ambiguity in understanding *hijras*. In India, in April 2014, the Supreme Court of India formally recognized the existence of the "third gender," affirming that the fundamental rights granted under the Constitution of India are equally applicable to them and giving them the right to self-identification as male, female, or third gender.[199] There are no formal definitions for this group in Bhutan and Sri Lanka. In Bangladesh, Maldives, and Sri Lanka, there are laws that punish same-sex sexual activities. Despite the existence of supportive laws, not one country in the region has ample legal framework to protect people with diverse SOGIESC (Table 1.10).

B.   Status of People with Diverse Sexual Orientation and Gender Identity and Expression in the Six South Asia Department Developing Member Countries

Demography

187.   In Bangladesh, estimates put the number of *hijras* at 10,000 to 500,000.[200] In Bhutan, 316 people were registered as people with diverse SOGIESC in 2019.[201] In India, 0.04% of the population was recorded as third or "other" gender in the census of 2011.[202] In Nepal, the 2021 census reported 2,928 individuals (0.01% of the population) identifying their gender identity as "other."[203] No official estimates are available for Maldives and Sri Lanka where same-sex sexual activities are punishable by law (Box 6. 1 and notes 2 and 3 of Table 1.10). Globally, the United Nations (UN) Office of the High Commissioner for Human Rights provides reliable estimates on the size of the global intersex population: 0.7%–1.7% of the entire population is born with intersex traits.[204]

---

[195] Cisgender individuals refer to those whose gender identity corresponds to their sex assigned at birth. Adapted from UN Free and Equal. Definitions.
[196] M. Bochenek and K. Knight. 2012. Establishing a Third Gender Category in Nepal: Process and Prognosis. *Emory International Law Review.* 26 (1). pp. 11–41.
[197] *Bdnews24.com.* 2013. "Third gender" gets state recognition. 11 November.
[198] Climate and Development Knowledge Network. 2020. Bangladesh: Radical Change Needed to Ensure Justice for Hijra Communities. 16 November.
[199] Human Rights Law Centre. 2014. Indian Supreme Court recognises third gender. 15 April.
[200] S. Chowdhury. 2020. Transgender in Bangladesh: First school opens for trans students. *BBC.* 6 November.
[201] *Kuensel.* 2019. Feeling recognised and included. 15 June.
[202] Government of India, Ministry of Social Justice and Welfare. Draft Transgender People (Protection of Rights) Rules, 2020. New Delhi.
[203] In Nepal, the legal term used for people with diverse SOGIESC is "other," which means not male or female. National Statistics Office. National Population and Housing Census 2021: National Report.
[204] UN Office of the High Commissioner for Human Rights. Intersex People: OHCHR and the Human Rights of LGBTI People.

Box 6. 1: Legal Status of People with diverse Sexual Orientation, Gender Identity and Expression, and Sex Characteristics in South Asia Department Developing Member Countries

The legal framework for people with different sexual and gender identities varies in the six countries. Nepal has recognized the rights of sexual and gender minorities in its constitution, included them in the census of 2011, and included a third gender category in official documents. India included the third gender option in passports in 2005, in the census of 2011, in voter identity cards in 2013, and ration cards in 2015. It decriminalized same-sex relations in 2019. In 2019, Bhutan's Parliament approved the amendment of the penal code, removing the sections that made same-sex sexual activities punishable by law.

In Bangladesh, *hijras* (intersex persons) are legally recognized, and official documents now have space for "others" as a third gender category. However, as *hijra* is legally defined as referring to intersex people, non-*hijra* transgender individuals cannot apply for a national identity card and, therefore, cannot register as a voter. Also, there is no separate voter list for hijras, and the election manifestos of the political parties do not include commitments toward protecting *hijras'* rights.[a] To have valid official documents, gender-diverse individuals who are non-*hijra* must choose the *"hijra"* option, which is not a true reflection of their gender identity. Moreover, same-sex sexual activities are still punishable by law in Bangladesh.

Sri Lanka prohibits same-sex sexual activities, which are punishable under sections 365 and 365A of the Penal Code of Sri Lanka. Section 399 of the same penal code prohibits the personation of a real or imaginary individual, a practice common to transgender groups. The Penal Code of Maldives prohibits and penalizes same-sex sexual activities. However, issues pertaining to intersex people appear to be invisible in South Asia in both public discourse and in the law.[b]

[a] ASM Amanullah, G. Ahmed, and T. Abir. 2019. *Political Economy Analysis for Gender Diverse Communities in Bangladesh*. Dhaka: Bandhu Social Welfare Society.
[b] G. Shankar. 2020. Law-making in South Asia on intersex rights: Breaking free from the binary. *Shuddashar*. 1 August.

Source: Extracted from the laws and/or policies of Bangladesh, Bhutan, India, Maldives, Nepal, and Sri Lanka.

Access to Social Resources and Services

188.   The consultation participants belonging to the diverse SOGIESC community across the six DMCs quoted instances of bullying and mockery from others (including service providers) as one of the barriers that prevent them from accessing education and health care services. They said that in educational institutions, bullying by peers for not conforming to gender norms (appearance and behavior, uniforms, dress codes) and absence of non-heteronormative outlook[205] (e.g., male–female binary in sporting events, sex education, access to toilets, seating arrangements in classrooms) often result in inadequate accommodation of transgender people, leading to academic underperformance, high dropout rates, and increased mental health problems. For instance, a study in Bangladesh noted that members of the *hijra* community often dropped out of school because of the hostile environment and lack of friendly behaviors exhibited by their peers and teachers alike.[206] Similarly, a survey by Pride Bhutan found that 93 of 106 trans men had less than higher-level schooling, and only 10 had university education.[207] The survey found transgender individuals in Bhutan to drop out of school early because of bullying

[205] The outlook according to which heterosexuality is the preferred or normal mode of sexual orientation.
[206] T. Habib. 2012. *A Long Journey towards Social Inclusion: Initiatives of Social Workers for Hijra Population in Bangladesh*. University of Gothenburg.
[207] *Kuensel*. 2021. Being a transgender in Bhutan. 10 July.

and having to live with the traditional gender norms (e.g., wearing *kira*, the national dress for women in Bhutan, and growing long hair) in schools. In Nepal, there are reported cases of people with diverse SOGIESC being bullied in school and expelled because they did not want to follow the expected gender dress norms. When the people with diverse SOGIESC choose to dress according to their preferred sex or gender identity and not as per their ascribed identities, they are accused of disobeying the school rules and are reprimanded.[208] In Sri Lanka, social and cultural prejudice against homosexuality and gender nonconformity is underpinned by inadequate sex education in schools.[209] There are reports indicating that intersex people in India face issues in obtaining education and employment because of bullying, or of parents refusing to send intersex children to school for fear of stigma. Still in India, intersex persons face difficulties with getting their marriage recognized and registered.[210]

189.   In Bangladesh, the government provides *hijras* and transgender communities with better access to social assistance by explicitly including them in the social assistance schemes under its social safety net program, with monthly old-age allowance to individuals aged 50 years and older, scholarships in four stages for *hijra* children, and skills and capacity development in alternative income-generating activities. However, their legal service support is limited, and they provide almost no support for *hijras'* access to financial services, alternative livelihoods (economic empowerment), or housing services.[211] In addition, the nationwide behavioral and serological surveillance in Bangladesh demonstrated the vulnerability of *hijra* to sexually transmitted infections, including HIV, because of selling unprotected sex to multiple clients.[212] In this aspect, the government has limited medical assistance. For housing services, shelter homes for the underprivileged run by Bangladesh's Department of Social Services are open to *hijras* but have no specialized shelter support for *hijras*.

190.   Access to and utilization of health care remains low for the people with diverse SOGIESC because of discrimination faced at facilities; lack of awareness (of specific needs of people with diverse SOGIESC, like hormone supplements); insensitivity of health care professionals; absence of certain services like mental health care; and general unavailability of hospitals equipped to serve their needs. Many intersex people are subjected to unnecessary and intrusive

208   Mitini Nepal. *National Parallel Report B +25: Issues, Achievements, Gaps and Recommendations of LBTQ of Nepal 2019.* Kathmandu.

209   Human Rights Watch. 2016. *"All Five Fingers Are Not the Same": Discrimination on Grounds of Gender Identity and Sexual Orientation in Sri Lanka.* New York.

210   Sristhi Madurai. 2020. *Human Rights of Intersex Persons in India: Information Toolkit.* Report prepared for the First National Intersex Human Rights Conference. Delhi. 22 December.

211   Government of Bangladesh, Ministry of Social Welfare, Department of Social Services. 2020. *Impact Analysis on Development Program for Improving the Living Standard of Hijra Community.* Dhaka. In 2012–2013 the Department of Social Services under the Ministry of Social Welfare supported the Program for Improving the Living Standard of Hijra Community (initially in seven districts) as a pilot program; the program was evaluated in 2020. The number of beneficiaries was 485 in the first year (2012–2013). Initially, a student stipend and training program were carried out. In 2014, the number of districts was increased to 21 and the tools of the program were also increased. It included old age, disabled or insolvent allowances, student stipend, imparting training, and post-training financial support schemes. As a result, the number of beneficiaries also increased, reaching a maximum of 7,650 people during 2017–2018 and 2018–2019. However, in 2019–2020 the number of program beneficiaries plummeted to 5,767 people, and the post-training financial support seemed absent. The number of beneficiaries remained higher for old age, disabled, or insolvent allowances and lower for the student stipend

212   The *hijras* in Dhaka, the capital city, had the highest recorded rate of active syphilis (10.4%) among other most at-risk populations. These findings warranted immediate HIV interventions. Several NGOs and community-based organizations implement HIV interventions, primarily promoting condoms and lubricants and mainly providing treatment of sexually transmitted infections. S. I. Khan et al. 2009. Living on the Extreme Margin: Social Exclusion of the Transgender Population (Hijra) in Bangladesh. *Journal of Health, Population, and Nutrition.* 27 (4). pp. 441–451.

medical interventions. In many countries without adequate access to pediatric care, there are reports of infanticide or abandonment of intersex children.[213] Fear and shame create hesitancy in accessing medical services. In India's health sector, according to the consultation participants, the discrimination suffered by transgender people is high; harassment is either in physical or verbal form, or in the form of judgmental looks or comments, or denial of treatment or equal treatment. A key barrier is the lack of health service providers who are sufficiently knowledgeable about transgender medicine and care.[214] In Nepal, the health-related requirements (e.g., medical needs, hormonal injections, sex-reassignment surgeries, and mental health counseling) are inadequate, with various barriers that prevent this disadvantaged group from fully accessing and utilizing health services.[215] There are three clinics in Sri Lanka for sex change. However, they are hardly accessible to transgender people because of the high cost implications and the challenging process. Discrimination in accessing health care exists, including being labeled mentally ill, lack of privacy from medical staff, and unwillingness by some medical staff to attend to them (footnote 212). At times, people with diverse SOGIESC cannot access welfare schemes because of the requirement of identity cards. In Bangladesh, for instance, most lack government-issued identity cards, which makes it hard for them to access social benefits.[216]

Access to Economic Resources and Services

191.   Inequalities and discrimination faced in schools force students with diverse SOGIESC to drop out, which translates into lack of employment opportunities in the future. Lack of legal identification documents, discrimination during recruitment processes, job harassment in the workplace, and a lack of job security for people with diverse SOGIESC exist in all the countries. Discrimination exists even in national subsidy programs as there is hardly any data regarding the people with diverse SOGIESC, and many government relief efforts separate those in need by gender, leaving transgender people out. The consultation participants assessed that people with diverse SOGIESC suffer from financial difficulties and are forced to live in poverty and distress because of these barriers.

192.   In Bangladesh, many *hijras* are forced to engage in sex work for a living and experience harassment and are at risk of unprotected sex. The *hijra* sex workers who are exploited by clients or mugged and beaten by hooligans do not seek police support because of fear of further harassment.[217] A small rapid impact assessment survey on the impact of the coronavirus disease (COVID-19) crisis on the third gender community in Bangladesh found that 82% of the 51 respondents had not earned at all in the past 2 weeks, 59% did not receive any support, and 86% did not have any savings.[218] The education and economic participation of *hijras* and transgender individuals remains a challenge.

[213] UN Office of the High Commissioner for Human Rights. *Human Rights for Hermaphrodites Too! Submission for OHCHR Study on Youth and Human Rights (HRC39)*. New York.

[214] J.D. Safer et al. 2016. Barriers to Health Care for Transgender Individuals. *Current Opinion in Endocrinology and Diabetes and Obesity.* 23 (2). pp. 168–171.

[215] Blue Diamond Society. 2018. *Discrimination and Violence Against Lesbian and Bisexual Women and Transgender People in Nepal: Shadow Report.* Kathmandu.

[216] K. Knight. 2020. The Most Vulnerable People in the World Right Now. *The Advocate.* 7 May.

[217] K. Knight. 2016. I Want to Live with My Head Held High: Abuses in Bangladesh's Legal Recognition of Hijras. Human Rights Watch. 23 December.

[218] Innovision Consulting Private Limited. 2020. *Economic impact of COVID-19 crisis on Third Gender community in Bangladesh.* Dhaka.

193.   In India, eligibility requirements may indirectly lead to gender restrictions on some jobs.[219] For instance, some jobs (e.g., navy, army, flight crews) may require a person to undergo invasive medical tests or submit identity documents, which are difficult to obtain for people with diverse sexual and gender identities.[220] A study conducted in 2015 by Sangama, based on interviews with 3,619 transgender people in Kerala, found that only 12% of the transgender people surveyed were employed, and half of those respondents earned less than $67 per month.[221]

194.   In cases where the identity of people with diverse SOGIESC is known in the workplace, they are susceptible to discrimination and harassment, including bullying, sexual harassment, assault, and misgendering. In addition, because of constraints in accessing formal sector employment, transgender and nonbinary people often take up work in the informal sector and work in precarious conditions or as sex workers and resort to begging, which further exposes them to rights violations.[222] This discrimination can be so pervasive that it can be better understood as "occupational segregation," whereby select social groups are not distributed throughout the labor market by their merit or skills, but rather by the bias and prejudices of employers. For people with diverse SOGIESC, occupational segregation first filters them into the informal market and out of the formal market. Secondly, even for those who can find employment in the formal market, the filtering keeps them out of higher-paying more senior-level jobs.[223] This systemic discrimination and segregation is not only harmful to the people who experience it, but presents a significant loss to businesses (in the form of less productivity) as well as diminished economic outcomes (in the form of less labor output).[224]

195.   People with diverse SOGIESC in Nepal continue to face discrimination from society because of prevailing mindsets. They are also deprived of employment in state institutions, including the civil service, army, and police, as the recruitment criteria do not accept the "Other" (i.e., the gender and sexual minorities) category as a gender choice.[225]

Social Practices, Participation, and Decision-Making

196.   Challenges exist for people with diverse SOGIESC in all six DMCs. Many experience difficulties in recognizing and accepting their own gender identity and sexuality and getting their family and community to accept them. Hence, they tend to hide their identity to avoid being misunderstood by their families and communities. Many are subjected to "conversion" therapy, forced marriages, and "corrective rape." Violence in the family can take the form of physical force (including honor killings), sexual abuse, wrongful confinement, and involuntary institutionalization. Usually, they are forced to either accept their sexuality and gender identity and leave their family, or ignore it and stay with the family. When compelled to leave, they are forced into sex work or begging to meet their basic needs despite the risk of criminal prosecution. Political representation remains almost absent in all countries. Nepal had members of Parliament

[219]   International Commission of Jurists. 2019. *Living with Dignity: Sexual Orientation and Gender Identity-Based Human Rights Violations in Housing, Work, and Public Spaces in India.* Geneva. p. 9.
[220]   Footnote 219, pp. 9 and 80.
[221]   Sangama. 2015. *Transgender Survey Kerala 2014–15.* Kerala.
[222]   Government of United Kingdom, Home Office. 2021. *Country Policy and Information Note—India: Sexual Orientation and Gender Identity and Expression.* Version 4. London.
[223]   P. Crehan et al. 2021. The Economic Case for LGBT+ Inclusion in the Caribbean. *Open for Business.* London.
[224]   M.V.L. Badgett. 2014. *The Economic Cost of Stigma and the Exclusion of LGBT People: A Case Study of India.* Washington, DC: World Bank Group.
[225]   S. Gurung. 2021. Nepal, the Beacon of LGBTQ+ Rights in Asia? Not Quite. *The Diplomat.* 10 February.

from the SOGIESC community during 2008–2013 but not in later years. In Bangladesh, a transgender mayor was elected in 2021. Currently, policy discourse is mostly from the perspective of HIV and AIDS rather than equal rights, which adds to the stigmatization of persons with diverse SOGIESC because of stereotyping.

197.   According to the Integrated Biological and Behavioral Surveillance Survey of 2016, violence, discrimination, and social stigma faced by people with diverse SOGIESC forced more than 42% of transgender women and 23% of gay and bisexual men in Bhutan to attempt suicide.[226] A survey conducted in 2015 in Kerala highlighted high rates of violence against transgender people, as more than half (52%) of the respondents of the survey reported to had been harassed by the police, and nearly all (96%) said they had not raised a complaint because of their gender identity (footnote 221). In Nepal (footnote 215) and Sri Lanka,[227] they are often subjected to police harassment, extortion, arrests, and arbitrary detention. They are detained in hospitals and forced to receive treatment against their will, e.g., sex corrective treatment as part of "conversion therapy." According to the consultation participants, there is a lack of safe spaces for those facing abuse and harassment at home or by service providers.

Intersectionality

198.   The dominant patriarchal family structure in SARD countries impacts the nature of discrimination and violence against lesbian, bisexual, and trans women. This increases their stress and impacts their mental health. In the assessment of the consultation participants, the violence faced by lesbians starts in the family since it is where control is exerted over a woman's sexuality, mobility, and access to resources.

199.   A study conducted in India found the immediate and extended families as the main perpetrators of violence against lesbian and bisexual women.[228] Studies conducted by the India Forum during the pandemic also show that trans women experience greater harassment and denial of dignity than trans men or homeless queer people.[229] In a survey conducted by Pride Bhutan, only 10 of 106 surveyed trans men had a university education, and most trans women were in the entertainment business (footnote 207). In Sri Lanka in general, women have been historically underrepresented at all levels of government, and non-binary women have been completely invisible in the political arena. No affirmative action has been taken to redress this situation for women of diverse gender identities and sexual orientations.[230]

200.   In Bangladesh, the *hijra* and transgender population belonging to small ethnic minority communities also experience poor access to services, isolation, and lack of dialogue about their livelihood issues because of the discrimination against their social identity. Similarly, according to the consultation participants, *hijra* and transgender individuals belonging to low-income groups cannot avail themselves of health care services unlike those from the higher income groups.

[226]   School of Planning Monitoring Evaluation and Research. 2016. *Integrated Biological and Behavioral Surveillance (IBBS) Surveys Among Vulnerable and Key Populations at Higher Risk in Bhutan, 2016: Final Report.* Kathmandu.
[227]   3CR. 2019. Intersex Human Rights and Queer Sri Lankan Identity. Podcast. 17 February.
[228]   K. Zaman, N. Chad, and I. Schneeweis. 2016. *India LGBTI: Landscape Analysis of Political, Economic and Social Conditions.* New York: Astraea Lesbian Foundation for Justice.
[229]   *The India Forum.* 2021. The Pandemic and the LGBTQ Community: The Need for Collective Action. 7 May.
[230]   The Women and Media Collective. 2017. *Discrimination of Lesbians, Bisexual Women and Transgender People in Sri Lanka: Shadow Report.* Report prepared for the 66th Session of the Committee for the Elimination of All Forms of Discrimination Against Women. Geneva. 13 February–3 March.

C.   Policy Analysis

201.   Not all six DMCs have laws and policies fully promoting and protecting the rights and welfare of people with diverse SOGIESC. In Bangladesh, while the third gender is recognized and since 2013 there have been policies to empower them, same-sex sexual activities remain punishable by law. Bhutan, India, and Nepal have recognized and decriminalized same-sex relationships and activities. However, only India and Nepal have developed guidelines for the implementation of these policies. Maldives and Sri Lanka do not have any policies or institutional frameworks for people with diverse SOGIESC, and in these countries, same-sex sexual activities are punishable by law. Table 6.1 provides a list of policies for people with diverse SOGIESC in four SARD DMCs.

Table 6.1: Policies and Acts for People with Diverse Sexual Orientation, Gender Identity and Expression, and Sex Characteristics in Selected Countries

DMC	Policies
Bangladesh	The Government of Bangladesh started to recognize the *hijra* (transgender persons) community as the *hijra* sex on 26 January 2014, although no formal definition is available.
	Proposal to fix the tax-free ceiling at Tk350,000 for the third gender community
Bhutan	Section 213 and 214 of the Constitution of Bhutan have been repealed, thereby decriminalizing homosexuality.
India	The Transgender People (Protection of Rights) Act, 2019 (came into effect January 2020).
	Census 2011 collected the data on the "third gender" population in the country (census 2021 will be conducted in 2023). Same-sex relations were decriminalized in 2019. India included the third gender option in passports in 2005, in the census of 2011, in voter identity cards in 2013, and ration cards in 2015.
Nepal	Article 12 of the Constitution of Nepal states that people have the right to have a citizenship identity card that reflects their preferred gender.
	Article 18 of the Constitution of Nepal guarantees the protection, empowerment, and development of LGBTI+ communities, along with other socially oppressed groups
	The government has added a separate category "O" for LGBTI+ persons on the citizenship certificate.
	A separate category "other" for LGBTI+ was also added to the 2011 census by the Central Bureau of Statistics.

DMC = developing member country; LGBTI+ = lesbian, gay, bisexual, transgender, intersex, and others; SOGIESC = sexual orientation, gender identity and expression, and sex characteristics.

Source: Extracted from the laws and/or policies of Bangladesh, Bhutan, India, and Nepal.

202.   Overall, while Bangladesh, Bhutan, India, and Nepal have made efforts to protect and promote the rights and welfare of this community, there are still many barriers to their development. Therefore, according to the consultation participants, it is important to reduce the gap in the implementation of policies and ensure greater political representation of the group so that the difficulties experienced by its members are effectively identified and addressed.

Furthermore, it is essential to recognize that official documents that recognize one's gender identity comprise one of the main concerns of people with diverse SOGIESC. For example, in many countries transgender individuals can change the gender marker in official certificates, but the process is long, costly, and often requires various court orders and medical examinations. The same applies to obtaining government-issued documents, such as identification cards and passports. With some exceptions, the gender option in these documents remains binary (either female or male).[231]

D.   South Asia Department Projects Aiming to Benefit Individuals with Diverse Sexual Orientation and Gender Identity

203.   None of the reviewed 19 selected projects of SARD for this gender equality and social inclusion (GESI) assessment included actions explicitly and specifically aiming to benefit people with diverse SOGIESC. Also, none of the reviewed second set of 15 projects of SARD (the same list of projects assessed for other disadvantaged groups: older people, people with disabilities, and excluded and vulnerable social identity groups) provided good practices in addressing the issues of people with diverse SOGIESC.

E.   Good Practices in Responding to the Issues of Individuals with Diverse Sexual Orientation and Gender Identity

204.   While the Asian Development Bank (ADB) has not engaged in issues of individuals with diverse SOGIESC, other stakeholder organizations in the DMCs have initiated programs to assist and empower this disadvantaged group. The following are examples of these initiatives:

(i)   **Empower for change**

    (a)   In Bangladesh, the Ministry of Social Welfare provides direct cash transfer and financial support for education. Transgender individuals are entitled to a direct monthly cash transfer of Tk600 ($5.82). The ministry also provides scholarships to transgender students at the primary level in the amount of Tk800 ($7.76) and at the secondary level in the amount of Tk900 ($8.73). At the university level, the amount of scholarship is Tk1,300 ($12.61). In addition, the ministry provides training in business development and has trained 900 transgender individuals and provided business start-up assistance of Tk10,000 ($97.00) per trainee.

[231]   C. Cortez, J. Arzinos, and C. De la Medina Soto. 2021. *Equality of Opportunity for Sexual and Gender Minorities.* Washington, DC: World Bank.

(b)   Rainbow Bhutan,[232] a nongovernment organization (NGO), provided virtual and tele-counseling to people with diverse SOGIESC who need help. It has partnered with Save the Children and the Ministry of Health for the skills development of trans women.

(c)   In India, the Humsafar Trust, an NGO, assists individuals with diverse SOGIESC in the Mumbai metro area and surrounding areas to face issues, such as conflicts with their families, extortion, blackmail, legal problems, and violence. During the COVID-19 pandemic, the Humsafar Trust provided necessities (e.g., food rations, medical services) to about 25,000 people with diverse SOGIESC.

(d)   In Nepal, the Blue Diamond Society operates drop-in centers that provide LGBT-friendly HIV prevention, education, testing, counseling, and treatment.

(e)   Mitini Nepal runs capacity building programs, such as jewelry-making and other skills, and educational and personal development, including counseling services for people with diverse SOGIESC.

(f)   In Sri Lanka, the Grassroots Trust provides support through shelters and safe houses to people with diverse SOGIESC and runs a trilingual portal (Bakamoono.lk) to promote its (and marginalized youth's) access to information.

(g)   The National Transgender Network in Sri Lanka provides socioeconomic, legal, medical, and emotional support to transgender individuals.

(h)   Equal Ground in Sri Lanka conducts awareness programs and consultations in rural areas and engages in career development initiatives for people with diverse SOGIESC.

(ii)   **Include for opportunity**

(a)   Mitini Nepal partners with schools to train teachers and educate students about the struggles and violence that people with diverse SOGIESC face. They also conduct awareness-raising campaigns through radio programs and academic institution orientation classes. In addition, every year on International Day Against Homophobia, Biphobia and Transphobia, they work with rural and urban communities across Nepal to celebrate and educate locals about the rights and experiences of people with diverse SOGIESC. Mitini Nepal plans to build a central home with services and shelter for homeless people with diverse SOGIESC as they have no safe spaces where they can gather and receive support and services.

(b)   Being LGBTI in Asia and the Pacific is a United Nations Development Programme (UNDP) regional program that aims at addressing inequality, violence, and discrimination on the basis of sexual orientation, gender identity, or intersex status. It is a collaboration between governments, civil society, regional institutions, and other stakeholders.[233] The program also strives to address the research gaps that exist on the stigma, violence, and rights violations experienced by sexual and gender minorities in Asia and the Pacific.

---

[232]   Rainbow Bhutan is now separated into two NGOs: Queer Voices of Bhutan and Pride Bhutan.
[233]   UNDP. Being LGBTI in Asia and the Pacific.

205.   The UNDP and World Bank have started responding to the issues of individuals with diverse SOGIESC toward their inclusion.

(i)   In India, UNDP assists the Ministry of Social Justice and Empowerment, which is the nodal ministry for promoting the welfare of transgender people in the country. In collaboration with other agencies and in consultation with civil society organizations (CSOs), UNDP helped the ministry develop a full-fledged framework, which seeks to address the gaps in transgender inclusion in government welfare measures and the vulnerabilities and risks faced by the transgender population.

(ii)   In Bhutan, UNDP advocated for decriminalization of diverse SOGIESC and worked closely with the Parliament for policy making.

(iii)   In 2019, the World Bank developed its Good Practice Note on Non-Discrimination: Sexual Orientation and Gender Identity to accompany its Environmental and Social Framework and the Bank Directive on Addressing Risks and Impacts on Disadvantaged or Vulnerable Individuals or Groups.[234] The objective of the Good Practice Note is to guide its staff and development partners in responding to the issue of discrimination based on SOGIESC.

(iv)   In 2019, the World Bank launched a study to examine the laws and regulations that affect the lives of people with diverse SOGIESC in 16 countries (including Bangladesh and India) and offer policy recommendations designed to prevent and eliminate discriminatory practices. The results of the study were published in 2021, under the title Equality of Opportunity for Sexual and Gender Minorities (footnote 231). The study measured six indicators: criminalization and SOGIESC, access to inclusive education, access to the labor market, access to public services and social protection, civil and political inclusion, and protection from hate crimes.

(v)   Another important study (footnote 234) carried out by the World Bank develops a model—applied to India—to estimate the economic cost of stigma, negative attitudes toward lesbian, gay, bisexual, and transgender (LGBT) people, and their exclusion in social institutions, such as education, employment, families, and health care. The model is applied to a case study of India, which had three major findings. First, there is clear evidence of stigma and exclusion of LGBT people in India. Second, the effects of stigma and exclusion are potentially costly to economies. Third, existing research does not allow for a precise estimate of the cost of LGBT exclusion, but the cost could be substantial.

---

[234] World Bank. 2019. Environmental and Social Framework for IPF Operations—Non-Discrimination: Sexual Orientation and Gender Identity (SOGI). *Good Practice Note*. Washington, DC.

F.   Conclusions and Way Forward

Summary of Findings

206.   The assessment found people with diverse SOGIESC to be extremely excluded and vulnerable. The following are the highlights of the assessment:

- People with diverse SOGIESC across the six DMCs experience various types of discrimination in different realms: private (e.g., difficulty in accepting own identity, conflict with family, bullying) and public spaces (e.g., bullying in schools, lack of sensitivity of health providers to their distinct needs, lack of access to employment, poor legal protection, sexual harassment and/or violence).
- Four of the six DMCs (i.e., Bangladesh, Bhutan, India, and Nepal) have laws and policies for people with diverse SOGIESC.
- SARD has no projects that explicitly and specifically address the issues of people with diverse SOGIESC.
- Stakeholders (government, CSOs, and international development partners) have responded to the call of people with diverse SOGIESC for assistance in promoting and protecting their rights and developing their capacity for economic and political development.

Way Forward for the South Asia Department

207.   ADB has started to recognize the importance of responding to the discrimination and vulnerability faced by people with diverse SOGIESC. This recognition is made explicit in the stakeholder engagement plan for the review and updating of its Safeguard Policy Statement (2009).[235] Also, ADB is conducting research on the legal barriers to SOGIESC inclusion in 23 of its DMCs, including Bhutan, Nepal, and Sri Lanka. Plans are underway for the conduct of a study on the economic cost of discrimination against people with diverse SOGIESC and the development of grant and technical assistance (TA) projects supporting people with diverse SOGIESC in Bangladesh, Bhutan, and Nepal.

208.   During the stakeholder consultations, representatives from the government and CSOs expressed the need for ADB to also engage people with diverse SOGIESC and articulated the following potential areas of SARD's assistance:

(i)   **Understand for action**
   (a)   Conduct a survey on the status of people with diverse SOGIESC and the distinct issues they face (Nepal).[236]
   (b)   Work to include questions on SOGIESC in larger diagnostics, thus allowing the ability to disaggregate data later and uncover new patterns of exclusion for this community, particularly by comparing with the general population.

[235] ADB. 2021. *Safeguard Policy Statement Review and Update: Stakeholder Engagement Plan. Draft for Consultation.* Manila.
[236] The Central Bureau of Statistics of Nepal is preparing to conduct a sample survey of the SOGIESC community in Nepal with possible support of ADB and other development partners in 2023.

(ii) **Empower for change**

    (a) Provide business development programs (including entrepreneurial skills development and access to business capital).

    (b) Expand the access of people with diverse SOGIESC to health facilities and services.

    (c) Provide vocational training to people with diverse SOGIESC and create a conducive environment for their employment in the private sector (Sri Lanka).

(iii) **Include for opportunity**

    (a) Facilitate specific policy reforms for transgender people (Bangladesh), formulate anti-harassment in the workplace law (India), and carry out judicial reform to decriminalize homosexuality (Sri Lanka).

    (b) Support educational and community awareness or sensitization programs (in schools, communities, and families) that will address education-related obstacles and promote the social acceptance of transgender people (Bangladesh) and individuals with diverse SOGIESC (India, Nepal, and Sri Lanka).

    (c) Improve the gender certification process (Sri Lanka).

    (d) Encourage partner private sector organizations (employers) to follow global practices on treating people with diverse SOGIESC.

    (e) Facilitate global networking and knowledge sharing among organizations working on the issues of people with diverse SOGIESC (Nepal).

VII. GEOGRAPHIC LOCATION AND INCOME POVERTY IN SOUTH ASIA: ISSUES AND RESPONSES

A. Introduction: Definitions

209. This chapter deals with both geographic location and income poverty, as evidence points to the strong linkage between them. Geographic exclusion occurs when accessibility to certain areas is difficult because of distance (remote and rural areas away from towns and cities); terrain (mountain and hilly areas, or remote islands); and seasonal hazards (wetlands, areas prone to floods, and landslides). Table 7.1 presents the definitions of geographically excluded areas in each developing member country (DMC) of the Asian Development Bank (ADB) in South Asia.

Table 7.1: Exclusionary Geographic Locations

DMC	Exclusionary Geographic Areas
Bangladesh	Rural and remote areas, hilly terrain, and wetlands
Bhutan	Rural and remote areas, and areas with difficult geographical terrain
India	Rural and remote areas with difficult geographical terrain, coastal communities, disaster-prone areas, informal settlements in urban areas (with homeless urban households)
Maldives	Islands other than those in the capital city of Malé and Addu
Nepal	Mountain and hill terrain with poor transport links. The government identified districts and palikas (municipalities and rural municipalities) as "backward areas"[a]
Sri Lanka	Eastern and northern provinces, estate sector, and rural areas

DMC = developing member country.

Note: These definitions were developed for the study in lieu of official government definitions.

[a] Government of Nepal, Election Commission. 2017. *Guidelines for the Proportional Representation Members in Provincial Election.* Kathmandu. The government identified Accham, Bajhang, Bajura, Dolpa, Humla, Jajarkot, Jumla, Kalikot, and Mugu, and districts as "backward areas" in the 2007 amendment of the Civil Service Act, 1993. Since all *palikas* (municipality or rural municipality) of a district could not be automatically treated as backward, the Election Commission identified 57 municipality and rural municipality as "backward" to enable candidates from backward areas to take part in the 2017 elections. The basis for selecting backward areas was unclear in the guidelines.

Source: Asian Development Bank (South Asia Department).

210.   In the South Asia Department (SARD) DMCs, official poverty lines and the subsequent national poverty rates are generated using consumption levels and, hence, are not comparable across countries. The international poverty line, created by the World Bank and last updated in 2015, is defined as $1.9 per person per day.[237]

B.   Status of the Geographically Excluded and Income Poor

Demography

211.   The nexus of poverty has come to be intrinsically linked with geographic location. Most poor South Asians still live in rural areas, and the proportion of chronic poor is greater in rural areas, given the greater opportunities in towns and cities (Table 7.2). Geographically difficult areas are also more affected by natural disasters (like floods in low-lying areas of *char*, the floodplain sediment islands, in Bangladesh), which further push inhabitants into poverty.[238]

212.   Table 7.2 shows that, in all six DMCs, the incidence of poverty is significantly higher in rural areas than in urban areas. The highest disparity exists in Nepal, where more than 40% of the rural population resides in poverty compared to 9% of the urban population, followed by India and Bhutan. East and central Bangladesh have fared much better: poverty has fallen moderately in Chittagong and declined rapidly in Barisal, Dhaka, and Sylhet. The differences between the country's east and west have occurred largely in rural instead of urban areas.[239] Poverty in Bhutan is still a rural phenomenon. Among the *dzongkhags* (administrative and judicial districts), the *dzongkhags* of Dagana (14%), Samtse (14%), and Monggar (13%) had the highest share of the entire poor population in the country, with 40% of poor people residing in these three rural *dzongkhags*.[240] Much of India's poverty is concentrated in rural areas, and India's wealthiest households were concentrated in urban areas in 2016. The two highest wealth quintiles had a 74% urban population. More than half of the rural population (55%) fell in the two lowest wealth quintiles.[241] In Maldives, in 2016, a large majority of poor people (9% under the low poverty line) lived in the atolls, outside of Malé.[242] In Nepal, 48 rural municipalities and 9 urban municipalities in 23 districts were identified as backward areas. Both the mountains and *tarai* (lowland areas) regions had Human Poverty Index values less than the national average (footnote 152). Geographic pockets of poverty exist in Sri Lanka. Colombo and the Western Province, as the main engines of economic growth, are relatively prosperous, while the Southern Province and former war-affected areas in the north and east are less developed. Districts in these less-developed areas have higher poverty rates, e.g., Mullaitivu (29%), Mannar (20%),

[237] TM T. Islam, D. Newhouse, and M. Yanez-Pagans. 2021. International Comparisons of Poverty in South Asia. *Asian Development Review*. 38 (1). pp. 142–175.

[238] U. Grant et al. 2004. Understanding Chronic Poverty in South Asia. In *The Chronic Poverty Report 2004–05*. Manchester, United Kingdom: Chronic Poverty Research Centre.

[239] R. Hill and M.E. Genoni. 2019. *Bangladesh Poverty Assessment: Facing Old and New Frontiers in Poverty Reduction*. Washington, DC: World Bank Group.

[240] Government of Bhutan, National Statistics Bureau. 2017. *Bhutan Poverty Analysis Report 2017*. Thimphu.

[241] NITI Aayog. 2019. *SDG India Index and Dashboard, 2019–20*. New Delhi.

[242] Government of Maldives, National Bureau of Statistics. 2018. *Household Income and Expenditure Survey 2016— Analytical Report IV: Poverty and Inequality*. Malé.

Table 7.2: Rural Population, Poor Population, and Rural and Urban Poor Population (%)

DMC	Share of Rural Population	Share of Population Below National Poverty Line	Share of Rural Poor	Share of Urban Poor
Bangladesh	61.1	24.3	26.5	18.9
Bhutan	56.9	08.2	11.9	0.8
India	64.6	21.9	25.7	13.7
Maldives	58.8	08.2	-	-
Nepal	78.9	25.2	42.3	08.7
Sri Lanka	81.1	04.1	07.6	02.1

- = data not available, DMC = developing member country.
Sources: World Bank. Open Data. Rural population (% of total population) (accessed 3 March 2022); and for poverty: United Nations Development Programme. 2020. *Human Development Report 2020—The Next Frontier: Human Development and the Anthropocene*. New York.

Kilinochchi district (13%), and Batticaloa district (19%) in Eastern province; and Monaragala district (21%) in Uva province.[243]

Access to Social Resources and Services

213.   In each of the six countries, people in rural areas, disaster-prone areas (like the *haor*, wetlands found in northeastern Bangladesh); remote areas; and places difficult to access because of physical terrain (e.g., outer atolls of Maldives, mountains of Nepal) are left behind. People in these areas experience multiple levels of exclusion and have lower literacy, health, water, sanitation, and hygiene indicators compared to less isolated areas. Social infrastructure like schools and health care centers is limited in *chars*[244] and *haors* of Bangladesh, mountainous regions of Bhutan and Nepal, remote atolls of Maldives, rural India, and the war-affected northern and eastern provinces in Sri Lanka. According to the consultation participants, connecting infrastructure to metropolitan areas is also severely limited in the DMCs, where most services tend to be centralized. In Bhutan, the government has expanded the road network, but transport connectivity remains poor in many parts of the country.[245] In Maldives, transport costs are high. Almost half of the inhabited islands do not have proper harbors and access facilities, and 25 islands have no harbors at all.[246] As a result, it is extremely challenging for inhabitants of geographically dispersed areas to access these services. In Bangladesh, the remoteness of the Chittagong Hill Tracts (CHT), poor communication, and CHT's unique socioeconomic characteristics have made providing basic social services to inhabitants difficult.[247] In Sri Lanka, health outcomes are worse in war-affected northern and eastern provinces, partly because of

---

[243] Footnote 171. p. 40.
[244] The *chars* (referring to midstream islands and others attached to the mainland) are created from river sediment. Emerging *chars* create new areas for settlement and cultivation, an important resource in a land-scarce country such as Bangladesh. However, a constant threat of riverbank erosion and flooding, combined with a lack of physical infrastructure, government services, and employment opportunities, makes for a vulnerable and difficult way of life. *Char* dwellers are considered poorer than the mainland population and are becoming the targets of efforts to reduce poverty. Government of Bangladesh, Planning Commission. Social Security Policy Support Programme.
[245] ADB. 2014. *Country Partnership Strategy: Bhutan, 2014–2018*. Poverty Analysis (Summary) (accessible from the list of linked documents in Appendix 2). Manila.
[246] ADB. 2015. *Maldives: Overcoming the Challenges of A Small Island State*. Manila.
[247] UNICEF Bangladesh. 2019. *Many Tracts One Community: UNICEF's Work in the Chittagong Hill Tracts*. Dhaka.

the delay in rebuilding destroyed infrastructure, and medical infrastructure is available only in far-off districts.[248]

214.   Access is further constrained by the non-affordability of these services because of widespread poverty in the region. In Bangladesh, to be near their workplaces, many poor households in Dhaka live in slums with poor housing, insecurity, and overcrowding.

215.   Poverty is not limited to geographically excluded and hard-to-reach areas. Slums have much higher levels of monetary poverty, more children out of school, and lower levels of access to water and sanitation services (footnote 237). In Bhutan, 57% of poor people were literate as compared to 69% of the nonpoor in 2017 (footnote 240). In India, the percentage of the population with no schooling was higher in rural areas (37% for women and 18% for men) than in urban areas (19% for women and 9% for men)in 2014–2015.[249] In Maldives, the proportion of 3- and 4-year-olds who attend an organized early childhood education program was 69% in the lowest wealth quintile and 87% in the fourth quintile in 2016–2017.[250] Different human development indicators illustrate the disparity that people of poor income levels experience in Nepal. The National Household survey of Nepal for 2016-17 reported that households of the richest quintile using piped water were more than double that of households of the poorest quintile and the households with no toilet facilities were 33% of the poorest group, while the households in the richest quintile with no toilets were 0%.[251] The estate sector is the poorest sector in Sri Lanka because of limited market access, poor infrastructure, and low levels of education. The Household Expenditure and Income Survey in 2012 showed that 82% of youth (5–20 years) in the estate sector were attending school as compared to 85% each for urban and rural youth.[252]

Access to Economic Resources and Services

216.   The stakeholder consultations highlighted the situation of the economy in rural and remote areas of the DMCs as highly dependent on traditional agriculture, making the inhabitants susceptible to poverty. Lack of market linkages, proper irrigation systems, and microcredit; low land fertility; and increasing incidence of natural disasters have made inhabitants' incomes highly vulnerable. According to the consultation participants, opportunities for employment in nonagricultural occupations remain limited.

217.   With a poverty incidence of more than 50%, CHT is one of the least economically developed regions in Bangladesh. Most of the population relies on subsistence farming, particularly *jhum* (a form of shifting cultivation) farming practices. With increased environmental degradation and a low capacity to adapt to the impacts of climate change, the agricultural practices can no longer sustain the population of the region.

---

[248] Government of Australia, Department of Foreign Affairs and Trade. 2021. *DFAT Country Information Report: Sri Lanka.* Barton, Australia.

[249] Government of India. Ministry of Housing and family Welfare. *National family Health Survey 2015-16.* p. 20.20

[250] Government of Maldives, Ministry of Health and ICF. 2018. *Maldives Demographic and Health Survey 2016–17.* Malé and Rockville, Maryland, United States.

[251] Government of Nepal, Central Bureau of Statistics. 2017. *Annual Household Survey 2016/17 (Major Findings).* Kathmandu.

[252] Independent Evaluation Department. 2016. *Country Assistance Program Evaluation: Sri Lanka, 2006–2015.* Sector Assessment: Education (Accessible from the list of linked documents in the Appendix). Manila: ADB.

218.   In India, 70% of rural Indian households are dependent on agriculture, yet the increase in farm productivity and farmers' incomes, job creation, and skills development to provide for nonfarm livelihood options in rural areas have been inadequate. According to the National Institution for Transforming India (NITI) Aayog Action Plan, in 2017 almost three-fourths of the rural households lived with a monthly income of less than ₹5,000 ($61.53).[253] In 2011, 56% of the rural households did not own land and 51% were casual laborers.[254] In Maldives, households whose heads worked in fisheries were poorer than those living in households whose heads worked in industries or services. Poverty incidence was lowest among households whose heads worked as managers, technicians, or clerical support workers (footnote 246). In Sri Lanka, the northern and eastern provinces reported the lowest median household income per capita in the 2016 Household Income and Expenditure Survey.[255] Unemployment rates are high as livelihood opportunities in the north and east provinces are limited. The private sector investments in the north and east have not been adequate to provide decent jobs and secure livelihoods for people struggling to survive as per the report by the UN Office of the High Commissioner for Human Rights in 2017. The Government of Sri Lanka promotes microcredit and self-employment schemes for day-to-day survival, but because of indebtedness and other forms of dispossession, large populations of these provinces are unable to benefit from them.[256]

Social Practices, Participation, and Decision-Making

219.   Consultation participants from civil society organizations (CSOs) highlighted limited participation and engagement of the rural community in their programs because of time poverty, low interest in themes they believed were not for them, and reluctance to voice their concerns with project teams. In many cases, even CSO projects are designed and implemented without consultations with the rural community they are seeking to benefit.

Intersectionality

220.   Exclusion based on geographical location and poverty is further compounded by other vulnerabilities, such as gender, old age, disability, social identity, geographic location, income, young age (disadvantaged youth), and migrant status. Discrimination and inequalities in everyday life are worse for poor and rural women. According to the consultation participants, restricted mobility because of concerns of safety, lack of economic opportunities beyond agriculture, time poverty, gender-based violence (GBV), and limited decision-making power are more severe for women in rural and geographically excluded areas and poor women in all DMCs. According to the Human Development Report 2020, among the ecological belts, the degree of gender disparity in human development is highest in the Tarai region of Nepal.[257] In Bangladesh, women's mobility is constrained. While 84% of men in slums and low-income communities go outside

[253] NITI Aayog. 2017. *India Three Year Action Agenda 2017–18 to 2019–20*. New Delhi.
[254] Government of India, Ministry of Rural Development. Socio Economic and Caste Census, 2011.
[255] Department of Census and Statistics, Ministry of National Policies and Economic Affairs Sri Lanka. 2018. *Household Income and Expenditure Survey - 2016: Final Report*. Battaramulla. Table 2.1, p. 7.
[256] UN Human Rights Treaty Bodies. 2017. *The State of Economic, Social and Cultural Rights in Sri Lanka: A Joint Civil Society Shadow Report to the United Nations Committee on Economic Social and Cultural Rights*.
[257] Government of Nepal, National Planning Commission and UNDP. 2020. *Nepal Human Development Report 2020— Beyond Graduation: Productive Transformation and Prosperity*. Kathmandu.

their community every day, only 40% of women do so in 2018.[258] According to the Demographic and Health Survey 2009, girls in remote atolls of Maldives are at a disadvantage as parents are less willing to send daughters, compared to sons, to Malé to continue their higher or technical education. Lower incomes, combined with a limited control of household assets and productive resources, were also particular challenges for women-headed households.[259] In rural India, while 75% of women workers were engaged in agriculture, women's operational landholding was only 14%. As per India's National Family Health Survey 2015-16, one-third of rural women had never attended school, compared with 16% of urban women. Additionally, rural women were more likely to have no regular exposure to any form of mass media than urban women (34% versus 8%) and the experience of physical violence was more common among women in rural areas (32%) than those in urban areas (25%).[260] In Sri Lanka, based on the Household Income and Expenditure Survey (HIES), 2016, women in rural areas are burdened with subsistence farming and household care responsibilities and are deprived of other decent employment opportunities that could contribute to a better quality of life.[261] This is true for the other DMCs too.

221.   Unemployment rates of women were comparatively higher in rural (7.7%) than in urban (6.6%) areas.[262] Older people in rural areas do not often get the same support or services as the older people living in urban areas because of limited infrastructure and services. According to the consultation participants, older people in rural areas who have any form of disability or health problem face additional challenges. In Sri Lanka, war widows of all ethnic groups and ages suffer from problems, such as lack of livelihood and income options and mental health issues, with older women being particularly affected.[263] In Bhutan, with high rural–urban migration, older people continue to live alone in villages, thus affecting the care and support system they receive.[264]

222.   Poverty incidence and geographic isolation are linked with social identities. In India, chronic poverty was disproportionately high among historically marginalized groups, such as scheduled castes and scheduled tribes. The two lowest wealth quintiles included 50% of the scheduled caste households and 71% of the scheduled tribe households.[265] In Nepal, chronic poverty is concentrated among excluded ethnic groups, such as the Dalits. Exclusion based on cultural practices or languages force various Adivasi Janajatis groups to higher levels of poverty. Some Madhesi groups (especially for Madhesi Dalits) have strong conservative practices that impact both women (such as mobility restrictions, strict norms about staying within the household and not mixing with others) and men (e.g., social acceptance of certain tasks allowed to men of different caste groups) and force them into deeper poverty because of gender and caste-based occupational segregation (footnote 66).

[258] World Bank. 2019. *What Works for Working Women? Understanding Female Labor Force Participation in Urban Bangladesh*. Dhaka. p.34

[259] J. El-Horr and R. P. Pande. 2016. *Understanding Gender in Maldives: Toward Inclusive Development*. Washington, DC: World Bank Group. p. 30.

[260] International Institute for Population Sciences and ICF. 2017. *National Family Health Survey (NFHS-4), 2015–16: India*. Mumbai: International Institute for Population Sciences.

[261] W. Nanayakkara. 2018. A Balancing Act: Can Sri Lanka Overcome Regional Income Inequalities? *Talking Economics*. Blog of the Institute of Policy Studies of Sri Lanka. 27 December.

[262] Government of Sri Lanka, Department of Census and Statistics. 2019. *Sri Lanka Labour Force Survey: Annual Bulletin 2019*. Battaramulla, Sri Lanka.

[263] International Crisis Group. 2017. *Sri Lanka's conflict affected women: Dealing with the legacy of war*. Belgium.

[264] Government of Bhutan, National Assembly of Bhutan, Social and Cultural Committee. 2018. *Report by Social and Cultural Committee.*. Thimphu. p.5

[265] A.K. Mehta et al. 2011. *India Chronic Poverty Report: Towards Solutions and New Compacts in a Dynamic Context*. New Delhi: Indian Institute of Public Administration.

C. Policy Analysis

Geographic Location

223. All six SARD DMCs have dedicated policies and acts to protect the welfare of those living in geographically difficult terrain or underdeveloped regions. Table 7.3 provides a list of some of these key policies.

Table 7.3: Key Acts and Policies for Geographically Excluded People

DMC	Policies
Bangladesh	National Rural Development Policy, 2001
	Chittagong Hill Tracts Land Dispute Resolution Commission
Bhutan	Bhutan National Urbanization Strategy, 2008
India	Mahatma Gandhi National Rural Employment Guarantee Act, 2015 Rehabilitation and Resettlement Act, 2013
Maldives	Strategic Action Plan, 2019–2023
Nepal	The Fifteenth Plan (2019-2024) National Employment Policy 2071 International Development Cooperation Policy, 2019
Sri Lanka	Regional Rural Development Banks Act, 1985

DMC = developing member country.

Source: Extracted from the six countries' policy documents.

224. Furthermore, the National Social Protection Strategy, 2014 of Bangladesh has dedicated programs that are explicitly targeted toward the population in CHT.[266] Some of these programs include allowances for beneficiaries, food assistance, and rehabilitation of non-Bengali people in the area through income and housing support. Other than the existing policies, the government also runs two projects: (i) the Sustainable Social Services Project to create a network of "para centers" (small villages) in the remote areas of CHT, making all the basic services available at the doorsteps of the marginalized communities; and (ii) the Strengthening Inclusive Development Project in CHT to build resilience among the community. These projects also have specific provisions for the empowerment of women.

225. Stakeholders in Sri Lanka assessed that despite a dedicated department for rural housing within the Ministry of Urban Development and Housing, a national policy for rural development, and well-defined projects in the country, various barriers (including low resource allocation) exist that prevent effective implementation. Despite these barriers, the government has been largely successful in addressing the housing issue in the country. In Bhutan, the government has taken a comprehensive approach through poverty alleviation programs in the 12th Five-year Plan to address barriers faced by the rural population. For instance, during the COVID-19 pandemic, loan interest charged for loans was waived temporarily (from April to September 2020) to reduce financial stress on the rural population. In Maldives, connectivity and limited access to resources and services are the two major barriers faced by people living in remote areas. To address this problem, the government has focused mainly on two aspects: connecting the

[266] Government of Bangladesh, Planning Commission, General Economics Division. 2014. *National Social Protection Strategy of Bangladesh*. Dhaka.

entire country through the public transport network and increasing access to essential services through the creation of regional hubs. However, according to the stakeholder participants, while these programs aim at universal access, there is a need for further dedicated provisions for the protection and uplifting of disadvantaged groups.

226.   Nepal has focused on rural development since its first Five-Year Plan, 1956–1961. Various policies and schemes have always been implemented for the rural and backward regions. For instance, the government has implemented rural development programs with the support of external development partners.[267] Affirmative actions have been taken for identified backward districts in civil service recruitment and social security allowances for all children under 5 in 14 geographically underdeveloped and excluded districts.

227.   Pradhan Mantri Gram Sadak Yojana is a nationwide plan in India to provide good all-weather road connectivity to unconnected villages. The program guidelines have set inclusive measures like mandatory transect walks with the participation of the communities to set road alignments and to identify road safety problems of pedestrians, including schoolchildren, or at pedestrian crossings.

Income Poverty

228.   All six SARD DMCs have dedicated nodal agencies and key acts and policies that work toward poverty alleviation (Table 7.4).

Table 7.4: Key Acts and Policies for Poverty Alleviation

DMC	Policies
Bangladesh	Sixth Five-Year Plan: Accelerating Growth and Reducing Poverty, 2011-2015
Bhutan	Poverty alleviation programs in the 11th Five-Year Plan (Rural Economy Advancement Programme), 2013–2018
India	Mahatma Gandhi National Rural Employment Guarantee Act, 2015
	National Land Acquisition and Rehabilitation and Resettlement Act, 2013
	Street Vendors Act, 2014
Maldives	Social Protection Act, 2014
Nepal	Poverty Alleviation Policy, 2019
	Poverty Alleviation Fund Act, 2006
Sri Lanka	Mahinda Chintana Vision for the Future, the Development of Policy Framework, Sri Lanka, 2010–2020

DMC = developing member country.

Source: Extracted from the six countries' policy documents.

[267]   K.P. Adhikari. 2015. Rural Development Policies, CBOs and their Sustainability in Nepal. In A. Adhikari et al., eds. *Sustainable Livelihood Systems in Nepal: Policies, Practices and Prospects*. Kathmandu: International Union for Conservation of Nature (IUCN) and Canada Foundation for Nepal (CFFN). pp. 237–263.

229.   Almost all the countries have specific provisions with an intersectional rural–urban lens for empowering excluded and vulnerable groups among the income-poor population. For example, the Rural Development and Cooperative Division in Bangladesh has the mandate to work with the rural poor, with a dedicated component for the empowerment of women and ethnic minorities. The focus is on livelihood empowerment and capacity building through organizing people into informal self-help groups. Offices at the *upazila* (subunit of a district) level are responsible for implementing these projects. With the high population of beneficiaries, monitoring policies and programs at the local level has proven difficult. Bhutan addresses poverty alleviation through five-year plans (like Bangladesh) as well as the Rural Economy Advancement Programme.[268] Besides these policies and programs, there were various initiatives to support poor people during the pandemic, e.g., waiving of interest on loans to reduce financial stress. In Maldives, access of vulnerable groups to products such as sanitary napkins and gloves was ensured during the lockdown period. A COVID-19 emergency response team was also active.[269]

230.   In Nepal, the fundamental rights and duties granted in the constitution and the provisions related to the economy and the agriculture, health, education, and social sectors all contribute to poverty alleviation in the country. Moreover, recognizing the need for a separate multisector policy for poverty alleviation, the government developed the Poverty Alleviation Policy in 2019 and established the Ministry of Land Management, Cooperatives, and Poverty Alleviation. The policy follows five main strategies: (i) identification of poor people population for developing more efficient and targeted programs; (ii) ensured easy access to basic needs, resources, and services for poor people; (iii) participation of poor people in the poverty alleviation program; (iv) employment generation; and (v) abolishment of all discrimination against poor people. According to the consultation participants, there is also a need for collecting disaggregated data.

231.   In Sri Lanka, the State Ministry of Rural Housing and Construction & Building Materials Industries attempted to address poverty by providing housing facilities to rural low-income and middle-income families. According to the consultation participants, insufficient funds are a major challenge. In India, the National Rural Livelihood Mission of the Ministry of Rural Development aims to alleviate rural poverty by creating sustainable livelihood opportunities for the rural poor. Toward this objective, the National Rural Livelihoods Mission seeks to promote sustainable community-based institutions that will facilitate the provision of financial services, economic services, and other entitlements to the rural poor, including rural women.[270]

D.   South Asia Department Projects Aiming to Benefit People in Difficult Geographic Locations and the Income Poor

232.   This section presents an assessment of the integration of actions targeting to understand and address the GESI-related issues of people in difficult geographic locations and the income

---

[268] Government of Bhutan, GNHC. 2019. *Twelfth Five Year Plan (2018–2023)*. Thimphu.
[269] L. Sherburne-Benz, S. Paternostro, and Z. Majoka. 2020. Protecting South Asia's Poor and Vulnerable Against COVID-19. *World Bank Blogs*. 2 July.
[270] Government of India, Ministry of Rural Development. National Rural Livelihoods Mission: Mission Document.

poor in 19 selected projects of SARD. These projects, which are in the three selected sectors (energy, transport, and water and other urban infrastructure and services), were selected based on the criteria listed in Chapter 1, paras. 17, 18 and 19. The assessment was on whether these projects have the key mainstreaming elements in four areas: (i) policies that seek to understand and address the issues of people in difficult geographic locations and the income poor; (i) institutional arrangements that locate responsibilities for ensuring the achievement of GESI targets focused on them; (iii) programming and budgeting directed at supporting them; and (iv) a monitoring and evaluation system that captures and reports project GESI results experienced by them.

233.   Overall, some projects across the three sectors have the following elements:

(i)   **Policies**

(a)   **Disaggregated data by geographic location and income poverty.** Of the 13 projects that had this element, 4 are energy projects, 3 are transport projects, and 6 are urban development projects. These projects are as follows:

- **Bangladesh:** Power System Enhancement and Efficiency Improvement Project (footnote 83) and Dhaka Environmentally Sustainable Water Supply Project (footnote 122)
- **Bhutan:** Secondary Towns Urban Development Project271 and Thimphu Road Improvement Project (footnote 86)
- **India:** Madhya Pradesh Energy Efficiency Improvement Investment Program (footnote 85), West Bengal Drinking Water Sector Improvement Project272, and Rural Connectivity Investment Program (footnote 121)
- **Maldives:** Preparing Outer Islands for Sustainable Energy Development Project273 and Kulhudhuffushi Harbor Expansion Project (footnote 87)
- **Nepal:** Third Small Towns Water Supply and Sanitation Sector Project (footnote 79) and South Asia Subregional Economic Coordination Road Connectivity Project274
- **Sri Lanka:** Local Government Enhancement Sector Project (footnote 123) and Supporting Electricity Supply Reliability Improvement Project (footnote 82)

(b)   **Policy provisions addressing the barriers to gender equality and social inclusion.** Of the 11 projects that had this element, 5 are energy projects, 1 is a transport project, and 5 are urban development projects. Examples of these policy provisions are developed energy and urban infrastructure services for poor income communities, communities living in rural areas, and women and other disadvantaged groups; improved market access through improved transport facilities; and improved health through access to quality drinking water. These provisions have the potential to increase

271   ADB. Bhutan: Secondary Towns Urban Development Project.
272   ADB. India: West Bengal Drinking Water Sector Improvement Project.
273   ADB. Maldives: Preparing Outer Islands for Sustainable Energy Development Project.
274   ADB. Nepal: South Asia Subregional Economic Cooperation Road Connectivity Project.

the overall productivity and income of the disadvantaged groups and capacity development of authorities. The projects that incorporated the aforementioned policy provisions are the same as those that collected disaggregated data.

(ii) **Institutional arrangements.** The responsibility for addressing GESI barriers is located within the executing agency or implementing agency project team. Of the seven projects that had this element, three are energy projects, two are transport projects, and two are urban development projects. Examples of these projects are the South Asia Subregional Economic Cooperation Dhaka–Northwest Corridor Road Project, Phase 2[275] and the Bangladesh Power System Enhancement and Efficiency Improvement Project (footnote 83); Bhutan's Secondary Towns Urban Development Project (footnote 271); India's West Bengal Drinking Water Sector Improvement Project (273); Nepal's Power Transmission and Distribution Efficiency Enhancement Project (footnote 80); and Sri Lanka's Supporting Electricity Supply Reliability Improvement Project (footnote 82) and Integrated Road Investment Program (footnote 120). Addressing GESI barriers is integrated into the functions of the executing agency and implementing agencies project team (apart from the GESI team or consultant).

(iii) **Programming and budgeting**

(a) **Activities aiming to empower people in remote geographic location and income poor.** Of the 10 projects that had this element, 5 are energy projects, 1 is a transport project, and 4 are urban development projects. Examples of project activities specifically targeting people in difficult geographic locations are improved meter water supply in Bhutan's **Secondary Towns Urban Development Project** (footnote 271) and encouraging increased employment of women and local poor in the **Kulhudhuffushi Harbor Expansion Project** (footnote 87). Other examples of these project activities are regularized water supply connections to low-income communities; gender- and disability-friendly footpaths (well-lit for women, girls, and people with disabilities); and training for households below the poverty line in the productive use of income opportunities that emerge from the electricity access, training them in technical skills, and providing them with support to establish microenterprises.

(b) **Activities aiming to create an enabling environment for gender equality and social inclusion.** Of the three projects that had this element, one is a transport project and two are urban development projects. Examples of these project activities are to ensure that poor people, vulnerable, and excluded are aware of grievance redress procedures and their entitlements according to the project entitlement matrix; ensure that women and other excluded groups are in the executive committees of water users' associations and enhance their leadership development.

[275] ADB. Bangladesh: South Asia Subregional Economic Cooperation Dhaka-Northwest Corridor Road Project, Phase 2 - Tranche 1.

(iv) **Monitoring and evaluation.** Some projects aiming to benefit income-poor people have monitoring and evaluation systems and reporting templates that capture and report their GESI-related benefits. Examples of these projects are Nepal's Third Small Towns Water Supply and Sanitation Sector Project (footnote 79) and Sri Lanka's Local Government Enhancement Sector Project (footnote 123).

E.   Good Practices in Responding to the Issues of People in Difficult Geographic Locations and the Income Poor

234.   The second set of 15 projects of SARD was assessed to identify their good practices in achieving GESI for people in difficult geographic location and the income poor along the pillars of the "Leave-No-One-Behind" (LNOB) framework. The following are the good practices identified:

(i) **Understand for action.** Certain ADB projects conducted surveys, including disaggregated data collection. For instance, as part of ADB's Skills Training and Education Pathway Upgradation Project in Bhutan, a comprehensive survey with disaggregated information was conducted before the project's inception. The survey results highlighted important insights on income inequality in the region. This data, providing evidence that the women trainees would not have any financing options for their higher education or training without support, helped set the rationale for the project and moved the Government of Bhutan to invest more in this sector.

(ii) **Empower for change**

(a) The Nepal **Supporting School Sector Development Plan**[276] implemented a pro-poor scholarship scheme in 15 districts of the country. Of the 699 poor students that received the scholarship, 324 (46%) were girls. The scholarship scheme aimed to increase girls' participation in science subjects in grades 11 and 12.

(b) The Nepal **Integrated Urban Development Project**[277] constructed GESI-sensitive community infrastructures based on the needs identified by women, income poor, and excluded groups (e.g., Dalits and Janajatis) in the project areas. Infrastructures included roads, drainage, culverts, sex-segregated community toilets, and small water supply works. For the construction of these community infrastructures, the project hired poor people in the project areas, 15% of whom were women. The project included a community development program to benefit poverty pockets in the project-covered municipalities and communities that could not benefit directly from the constructed infrastructures.

(iii) **Include for opportunity.** The Maldives Inclusive Micro, Small, and Medium-Sized Enterprise Development Project (footnote 95) established seven regional business

---

[276] ADB. Nepal: Supporting School Sector Development Plan.
[277] ADB. Nepal: Integrated Urban Development Project.

centers—some of which are in remote islands or atolls—to provide business development services to micro, small, and medium-sized enterprises (MSMEs), including women-led MSMEs. The project provided business development services (training on business start-up, business planning, business consultations, and technical visits) to 17,465 existing and aspiring entrepreneurs, of whom 8,729 (50%) were women, and business loans to 96 women-owned MSMEs.

235.   During the stakeholder consultations in the six DMCs, the participants from CSOs shared their related initiatives, some of which are as follows:

(i)   **Empower for change**
(a)   In Bangladesh, Friendship established women's weaving centers in the remotest parts of the *chars* and held awareness campaigns on how char dwellers can access government services.
(b)   In Bhutan, the Tarayana Foundation works with underserved communities in remote areas of the country. It started a microfinance company through which it proved the effectiveness of a unique approach called the "business in a box" model. In this model, people are provided cash loans and offering assistance in buying materials or machinery for their businesses and marketing their products.
(c)   The South Asian Association for Regional Cooperation Business Association of Home-based Workers Bhutan works with home-based workers, especially women, by enhancing their livelihood skills, such as in weaving, tailoring, and food processing, and linking them with the market. The organization also facilitates workers' travel to neighboring countries to participate in advanced training, such as on tailoring, weaving, and bookkeeping. Additionally, the business association provides the workers with materials, kits, and samples so that they can sell their finished products at piece rate and get paid directly. After being trained, some women workers start their own businesses, such as tailoring shops. The business association also has a trade facilitation center where any female worker can work if they face any issues while working at home.
(d)   Jeevan Rekha Parishad in India works with rural, tribal, and poor women in slums. To address their poverty and hunger, Jeevan Rekha Parishad implements a beekeeping project, through which 550 tribal women beekeepers produce, collect, process, and sell honey both online and offline. The organization also supports self-help groups in running Regenerative Ecotourism, which is a sustainable ecotourism project. The organization was able to sustain this project during the COVID-19 pandemic because many tourists preferred to stay in remote islands.
(e)   Pradan in India organizes self-help groups in the poorest regions of India to improve women's livelihood through better agriculture practices and water management, raise women's gender equality awareness and self-confidence, engage men in addressing GBV, address untouchability, and increase women's participation in household decision-making. The organization uses street play or theater held in public view (e.g., streets) as a method for raising awareness.

(iii)   **Include for opportunity.** The United Nations Development Programme (UNDP) in Bangladesh works in the CHT districts, home to 13 indigenous groups, in a very remote part of Bangladesh. UNDP's initial project was to prevent conflict in the area and support the government in implementing the Chittagong Hill Tract Peace Accord of 1997. Finding a high school dropout rate in schools, UNDP also introduced "teaching in mother language," where students are taught in their indigenous language. As recruiting teachers was a challenge, UNDP helped some people complete a secondary level of education and then hired them as teachers.

F.   Conclusions and Way Forward

Summary of Findings

236.   This study merged the GESI assessment of the situation in difficult geographic locations with income poverty, which are two dimensions of social exclusion, because of their interrelation. Most income-poor South Asians live in rural and disaster-prone areas. The highlights of the assessment are as follows:

(i)   **Situation**
   (a)   People in difficult geographic areas and the income poor have limited access to basic social services. The increased environmental degradation and low capacity to adapt to climate change have made current agricultural practices unable to sustain the population. Hence, these people's dependence on agriculture has made them more susceptible to poverty.
   (b)   Income-poor people in difficult geographic locations have limited participation in community development programs because of their time poverty, location, and lack of trust in the ability of these programs to lift them out of poverty.
   (c)   Among the income poor and those in difficult geographic locations, women are the most adversely affected because of restricted mobility because of concerns of safety, lack of economic opportunities beyond agriculture, time poverty, GBV, and limited decision-making power. As a result, women's unemployment rates are higher in rural areas than in urban areas.
   (d)   Poverty incidence and geographic location are also linked with social identities, as chronic poverty is disproportionately higher among historically marginalized social groups, such as scheduled castes and scheduled tribes in India and Dalits in Nepal.
   (e)   All six DMCs have dedicated policies and acts to protect the welfare of people in difficult geographic locations or underdeveloped regions, and for poverty alleviation.

(ii)   **Responses**
   (a)   SARD has responded to exclusion and vulnerability issues experienced by income-poor people in difficult geographic locations. In the three sectors covered in this assessment, SARD has examples of projects responding to these issues and a list of related good practices.
   (b)   In all six DMCs, the government and CSOs have initiatives or programs responding to the empowerment and inclusion needs of people in difficult geographic locations and the income poor.

Way Forward for the South Asia Department

237.   During the stakeholder consultation workshops, representatives from the government and CSOs shared the following as potential areas for SARD's assistance.

(i)   **Bangladesh**

    (a)   Support the building of partnerships between local communities and CSOs in developing and maintaining community infrastructures with government support.

    (b)   Assist in creating a formal information network or platforms where the income poor, especially those in difficult geographic locations, can raise their needs and access information on available resources, services, and opportunities for development.

(ii)   **Bhutan**

    (a)   Continue developing the capability of rural women farmers to access markets, which remains a challenge despite ADB's previous TA project, Advancing Economic Opportunities Of Women And Girls (2011-15).

    (b)   Facilitate policy dialogues to address issues faced by people with special needs (e.g., people with disabilities) in remote areas, as responding to these needs tends to be dropped or blocked at the local level, failing to reach the national level.

    (c)   Support the development of existing microfinance institutions, like the Bhutan Association of Women Entrepreneurs, into full-fledged micro banks to provide better services to poor women.

(iii)   **India**

    (a)   Increase the community's engagement in ADB-assisted projects by establishing community-based monitoring systems.

    (b)   Promote the convergence of efforts of the government, CSOs, and poor communities by helping key actors understand the importance of partnership and develop trust in each other.

    (c)   Support a bottom-up approach to development by engaging the target communities or social groups in identifying and designing development initiatives based on their needs and aspirations.

(iv)   **Sri Lanka**

    (a)   Support the staff demobilization when the mine action program in the eastern and western regions ends (expected to conclude in 2026).[278] More than 2,500 de-miners work in the sector and almost 50% are female de-miners (of which 95% of them breadwinners of their families).

    (b)   Include internally displaced people as a key vulnerable group and incorporate their needs in the SARD GESI framework.

---

[278] The informant interviewed for this study did not mention the end date of the mining action program. For clarity of this proposed way forward for SARD, the end date of the program was culled from Government of Sri Lanka, State Ministry of Rural Housing and Construction and Building Materials Industries Promotion, National Mine Action Centre. 2022. *Sri Lanka Mine Action Programme: Moving towards completion.* Colombo.

VIII.   YOUNG AGE AND MIGRANT STATUS IN SOUTH ASIA

A.   Introduction

238.   This chapter merges the discussion of issues of disadvantaged youth and migrant workers for three reasons. First, these two groups share the same type of disadvantage, which is situational (Figure 1. 2 of Chapter 1 of this report) and may be temporary (the conditions may change when the young person becomes an adult, and when the migrant worker returns to the country or place of origin or acquires full rights in the new location). Second, the discussion of the situation of these two groups is limited to some countries (disadvantaged youth in Bhutan, India, and Maldives, and migrant workers' situation in India and Maldives). Third, the initiatives of the South Asia Department (SARD) to assist these two disadvantaged groups are limited.

B.   Disadvantaged Youth

Definition

239.   The government and civil society stakeholders in Bhutan, India, and Maldives identified disadvantaged youth as a very vulnerable group.[279] Bhutan's National Youth Policy, 2011 defines youth as people from 13 to 24 years old.[280] In Maldives, the population aged 18–34 years is considered youth.[281] In India, the National Youth Policy, 2014 defines youth as people aged 15–29 years.[282]

---

[279] While youth are considered a vulnerable group across all DMCs, this study focused on discussing particularly the concerns of disadvantaged youth in selected countries where the issues were considered critical by the resident missions.

[280] Government of Bhutan, Ministry of Education, Department of Youth and Sports. 2011. *National Youth Policy.* Thimphu.

[281] A. Demmke. 2017. *Thematic Analysis on Youth in Maldives Based on 2014 Population and Housing Census Data.* Malé: UNFPA Maldives Country Office; and Government of Maldives, Ministry of Finance and Treasury, National Bureau of Statistics.

[282] Government of India, Ministry of Youth Affairs and Sports. 2014. *National Youth Policy, 2014.* New Delhi.

Status of Disadvantaged Youth in Bhutan, India, and Maldives

Demography

240.   In Bhutan, 60% of the population is below the age of 25.[283] Youth in Maldives represent 37% of the national population. Those aged 20–34 years remain the largest bulk of the youth population, one-third of whom lives in Malé.[284] Close to 28% of the population belongs to the "youth" category in India (footnote 282).

Access to Social Resources and Services

241.   The consultation participants in Bhutan, India, and Maldives highlighted various barriers limiting youth's access to education. The young population, specifically the ones from disadvantaged backgrounds, lack access to technology like smartphones and were hit hard by school closures after the onset of coronavirus disease (COVID-19) in Bhutan. The consultation participants also highlighted that youth-centric training programs on important skills, like computer knowledge or English speaking skills, were few and insufficient.

242.   Youth reproductive and sexual health is a major concern in the three countries because of their significant adolescent population. India has a high rate of child marriage that results in early childbearing and serious reproductive health problems.[285] One study found prevalence of reproductive tract infections and sexually transmitted infections among young women and men in India. Many lack information about or access to the treatment they need or are reluctant to seek treatment because of fear of stigma and discrimination. India also has one of the world's highest prevalence rates of iron deficiency anemia among women, including adolescents (footnote 285). Similarly, in Bhutan, early age marriages and pregnancies, low use of contraceptive methods, and sexually transmitted infections continue to be prevalent among adolescents and youth. Teenage pregnancy and early parenthood have been acknowledged as important social and health concerns in the country, as they pose a substantial challenge to young women's health and their access to education and other socioeconomic resources.[286]

243.   In Maldives, a study found that young people's perceptions and understanding of sexual and reproductive health are limited to the information received through the biology lessons and the life skills program conducted in schools by the Ministry of Education.[287] The same study also noted that there is a communication gap between parents and youth regarding sexual and reproductive health, and as a result, young people resort to seeking this information from friends, other family members, or electronic and print media, which is not always accurate. Moreover, premarital sexual activity is illegal in Maldives, which has led to limited data and has

---

[283] UNFPA Bhutan Country Office. What We Do: Young People.

[284] Government of Maldives, Ministry of Finance and Treasury, National Bureau of Statistics; and UNFPA Maldives Country Office. 2018. *Youth in Maldives*. Malé.

[285] R. Pande et al. 2006. *Improving Reproductive Health of Married and Unmarried Youth in India: Evidence of Effectiveness and Costs from Community-based Interventions*. Washington, DC: International Center for Research on Women.

[286] L. Dorji. 2009. Sexual and Reproductive Health of Adolescents and Youth in Bhutan. *Monograph Series*. No. 7. Thimphu: Government of Bhutan, National Statistics Bureau; and UNFPA.

[287] Asia-Pacific Resource and Research Centre for Women. 2019. *Sexual Reproductive Health Services Seeking Behavior Among Maldivian Youth Between the Ages of 18–25 Years*. Malé.

restricted certain services for unmarried youth.[288] Difficulties related to obtaining information and services are compounded for adolescents who are marginalized based on their sexuality, gender expression, or marital status.

244.   In Bhutan and Maldives, drug abuse is also a major cause of concern among the vulnerable youth, but rehabilitation facilities and trained personnel are inadequate. The consultation participants said that the drug court in Maldives has been functioning well, but because of insufficient support services, there remains a huge backlog of cases, and the rate of relapse after treatment is very high. There is only one treatment center and two detoxification centers, which are mostly full; there is also no national strategy or policy for prevention.[289]

245.   A survey conducted by the United Nations Children's Fund (UNICEF) found that about 14% (or one in seven) of 15- to 24-year-olds in India reported often feeling depressed or having little interest in doing things. It also found that young people seem reticent to seek support for their mental stress. Only 41% of young people aged 15–24 years in India said that it is good to get support for mental health problems, compared to an average of 83% in 21 countries covered in a UNICEF study.[290] In Bhutan, a study noted that young people aged 10–24 constituted 33% of the mental health outpatients.[291] While no formal estimates are available for Maldives, the national mental health policy of the country has recognized that suicide is an increasing problem, especially in the adolescent and young age group.[292] Inability to recognize symptoms, concerns of negative social perceptions, misinformation, lack of awareness, and inadequate availability of and access to services are challenges to the mental health of young people in these countries.

Access to Economic Resources and Services

246.   According to the consultation participants, while recent government interventions in all three developing member countries (DMCs) have aimed at providing skills training and more employment opportunities for the youth, gaps remain because of a lack of resources and poor implementation. Youth unemployment in Bhutan increased from 10.7% in 2015 to 12.3% in 2017, even though 93% of youth were literate then.[293] In India, 12.9% of youth (aged 15–29) were unemployed in 2021.[294] Of those employed, 47% were in the agriculture sector as cultivators and laborers.[295] In Maldives, unemployment among the young population aged 15–24 years was 16%, and 8% among the youth population aged 18–34 years, both higher than the national average of 6%.[296]

[288] S. Hameed. 2018. To Be Young, Unmarried, Rural, and Female: Intersections of Sexual and Reproductive Health and Rights in the Maldives. *Reproductive Health Matters*. 26 (54). pp. 61–71.
[289] A. Adyb. 2014. Maldives under the Burden of Drugs. *Journal of Alcoholism and Drug Dependence*. 2 (4).
[290] UNICEF. 2021. UNICEF Report Spotlights on the Mental Health Impact of Covid-19 in Children and Young People. News release. 5 October.
[291] L. Dorji et al. 2015. Crime and Mental Health Issues Among the Young Bhutanese People. *Monograph Series*. No. 8. Thimphu: Government of Bhutan, National Statistics Bureau; and UNFPA.
[292] Government of Maldives. 2017. *National Mental Health Policy 2015–25*. Malé.
[293] Royal Government of Bhutan. National Bureau of Statistics. *Harnessing Demographic Dividend in Bhutan*. p. 24. Youth unemployment refers to the share of the labor force ages 15–24 without work but available for and seeking employment.
[294] Government of India. Ministry of Statistics and Programme Implementation. Periodic Labour Force Survey. 2020-21.
[295] R. Chand and J. Singh. 2022. Workforce Changes and Employment Some Findings from PLFS Data Series. *NITI Aayog Discussion Paper*. No. 1/2022. New Delhi: NITI Aayog.
[296] World Bank Group. 2014. *Youth in the Maldives: Shaping a New Future for Young Women and Men through Engagement and Empowerment*. Washington, DC.

247.   In three DMCs, inadequate vocational skills and institutions for skills building and vocational training have resulted in limited economic opportunities and inability of the youth to find jobs. Related to this issue, in August 2020, India announced the National Education Policy, which aims to make awareness about vocational skill training accessible to nearly 50% of learners across the country by 2025. This policy seeks to address the issues of information asymmetry and dignity of labor that made vocational skilling non-aspirational in the past.[297]

248.   Drug abuse is a cause of concern in Maldives and has negative consequences for young people. The absence of adequate rehabilitation services creates problems for convicted men when they seek employment and reintegration into society. For instance, as per a Maldivian study, poor reintegration following drug-related offenses has resulted in young men seeking social support by joining or rejoining gangs.[298]

Social Practices, Participation, and Decision-Making

249.   The consultation participants observed that peer pressure, ignorance, lack of parental guidance, and incomplete information regarding the effects of drugs have pushed youth into drugs in the DMCs. In Bhutan, more than 60% of male students from higher secondary classes (IX-X and XI-XII) reportedly had friends using cannabis, alcohol, or solvents, while about one-third of the female students also agreed that they had friends who were using such substances. One-fourth of the students from senior high school classes (XI-XII) reported drug use-related problems in the family.[299] The consultation participants also highlighted that families, particularly parents, lack sensitivity and counseling skills in dealing with substance abuse problems. These children and young adults are shamed and "hidden" from the community, which only worsens the problem. In Maldives, drug users are often alienated from and stigmatized by their families, friends, and peers. Almost 44% of drug users in Malé and 53% in the other atolls reported having conflicts with family and friends.

Intersectionality

250.   Barriers faced by disadvantaged youth are compounded by their social identities and gender. For example, in India, consultation participants highlighted the exclusion of disadvantaged youth belonging to marginalized groups, such as scheduled castes and scheduled tribes, from regular community activities. They said that as a result, their only interaction with other people in their community is through the services expected of them based on their caste/ethnicity. According to a 2014 World Bank report, young women in the atolls of Maldives, outside of the capital city of Malé, were keen to work and earn a livelihood but did not participate in the labor force because of restrictive social and cultural norms (footnote 296). For these women, a key reason for being unemployed was the disproportionate burden of their care responsibilities. The average age of first marriage is 22.5 years for women, and by age 25, they have had their first child (footnote 284).

[297] A. Francis. 2021. The Need to Invest in Vocational Training. *India Development Review*. 5 March.
[298] United Nations Office on Drugs and Crime. 2013. *National Drug Use Survey Maldives—2011/2012*. Malé.
[299] United Nations Office for Drugs and Crime. 2012. Bhutan: Safeguarding Youth from the Perils of Drug Use.

Policy Analysis

251.   All three DMCs have dedicated policies and acts for the protection, uplifting and empowerment of disadvantaged youth (Table 8.1).

Table 8.1: Key Acts and Policies for Disadvantaged Youth

DMC	Policies
Bhutan	National Youth Policy, 2010
India	National Youth Policy, 2014 National Skills Development Mission, 2015
Maldives	Juvenile Justice Act, 2019
	National Youth Policy, 2003

DMC = developing member country.

Source: Extracted from the countries' policy documents.

252.   The National Youth Policy, 2010 in Bhutan seeks to support the youth population with educational and employment opportunities. It facilitates their access to entrepreneurial guidance, financial credit, and health information aimed at (i) preventing the use of alcohol, drugs, and other forms of substance abuse; (ii) preventing the spread of diseases like HIV; and (iii) ensuring measures for de-addiction, among other things. The policy also seeks to sensitize society to the needs, interests, opinions, ideas, and aspirations of its young people; and to sensitize national policy makers to identify and mainstream youth issues into national development. Similarly, in India, the civil society organization (CSO) participants observed that the National Youth Policy and other related policies are inclusive at all levels.

253.   Apart from enforcing existing policies and acts, the Government of Maldives implements various initiatives to engage youth and address their challenges, which was appreciated by the consultations' youth participants. Some of these initiatives include building infrastructural facilities like sports grounds, to increase youth activity, engaging in consultative policy making, and implementing skills development and youth leadership programs. However, according to the consultation participants, the COVID-19 pandemic adversely affected the implementation of these programs.

C.   Migrant Workers in India and Maldives

Definition

254.   A 2022 report of the Government of India's Ministry of Statistics and Programme Implementation defines a migrant as a household member whose last usual place of residence any time in the past is different from the present place of enumeration.[300] In Maldives, the 2014 census defined "migrant" as a person who at any time in their life had changed their island of

---

[300] Government of India, Ministry of Statistics and Programme Implementation. 2022. Migration in India, 2020–2021. News release. 14 June.

usual residence.[301] Internal migrants in India and international migrants in Maldives are identified as vulnerable groups.

Status of Migrant Workers in India and Maldives

Demography

255.   According to official estimates from PLFS survey 2020–2021, the migration rate (the percentage of migrants in the population) in India is 29% (rural: 27%, urban: 35%), and 88% of the migration takes place within the same state. Marriage was the prime reason behind migration for more than 71% of the migrants, with 87% of women and 6% of men migrating for marriage.[302] In the latest Maldivian census 2014, 44% of the Maldivians had changed their residence over the course of their lifetime. Such change mostly involved moving to Malé because of its relatively high level of development compared to the other atolls. If coupled with its nonadministrative islands, Malé had the largest proportion of internal migrants (56%), followed by Felidhu (47%) and South Nalindhe (45%). The Maldives census also enumerated 338,434 resident Maldivians and 63,637 resident foreigners, about 16% of the total resident population in Maldives. Foreigners come mostly from Bangladesh, India, and Sri Lanka and work in the tourism industry and the construction sector (footnote 301).

Access to Social Resources and Services

256.   Most migrants working in the informal sector in India are undocumented workers, which restricts their access to basic social services like vaccination and health care. Social security schemes (and programs on health, education, and upskilling) are usually linked with domicile status, thus making it difficult for migrants to access such benefits. According to the consultation participants, interventions like the One Nation One Ration Card plan in India, rolled out on 1 June 2020, are helpful (One Nation One Ration Card is an inclusive measure that can help migrant ration cardholders to obtain food grains from any fairly priced shops in India). However, such interventions require effective systems and higher awareness among the migrant population about the individual schemes.

257.   The consultation participants noted that the mechanisms to collect periodic data on migrants could be improved in India. In particular, contractors, who hire migrants as daily laborers, often do not want to register workers as this leads to additional costs per hire. In India, a study highlighted that migrant workers who largely form the informal labor market escape safety nets of employment laws because of the lack of specific provisions to recognize their mobile nature and temporary work tenures.[303]

258.   The Government of India has attempted to address these problems by introducing registration systems to regulate the inflow of migrant workers into each state, with Kerala as

---

[301] P. Plewa. 2018. *Migration in Maldives: A Country Profile 2018.* Malé: International Organization for Migration.

[302] Government of India, Press Information Bureau. Ministry of Statistics and Programme Implementation. 2022. *Migration in India 2020-21.* New Delhi.

[303] J. John et al. 2020. *A Study on Social Security and Health Rights of Migrant Workers in India.* New Delhi: Kerala Development Society.

the first state to enact a social security scheme (footnote 303). However, despite this crucial attempt of the Kerala state government, the nature of migration and the structural requirements of the scheme have limited its scope and implementation. The seasonal nature of labor, lack of motivation among the migrants, lack of regulation among the employers, and cultural and language barriers act as hurdles to the take-up of the scheme (footnote 303). In early 2015, the Government of Maldives estimated that at least 35,000 undocumented international migrants—the group most vulnerable to exploitation—were in the country. However, the real number of these irregular migrants is likely to be much higher (footnote 301).

Access to Economic Resources and Services

259.   In both India and Maldives, most migrant workers work in the informal sector, where they experience low job security and harsh work conditions. However, employers in Maldives reported a preference for migrant workers because of the lower wages and working conditions that they are willing to accept, and their job commitment and loyalty (footnote 301).

260.   Migrants have also been one of the most severely affected groups in the aftermath of the COVID-19 pandemic, as many were left out of jobs and income opportunities during the lockdowns. Within India, an estimated 40 million internal migrant workers, largely in the informal economy, were severely impacted by the government's COVID-19 lockdown.[304] They were retrenched in large numbers and became unemployed with their wages unpaid in the destination states, which forced them to return to their states of origin (a phenomenon popularly termed "reverse migration"). A few migrants reported that they received work under the same employer or contractor after the lockdown but complained of nonpayment of wages during the lockdown period. They were forced to return to their villages because of unpaid wages; lack of a place to live with basic facilities, such as electricity and water provided by the employer or contractor; and lack of immediate governmental protection for basic necessities. Those who returned home found, in some instances, villages refusing entry because of fear of COVID-19 transmission.[305] In Maldives, cases of deceptive recruitment practices, unsafe living and working conditions, and excessive work demands contributed to the problems of the migrant workers.[306]

Social Practices, Participation, and Decision-Making

261.   The consultation participants assessed that because of unfamiliarity with a new place and lack of secure employment and income, international migrants often have limited negotiation power in a new city and country. For instance, unskilled migrants in Maldives are met with xenophobia and discrimination and are looked down upon by the locals in the capital city. Since the onset of the pandemic in the country, there have been increasing reports of discrimination and stigma against migrants (footnote 306).

---

[304] A. Khan and H. Arokkiaraj, 2021. Challenges of Reverse Migration in India: A Comparative Study of Internal and International Migrant Workers in the Post-Covid Economy. *Comparative Migration Studies.* 9 (49).
[305] C. Patel. 2020. The Indian migration crisis: The hidden majority. *Routed.* 20 June.
[306] Human Rights Watch. 2020. Maldives: Covid-19 Exposes Abuse of Migrants. 25 August.

262.   Exclusion and vulnerabilities faced by migrant workers are compounded by gender identities. In Maldives, the admission of migrant domestic workers has helped many local women, replacing them in household chores. Migrant men coming into Maldives outnumber migrant women because of demand and supply factors, such as heightened demand for construction workers and Bangladesh's ban on female migration from the country. The stay period of women in Maldives was lower (0–1 and 1–2 years) than of men, who usually stayed for 3–4 and 5–9 years (footnote 281).

263.   In India, the consultation participants highlighted some of the difficulties faced by women migrants, including gender wage gaps (even in pre-pandemic times), lack of proper sanitation and health facilities, and safety concerns. It was observed that while male migrants can secure employment in the infrastructure sector, most women end up working as domestic workers or in the informal sector. In India, home-based women migrant workers who chose to stay back in their place of employment during the pandemic experienced a drop in daily wages and missed out on COVID-19 relief schemes.[307] According to the consultation participants, women migrants, in whichever occupation, were more vulnerable to sexual abuse and violence from spouses and contractors. A 2015 study by UKaid found high prevalence of spousal violence among women migrant workers in India.[308] According to the consultation participants, many scheduled caste women migrants do not have their ration cards and do not own land or financial assets, making them more vulnerable to abuse.

Policy Analysis

264.   Table 8.2 provides a list of some policies for migrant workers in India and Maldives.

Table 8.2: Key Acts and Policies for Migrant Workers in India and Maldives

DMC	Policies
India	The Inter-State Migrant Workmen (Regulation of Employment and Conditions of Service) Act, 1979
	The Building and Other Construction Workers (Regulation of Employment and Conditions of Service) Act, 1996
	Equal Renumeration Act, 1976
	Labour Code, 2022 The Right of Children to Free and Compulsory Education Act, 2009 (includes the provision of seasonal hostel for children whose parents are migrating) National Food Security Act, 2013 (One Nation One Ration Card for migrating families) e-shram card, 2021
Maldives	Expatriate Employment Regulations, 2020 (Regulation No. 2020/R-62)
	Regulation on Employment of Expatriates in the Maldives, 2021
	Immigration Strategic Plan, 2020–2024

DMC = developing member country.

Source: Extracted from the six countries' policy documents.

---

[307] S.I. Rajan et al. 2020. The COVID-19 Pandemic and Internal Labor Migration in India: A "Crisis of Mobility." *The Indian Journal of Labour Economics*. 63 (4). pp. 1021–1039.

[308] L.R. Saraswati, V. Sharma, and A. Sarna. *Female Migrants in India*. New Delhi: Population Council.

265.   In India, the Interstate Migrant Workmen (Regulation of Employment and Conditions of Service) Act of 1979 and the Building and Other Construction Workers (Regulation of Employment and Conditions of Service) Act of 1996 are some of the key acts and policies implemented by the Government of India for the protection of the rights and welfare of migrant workers. These acts aim to regulate the employment and working conditions of the workers. According to the consultation participants, more effective service delivery mechanisms; better utilization of funds (for example, the Building and Other Construction Workers Fund); more labor inspectors; and the presence of a coordinating body at all levels of the government would contribute to better implementation of the policies. Furthermore, the consultation participants assessed that more human and financial resources are required to close the gaps, as the Building and Other Construction Workers Fund is significantly underutilized and the number of labor inspectors to support India's large migrant labor population is disproportionately low. The participants also highlighted the need for a separate coordinating body at the national, state, and regional levels and for mainstreaming the rights of migrant workers into the existing acts and policies.

266.   The Constitution of Maldives upholds the fundamental rights of all its citizens and migrant workers. While the country has no comprehensive migration policy to address all the aspects of migration, their rights are guaranteed in the Employment Act, 2008 (Act No, 2/2008); the Immigration Act, 2007 (Act No. 1/2007); the Anti-Human Trafficking Act, 2013 (Act No. 12/2013); and the Regulation on Employment of Expatriates in the Maldives, 2021 (Regulation No. 2021/R-16).[309] The regulations on expatriate employment and individual guidelines and rules cover various issues for foreign migrant workers, such as registration with the online Xpat system, granting of quotas, collection of quota fees, granting of approval to work in the country, deposits and refunds, accommodation of service providers, arrangements and standards of accommodation, and disciplinary measures for breaches.[310]

267.   The country has also made efforts to regulate undocumented migrant workers through the amendment of the Decentralization Act, 2010 (Act No. 7/2010), which requires local councils to maintain a registry of migrant workers in the islands.[311] The Government of Maldives launched a strategic action plan in November 2020 that covers the immigration strategic action plan. The plan aims to streamline visa application and issuance through modern technology; establish regular migration channels; and prevent human trafficking, people smuggling, and other transnational crimes.[312] The consultation participants said that this is particularly important for the country, as it is surrounded by water and is a famous tourist spot.

[309] Government of Maldives, Labour Relations Authority. *Regulation on Employment of Expatriates in the Maldives 2021.* Malé (in Dhivehi).
[310] *Maldives Insider.* 2020. Maldives Enacts New Expatriate Employment Regulations. 17 August.
[311] Ministry of Finance. 2020. *Decentralization Act.* Malé (in Dhivehi).
[312] Government of Maldives, Maldives Immigration. 2021. *Strategic Plan 2020–2024.* Malé.

D.   South Asia Department Projects Aiming to Benefit Disadvantaged Youth and Migrant Workers

268.   This section presents an assessment of the planned and actual contributions of the reviewed 19 projects (under the energy, transport, and water and other urban infrastructure and services sectors) of SARD to uplifting the situation of the disadvantaged youth and migrant workers in the six DMCs. This list of SARD projects is the same as those reviewed in the previous chapters and selected based on the criteria presented in Chapter 1, paras. 17, 18, and 19 of this report. The assessment was on whether these projects have the key mainstreaming elements in four areas: (i) policies that seek to understand and address the issues of disadvantaged youth and migrant workers, (ii) institutional arrangements that locate responsibilities for ensuring the achievement of planned benefits for them, (iii) programming and budgeting directed at supporting them, and (iv) a monitoring and evaluation system that captures and reports project GESI results experienced by the two groups.

Disadvantaged Youth

269.   Of the reviewed 19 projects, only two projects, both under the energy sector and categorized effective gender mainstreaming (EGM) (footnote 21), explicitly incorporated in the project design disadvantaged youth as a target project beneficiary. One was the **Preparing Outer Islands for Sustainable Energy Development Project** (footnote 273) in Maldives. The other was the **Supporting Electricity Supply Reliability Improvement Project** (footnote 82) in Sri Lanka. These project features are related to the mainstreaming element, programming, and budgeting.

(i)   The **Preparing Outer Islands for Sustainable Energy Development Project** (footnote 273) sought to include the youth in remote atolls of Maldives among the participants of its gender-inclusive public consultations on the benefits of renewable energy, energy efficiency, and energy savings. A total of 5,462 students (47% females) in grades 8–10 in 85 islands and 841 students (58% females) in grades 11–12 in 31 islands participated in the awareness sessions. In these sessions, the project team encouraged the female students to take up technical or engineering vocational courses. The project's gender action plan also included the provision of internship programs in Fenaka Corporation Limited, a power utility supplying electricity to the communities of inhabited islands, for female students interested in careers in the energy sector. However, an internship program was deemed unrealistic for secondary education students. Hence, Fenaka offered visits or exposure to their sites to interested female students as an alternative way of encouraging them to pursue a career in the energy sector. The project team also identified other schools on the project-covered islands with female students interested in the internship program.

(ii)   The **Supporting Electricity Supply Reliability Improvement Project** (footnote 82) in Sri Lanka targeted to improve the energy-based technical skills of young women and men. Of the 615 youth trained in routine electrical repairs; operation and maintenance of hybrid renewable energy systems; and other employment skills (e.g., communication, bookkeeping, first aid, and occupational health and safety), 473 (77%) were women and 100% belonged to households below the poverty line.

Migrant Workers

270.   None of the reviewed 19 infrastructure sector projects of SARD aimed to respond to the needs and problems of migrant workers.

E.   Good Practices in Responding to the Issues of Disadvantaged Youth and Migrant Workers

271.   This section has two parts. The first part is a review of another set of 15 projects of SARD to identify SARD-assisted projects' good practices in responding to the needs and conditions of disadvantaged youth and migrant workers. The second part presents the good practices of CSOs and government organizations that participated in the stakeholder consultations held for this assessment. Most participants in these consultations were from CSOs. The good practices are classified into the three pillars of the LNOB framework.

Disadvantaged Youth

272.   Of the reviewed 15 projects of SARD, five had features aiming to benefit the youth, especially women and those from disadvantaged groups.

   (i)   **Understand for action.** The **Inclusive Micro, Small, and Medium-Sized Enterprise Development Project** in Maldives (footnote 95) included a study on the opportunities and barriers to youth's participation in micro, small, and medium-sized enterprises (MSMEs). Among the barriers identified were (a) lack of access to sufficient capital, (b) poor transportation and marketing, (c) tedious licensing procedures, and (d) problems in maintaining work-life balance among women with their rigid traditional gender roles.

   (ii)   **Empower for change**

      (a)   **Supporting Kerala's Additional Skill Acquisition Program in Post-Basic Education** (footnote 92) aimed to enhance the employability of the state's youth and create opportunities for their productive employment. As of March 2020, of the 198,912 students enrolled in the additional skill acquisition program's foundation course (e.g., communicative English, information technology, time and stress management, teamwork, interpersonal skills, organizational skills), 115,456 (58%) were females. With the employment skills learned from the program, by 2019, the employability index of female trainees of the additional skill acquisition program increased to 69 or by 21 percentage points (from 48 in 2016), and that of male trainees to 68 or by 17 percentage points (from 51 in 2016).

(b)   The Sri Lanka **Skills Sector Enhancement Program** (footnote 97) aimed to increase the number of students enrolled in technical programs to 224,000 and provided financial help to at least 60,000 students in disadvantaged situations.

(c)   The Nepal **Supporting School Sector Development Plan** (footnote 276) implemented a pro-poor scholarship scheme in 15 districts of the country. Of the 699 poor students that received the scholarship, 324 or 46% were girls.

(d)   The Maldives Inclusive **Micro, Small, and Medium-Sized Enterprise Development Project** (footnote 95) aimed to increase youth- and women-led businesses by providing training, business consultations, and business start-up loans. Of the 17,465 participants in 532 trainings in business development and 3,525 business consultations and technical business visits, 10,440 (60%) were youth, and 8,729 (50%) were women.[313] The beneficiaries of the project's line of credit facility included 37 youth-led MSMEs.

(e)   **Include for opportunity.** Under the Maldives **Inclusive Micro, Small, and Medium-Sized Enterprise Development Project** (footnote 95), youth and gender concerns were integrated as crosscutting themes in all activities, plans, and programs of the Ministry of Economic Development and seven business development service centers established in different regions (Fonadhoo, Hanimadhoo, Kudahuvadhoo, Kulhudhuffushi, Malé, Naifaru, and Thindadhoo) of the country.

273.   In the stakeholder consultations in Bhutan, India, and Maldives, the participants shared their initiatives to help address the issues of disadvantaged youth. Among these initiatives were the following:

(i)   **Understand for action.** The Bhutan Youth Development Fund engages young females as adolescent enquirers to identify the needs and issues of the young, and it uses the data as the basis of its projects.

(ii) **Empower for change**

(a)   The Bhutan Youth Development Fund aims to ensure that all youth have equal access to education, meaningful employment, and opportunities to develop their potential. Their initiatives are in the areas of (1) youth training on child protection through the Young Volunteers in Action project, which is being operated in all 20 regions; (2) awareness raising through the development of information and communication materials, which are shared with young people; (3) the bringing back of out-of-school youth to school through getting the support of their peer groups; and (4) youth livelihood and employment, in which the Youth Development Fund works with the International Youth Foundation to roll out training called Passport to Success to enhance the livelihood skills, employability, empowerment, and soft skills of youth.

---

[313]   ADB. 2019. *Completion Report: Inclusive Micro, Small, and Medium-Sized Enterprise Development Project in Maldives.* Manila.

(b)   The Organization for Youth Empowerment was set up to help Bhutanese youth find meaningful employment. Its primary focus is on students or youth enrolled in technical training institutes or those that have entered the labor market.

(c)   Save the Children in Bhutan promotes child rights and welfare. Some of its interventions are related to (1) job protection, where they work with the government and CSOs; and (2) youth with disability, particularly helping students with visual and hearing impairment get jobs.

(d)   Dream a Dream in India aims to empower young people from vulnerable backgrounds to overcome adversity and thrive in a fast-changing world. It has two programs: (1) **After-School Life Skill Program**, through which they train children ages 8 to 15 in more than 25 government-aided and low-income private schools in Bangalore in life skills, and (2) the **Career Connect Program** for students who participated in the **After-School Life Skill Program** and are experiencing difficulty in entering the formal market.

(e)   The Yuva Parivartan in India is a nongovernment organization (NGO) that helps out-of-school youth through vocational skills training, guidance, counseling, and financial assistance.

(f)   The responsible government agency in India, the Ministry of Youth Affairs and Sports, with its Department of Youth Affairs, implements a few schemes, including the Rashtriya Yuva Sashaktikaran Karyakram youth empowerment program, the National Service Scheme, and the Rajiv Gandhi National Institute of Youth Development. These schemes aim to organize youth of the country and enhance their capacities to develop democratic institutional mechanisms.[314]

(ii)   **Include for opportunity**

(a)   The Organization for Youth Empowerment in Bhutan works with concerned government agencies like the National Commission for Women and Children and the Royal Bhutan Police for the enactment or implementation of laws or policies that benefit the youth.

(b)   Save the Children in Bhutan helps the government establish emergency shelter facilities, including a child helpline, for children in difficult circumstances, and supports the strengthening of the child justice system.

(c)   Open Hand Maldives is an NGO that helps youth with drug addiction problems. They were the first to operate drop-in centers in Maldives.

Migrant Workers

274.   Among the reviewed 15 projects of SARD, only the **COVID-19 Active Response and Expenditure Support Program** (footnote 124) in Maldives explicitly included migrant workers as target beneficiaries. Under this program, migrant workers accommodation facilities were

---

[314]   Government of India, Ministry of Youth Affairs and Sports. *Annual Report 2021–22*. New Delhi.

constructed.[315] About 9,613 male migrant workers were given temporary accommodation by June 2021.[316] Women migrant workers were mostly in the service sector and got some type of accommodation from their employers. In addition, the National Social Protection Agency provided support to all foreigners (including migrant workers) who tested positive for COVID-19 (if their infections were not covered by either their own private insurance or other medical coverage) in accordance with the COVID-19 Special Measures Act that was passed by the Parliament in 2020.

275.   In the stakeholder consultations in India and Maldives, participants from CSOs shared the following initiatives to support migrant workers.

(i)   **Understand for action**

    (a)   The Disha Foundation in India includes in its strategy the profiling of migrant workers through software developed in-house, which it uses to identify the services migrant workers need, and a tracking mechanism to locate the migrant workers who are registered in its system.

    (b)   Jan Sahas is a community-centric organization working in nine states of India. It implements the India Migration Corridor Program, which covers both source districts and destination districts, and uses a tech platform called the longitude migration tracking system that tracks about 120,000 migrants for the provision of needed support, such as social security benefits. They are also launching an app called Jan Saathi that can collect information and track migrant families using the migrant workers' mobile numbers.

(ii)   **Empower for change**

    (a)   The Disha Foundation in India aims to make migration safer and more productive for the migrant workers by addressing issues related to their health, livelihood, food security, education, living conditions, and access to public services. Its model includes physical migration resource centers that have dedicated mobile applications with an integrated helpline that they use to reach out to migrant workers; and provision of membership cards to the workers, with which the foundation offers its main services (e.g., job linkage support; access to low-cost health care through a tie-up with [referral to] the government health system and services; and need-based legal support, especially for those exploited at their workplace).

    (b)   Jan Sahas works on safe migration and workers' protection, and assists migrant workers who are victims of trafficking or rape and sexual violence. Its interventions include the Migrant Resilience Collaborative, under which it provides social security benefits to migrant workers (currently being implemented in 84 districts across 12 states); and migrant worker protection and responsible recruitment.

---

[315]   ADB. 2022. *Report and Recommendation of the President to the Board of Directors: Proposed Countercyclical Support Facility Loan, Grant, and Technical Assistance Grant to the Republic of Maldives for the COVID-19 Active Response and Expenditure Support Program.* Environmental Monitoring Report (January–March 2022) (accessible from the list of linked documents in Appendix 2). Manila.

[316]   Temporary accommodation was provided to male migrant workers that were being repatriated, i.e., unregistered migrant workers, and those going back to their home country because of reasons such as unemployment and COVID-19 mitigation measures.

(c)   The Aajeevika Bureau and Jan Sahas in India work at both source and destination centers to support the migrant workers through skills development and legal support.

(d)   The Maldivian Red Crescent helps migrants in Maldives access basic services (including COVID-19 vaccination) and helps undocumented migrants with registration.

(iii) **Include for opportunity.** The International Organization for Migration established an office in Maldives in 2013. The organization's work is in three areas: (a) technical support to the government for the development of a policy on migrants' health, (b) close coordination with the national anti-trafficking steering committee, and (c) assistance in developing the government's capacity in an integrated approach to migration.

F.   Conclusions and Way Forward

Summary of Findings

276.   This chapter merged the assessment of the situation of disadvantaged youth and migrant workers because (i) the assessment of disadvantaged youth was limited to Bhutan, India, and Maldives, and the assessment of migrant workers to India and Maldives; and (ii) SARD has few initiatives engaging both disadvantaged groups. Hence, a single chapter was deemed sufficient for the results of the assessment. The highlights are as follows:

(i)   **Disadvantaged youth**
(a)   The youth in the three countries comprise a significant proportion of the national population: 60% in Bhutan, 35% in India, and 37% in Maldives.
(b)   Many youths, especially those from disadvantaged backgrounds and social identity groups, face various barriers to their access to education and economic opportunities. Examples are lack of access to information technology, which became more pronounced during the lockdown and school closures because of the COVID-19 pandemic; limited resources for the implementation of skills development and employment programs; inadequate rehabilitation services for youths with a substance abuse problem; and families' view of the education of their young women as a waste of resources because they are expected to eventually marry and be confined to their homes.
(c)   All three DMCs have dedicated policies and acts for the protection, uplifting, and empowerment of disadvantaged youth.
(d)   SARD's initiatives to respond to the situation of the disadvantaged youth— as reflected in 7 of 34 reviewed projects (19 projects reviewed to identify approaches to mainstream the concerns of youth and 15 projects reviewed to identify good practices)—are focused on encouraging more young women to take up careers in the men-dominated energy sector, developing the youths' employment skills, and assisting the youths to capture job opportunities or become entrepreneurs.

(e)   The government and CSOs in the three countries have good practices in responding to the issues of the youth and uplifting their conditions.

(ii)   **Migrant workers**

(a)   In India and Maldives, the term "migrants" refers to those who changed their place of residence from their place of birth. Based on this definition, 37% of the population in India and 44% in Maldives are migrants. Internal migrants in India and international migrants in Maldives are identified as vulnerable groups.

(b)   In both India and Maldives, many migrant workers work in the informal sector and are therefore not covered by employment laws, and experience low job security and harsh work conditions. They were among the groups severely affected by the COVID-19 pandemic. Unskilled migrants in Maldives are met with xenophobia and discrimination. Women migrant workers, who are mostly domestic workers, face more difficulties because of wage discrepancies, lack of proper sanitation and facilities, and extra vulnerability to sexual abuse and violence.

(c)   India and Maldives have laws and policies regulating the employment and protecting the conditions of migrant workers.

(d)   Of the 34 reviewed projects of SARD, only COVID-19 Active Response and Expenditure Support Program (footnote 124) in Maldives explicitly included migrant workers as target beneficiaries.

(e)   As SARD has limited support for migrant workers, it can draw potential entry points and lessons from the good practices of CSOs in the two countries.

Way Forward for the South Asia Department

277.   During the stakeholder consultations, representatives from CSOs and the government shared their recommendations for SARD's possible areas of assistance on the issues of disadvantaged youth and migrant workers as follows.

(i)   **Disadvantaged youth in Bhutan**

(a)   Assessment of youth's employment skills and available skills development and vocational training programs

(b)   Documentation of best practices

(c)   Reproductive health of teenagers

(d)   Capacity development of service providers to better serve young people with different needs

(e)   Awareness-raising on the rights of the youth

(ii)   **Disadvantaged youth in India**

(a)   Youth's timely access to accurate information

(b)   Awareness-raising of local officials and policy makers on the issues and needs of youth, and their engagement in promoting the welfare of youth

(c)   Training of trainers and role models for youth development

(d)   Livelihood programs for youth who dropped out of school early

(e)   Short-term (15–20 days) vocational and entrepreneurship courses

(iii) **Disadvantaged youth in Maldives**

(a)   Youth skills development program to better prepare youths for the job market

(b)   Strengthening of CSOs that help youths with substance abuse problems

(c)   Building of infrastructures (e.g., treatment centers, drop-in centers) for the recovery of youths with substance abuse disorders

(d)   Training of teachers, sports coaches, and officials on how to develop the sports sector for youth development, and strengthening of the Maldives National Institute of Sports

(iv)   **Migrant workers in India**

(a)   Development of guidelines for the recruitment, training, and contracting of migrant workers and modes of payment for their services (e.g., through bank transfer, not cash) to ensure compliance with existing laws

(b)   Establishment of a migration support center in every city (port of arrival) situated in an area with easy access to a train station or a bus station, where migrant workers can receive needed services

(c)   Construction or improvement of migrant hostels

(d)   Improvement of coordination between source and destination states to devise how migrant workers can avail themselves of existing schemes and services and social security benefits

(e)   Institutional strengthening through the development of the capacity to collect, store, and use data (social registry), such as the number of migrant workers, their needs, and characteristics; and design and administer programs, such as for social security, skills development, and the health and welfare of migrant women and children

(f)   Development of the capacity and expansion of the areas covered by the services of CSOs working for migrant workers

(g)   Empowerment of migrant workers so they can make demands for their rights, such as fair wages

(h)   Improvement of migrant workers' access to water, sanitation, and childcare facilities at their destinations

(v)   **Migrant workers in Maldives**

(a)   Assessment of the situation of migrants in the country

(b)   Strengthening of existing and development of new mechanisms for migrants to seek help without fear, such as migrant support centers

Photo credit: Practical Action,
Sri Lanka- Zul Mukhida

IX. OVERVIEW OF THE ASSESSMENT RESULTS AND ACTION POINTS

A.   Overview of the Assessment Results

278.   The assessment of the situation of different disadvantaged groups or different dimensions of exclusion and vulnerability in South Asia—presented in the other chapters of this report—spotlights the following general concerns and needed areas of action:

(i)   **There is strong evidence that in the six development member countries (DMCs), the most disadvantaged in each excluded and vulnerable group are women.** Many women experience different layers of exclusion and vulnerability. Understanding and confronting these layers or intersecting dimensions of inequality, exclusion, and vulnerability (e.g., gender, age, disability, social identity, sexual orientation, gender identity, expression and sex characteristics [SOGIESC]; income poverty, geographic location) separately or unevenly (e.g., more focus on one and negating or partially attending to others) may not resolve the barriers to women's access to services, resources, and opportunities, and their participation in different spheres of society on an equal basis with men.

(ii)   **Men and individuals with diverse SOGIESC of disadvantaged groups also experience intersecting inequality, exclusion, and vulnerability.** In line with the "Leave-No-One-Behind" (LNOB) principles, development interventions need to address their conditions too.

(iii)   In view of the first two bullet points, **social and gender analyses to inform the gender equality and social inclusion (GESI) features of South Asia Department projects have to include the identification and examination of the manifestations of intersecting inequalities, exclusion, and vulnerability** experienced by the projects' targeted beneficiaries, especially women and girls, in addition to the assessment of gender inequality experienced by women and poverty experienced by disadvantaged social groups.

(iv)   **Not all six DMCs have policies addressing the intersecting inequalities faced by women, girls, men, and boys of excluded and vulnerable groups.** As articulated during the stakeholder consultations, one potential area of action of SARD is to support multisector dialogues for GESI policy reform and to develop the capacity of government agencies to address the GESI policy implementation gaps. In acting on this call for support, SARD can build on its proven competencies in gender mainstreaming and other stakeholders' available resources and initiatives in the DMCs.

(v) **While the government, civil society organizations (CSOs), and other international development partners in the DMCs (except Maldives) have recognized and acted on the GESI issues of people with diverse SOGIESC, SARD has not yet been fully engaged as none of its assessed projects are explicitly targeted to benefit these people.** The inclusion of people with diverse SOGIESC in the review and updating of the Safeguard Policy Statement of the Asian Development Bank (ADB); ADB's research on the legal barriers to SOGIESC inclusion in 23 DMCs, including Bhutan, Nepal, and Sri Lanka; and the upcoming study on the economic cost of discrimination against people with diverse SOGIESC in South Asia and three grant or technical assistance projects supporting people with diverse SOGIESC in Bangladesh, Bhutan, and Nepal are good starting points. Also, given the strong demand of stakeholders for support, SARD may consider developing a program or project addressing their concerns and those of other excluded and vulnerable groups covered in this assessment and/or finding ways to integrate the issue of people with diverse SOGIESC into its pipeline projects. Along this line, SARD has identified pipeline programs and projects where actions to benefit people with diverse SOGIESC can be integrated. This move is in line with the SARD GESI framework, which adopts a nonbinary definition of gender and integrates diverse SOGIESC into the definition of gender equality.

(vi) **The assessment of stakeholder initiatives (including SARD projects) along the LNOB framework suggests an unequal or imbalanced focus on the three pillars.** As designing programs along the three pillars ensures a holistic or comprehensive response to inequality, exclusion, and vulnerability, this point is worth noting. For instance, while initiatives in line with "empower for change" need further strengthening (as they are critical to achieving GESI), equal attention and actions are also required on the two other pillars, "understand for action" and "include for opportunity" (paras. 9(ii) and 11 and Table 1.1 of Chapter 1 of this report provide definitions of these three pillars).

B.   Way Forward: 10-Point Guide for Designing and Operationalizing Gender Equality and Social Inclusion Programs

279.   The assessment of good practices of ADB SARD and stakeholder organizations in the six DMCs also provides a list of action points to consider in designing and operationalizing GESI programs. Some of these points are lessons (from success factors and challenges encountered), and some are affirmations of current practices. The lessons that emerge reiterate the importance of a transformative GESI mainstreaming approach, which cuts across the three pillars of the LNOB framework.

Point 1: Mainstream GESI in program or project design and operational frameworks and tools rather than treat it as a separate added activity.

280.   In designing programs and projects to achieve GESI results, SARD project teams and partner executing and implementing agencies need to ensure the following: (i) GESI features should be explicitly mentioned in all project documents, including the project's design and monitoring framework, project administration manual, stakeholder participation plan, and social safeguards plan; (ii) GESI functions should be explicitly stated in the job description of all staff; and (iii) all staff with or without direct roles in implementing the gender or GESI action plan should be oriented on the basic concepts of GESI and trained in mainstreaming GESI in organizations and programs or projects. This is because everyone has a role to play in applying GESI principles in the day-to-day operations of the project and in helping the project achieve its GESI results.

Pillar 1: Understand for Action

Point 2: Identify the disadvantaged groups (as defined in this assessment report) in program or project areas and consult them on how they can benefit and/or can be adversely affected by a proposed program or project. Integrate their views into the project's GESI features.

281.   Consultations with the target beneficiary groups (with significant representation and participation of women, men, and nonbinary individuals) provide essential insights into their needs and expectations from the project; possible impacts of the intervention (desired and undesired); and barriers that they, especially women of disadvantaged groups, may encounter in accessing project benefits. Some good practices are as follows:

   (i)   **Timing of consultations with target disadvantaged groups** should be scheduled throughout the project cycle, including design and evaluation, and not limited to the inception phase.
   (ii) **Going beyond consultations** and adopting innovative approaches, such as transect walks[317], and conducting participatory safety audits in accessing public infrastructures, help deepen a project's engagement with the target women and disadvantaged groups.

Point 3: Use participatory and reliable methods in collecting disaggregated data or information about the disadvantaged groups in ethical ways that do not place them into more vulnerable situation.

282.   GESI assessments during project design provide information about barriers to GESI experienced by disadvantaged groups in the program or project area and how the project can contribute to addressing these barriers. Official (government) disaggregated data on the different disadvantaged groups may not be available. Hence, it is a good practice for ADB to use alternative sources of disaggregated data, either by conducting its own surveys or by leveraging the surveys and studies of research institutions and CSOs. ADB should use ethical methods in conducting surveys or other types of research about people with diverse SOGIESC, especially in countries where they are not legally recognized or experience stigmatization or discrimination, to avoid disclosing their identity and exposing them to danger.

---

[317] Transect walk is a participatory action research method where community members and planners from the government and/or development partners walk through different community areas to map community resources and areas needing development or identify appropriate locations for project resources or services.

Pillar 2: Empower for Change

Point 4: In designing the GESI features of a project, consider the distinct empowerment needs of women, girls, men, and boys experiencing overlapping exclusion and vulnerabilities due to their intersecting disadvantaged identities (e.g., age, disability, social identity, SOGIESC, geographic location, income status, and migrant status).

283.   The intersectionality framework, which this assessment adopted, recognizes the diversity of women and the excluded and vulnerable groups, and the different forms and degrees of inequality, exclusion, and vulnerability they experience, depending on their intersecting disadvantaged identities. These differences call for different or context-specific responses, not uniform or fixed approaches. Hence, the program GESI strategy or project GESI action plan should not have uniform activities and targets for all women and excluded and vulnerable groups but should consider their distinct empowerment needs. The consultations and situational analyses during project design can be designed to provide a comprehensive view of the distinct empowerment needs and aspirations of women, men, and nonbinary beneficiaries.

Point 5: Incorporate skills development and capacity building in project design and interventions, as it helps address the livelihood difficulties experienced by women and excluded and vulnerable groups.

284.   Incorporating interventions for capability or skills development of women and girls, especially those from excluded and vulnerable groups, in project designs is effective in addressing the livelihood barriers and other barriers they face. Moreover, without proper training and skills, recruiters might not have adequate incentives to hire women during project activities, even if the project design contains specific targets to include them. Some lessons in promoting economic empowerment are as follows:

(i)   **Partnerships with private firms** can help create more employment opportunities for women, youth, and other excluded and vulnerable groups. It also allows CSOs to provide vocational training and skills building to help women, youth, and other disadvantaged groups access meaningful job opportunities.

(ii)   **Professional certifications add credibility to training** and help the target women and disadvantaged groups secure employment.

(iii)   **Building a GESI-supportive infrastructure and conducive environment encourages participation in training.** Well-designed training and skills development programs should address the existing gender and social norms that constrain the involvement of women, especially those from disadvantaged groups and excluded and vulnerable groups, in different events. For instance, for women responsible for household chores and child-rearing, one response is to take the training to the women's locations to ensure their easy access and wider participation. Further, on-site childcare facilities should be arranged. Disability-friendly infrastructure and support enable participants with disability to access training events. Appropriate toilet facilities support the SOGIESC community.

(iv)   **Foster a culture of entrepreneurship among women and disadvantaged groups.** With the provision of relevant skills and capacity development, women, especially people from disadvantaged groups (including those with diverse SOGIESC), can start small businesses to enhance their livelihoods. Various development partners and CSOs involved in developing the entrepreneurship capacities of women, people with disabilities, people with diverse SOGIESC, rural populations, and youth have recognized the need to extend their efforts beyond training. For instance, they also see the need to improve access to markets.

Point 6: Organize or strengthen self-help groups that can provide a common platform for women's and excluded and vulnerable groups' empowerment.

285.   Self-help groups can be an effective means to build confidence and develop skills and capacity, including to influence policies of relevance, of group members. Various NGOs across the SARD DMCs help vulnerable communities organize themselves into self-help groups that enable people, especially women of excluded and vulnerable groups, and people of disadvantaged groups, to earn a decent living for themselves and their families. NGOs' expertise and understanding of community dynamics enable them to work effectively with community groups.

Point 7: Enhance the accountability of service providers for GESI.

286.   Developing the capacity of service providers, particularly those working in critical sectors such as health care and education, in mainstreaming GESI in their operations, and in practicing GESI principles in their relations with clients, is essential. However, to enhance the effectiveness of these interventions, the capacity of women, especially those from excluded and vulnerable groups and people of disadvantaged groups, to hold service providers accountable or responsible for upholding GESI principles and policies must be developed. The steps include raising the awareness of these women and excluded and vulnerable groups about their rights, and organizing them to have a collective voice.

Pillar 3: Include for Opportunity

Point 8: Develop the awareness and sensitivity of communities and service providers to the GESI needs of women, girls, and excluded and vulnerable groups to challenge discriminatory gender and social norms and address the structural inequalities that create stigma and discrimination.

287.   Many CSOs and development partners, including ADB, are focusing on awareness generation and community sensitization to address the deeply embedded attitudes and structural inequalities that create social stigma and discrimination. Some good practices are as follows.

(i)   **Collaborating with influential community members improves the reach and impact of awareness programs.** Awareness generation campaigns are more likely to succeed when supported by influential community members. For instance, Sri Lankan CSOs have been conducting awareness programs in rural areas with religious leaders and government officials for greater inclusion of people with diverse SOGIESC.

(ii)   **Engage people of advantaged groups (including men and boys) to make them aware of the benefits of reducing gender inequality and other forms of discrimination.** Merely providing development opportunities to women from excluded and vulnerable groups and people of disadvantaged groups is insufficient. Sensitizing family members, including men and boys, is essential to transforming unequal social structures and deeply rooted discriminatory practices.

(iii) **Awareness generation and sensitization of service providers bring positive attitudinal changes in the community.** Raising the GESI awareness of service providers and developing their capability to observe GESI principles in dealing with their clients is essential to ensuring that the disadvantaged groups receive the benefits they are entitled to from a project.

(iv) **Challenging social and gender norms expands the opportunities available to excluded and vulnerable groups.** Traditional social and gender norms can result in lack of confidence among women and disadvantaged groups in engaging in nontraditional types of work and in participating in public affairs.

Point 9: Incorporate GESI elements in infrastructure design, as it enhances the infrastructure's utility and impact on women and disadvantaged groups.

288.   Several ADB projects in the six DMCs constructed GESI-sensitive infrastructures as part of project activities to ensure that the needs of women and other disadvantaged groups were met. These infrastructures include streetlights, gender-segregated toilets, and bathing facilities that are safer for use of women, older people and people with disabilities.

Point 10: Seek government buy-in and collaboration and build on existing institutional mechanisms.

289.   Engaging, collaborating, and partnering with the government to mainstream GESI in development sector programs and projects is critical; hence, the following should be considered when developing a GESI strategy:

(i) **Alignment with government priorities and development agendas increases the chances of government buy-in.** Interventions aligned with the government's development priorities are likely to secure stronger government interest and collaboration.

(ii) **Collaborating early with allied sector agencies improves project efficiency and can enhance the sustainability of project outcomes**. Early collaboration with stakeholders helps develop a sense of shared ownership, trust, and understanding. For this purpose, ADB ensures that the gender action plan or GESI action plan of a project is a product of collaborative work with the executing and implementing agencies.

(iii) **Strengthening the institutional capacity of the government is essential for mainstreaming GESI.**

APPENDIX 1

LIST OF REVIEWED PROJECTS OF THE ASIAN DEVELOPMENT BANK'S SOUTH ASIA DEPARTMENT

Table A1.1: Reviewed Projects in Three Infrastructure Sectors Across the Six Developing Member Countries

DMC	Energy	Transport	Water and Other Urban Infrastructure and Services
Bangladesh	Bangladesh Power System Enhancement and Efficiency Improvement Project (EGM)	South Asia Subregional Economic Cooperation Dhaka-Northwest Corridor Road Project, Phase 2 (EGM)	• Dhaka Environmentally Sustainable Water Supply Project (EGM) • Second City Region Development Project (EGM)
Bhutan	No project in the energy sector was selected	Thimphu Road Improvement Project (SGE)	• Secondary Towns Urban Development Project (EGM) • Phuentsholing Township Development Project (SGE)
India	Madhya Pradesh Energy Efficiency Improvement Investment Program – Tranche 1 (EGM)	Second Rural Connectivity Investment Program – Tranche 1 (EGM)	West Bengal Drinking Water Sector Improvement Project (GEN)
Maldives	Preparing Outer Islands for Sustainable Energy Development Project (and additional financing) (EGM)	Kulhudhuffushi Harbor Expansion Project (SGE)	Greater Male Environmental Improvement and Waste Management Project (EGM)
Nepal	Power Transmission and Distribution Efficiency Enhancement Project (EGM)	South Asia Subregional Economic Cooperation Road Connectivity Project (EGM)	Third Small Towns Water Supply and Sanitation Sector Project (GEN)
Sri Lanka	Supporting Electricity Supply Reliability Improvement Project (EGM)	Integrated Road Investment Program, tranches 1–4 (EGM)	Local Government Enhancement Sector Project (and additional financing) (EGM)

DMC = developing member country, EGM = effective gender mainstreaming, GEN = gender equity theme, SGE = some gender elements.

Source: Asian Development Bank (South Asia Department).

Table A1.2: Fifteen Reviewed Projects Across the Six Developing Member Countries for Identification of Good Practices

DMC	Projects
Bangladesh	• Bangladesh Emergency Assistance Project • Second Chittagong Hill Tracts Rural Development Project, Phase 2
Bhutan	• Health Sector Development Program • Skills Training and Education Pathway Upgradation Project
India	• Madhya Pradesh Urban Services Improvement Project • Kerala's Additional Skills Acquisition Program in Post-Basic Education • Rajasthan Urban Sector Development Program • Bengaluru Metro Rail Project • Delhi-Meerut Regional Rapid Transit System Investment
Maldives	• COVID-19 Active Response and Expenditure Support Program • Inclusive Micro, Small, and Medium-Sized Enterprise Development Project
Nepal	• Skills Development Project • School Sector Development Plan • Integrated Urban Development Plan
Sri Lanka	• Skills Sector Enhancement Program

COVID-19 = coronavirus disease, DMC = developing member country.

Source: Asian Development Bank (South Asia Department).

APPENDIX 2

UNITED NATIONS TREATY RATIFICATION STATUS OF SOUTH ASIA DEPARTMENT COUNTRIES

Human Rights Instrument	Bangladesh	Bhutan	India	Maldives	Nepal	Sri Lanka
International Convention on the Elimination of All Forms of Racial Discrimination (1969)	Ratified (1979)	Signed (1973)	Ratified (1968)	Ratified (1984)	Ratified (1971)	Ratified (1982)
International Covenant on Civil and Political Rights (1976)	Ratified (2000)		Ratified (1979)	Ratified (2006)	Ratified (1991)	Ratified (1980)
International Covenant on Economic, Social and Cultural Rights (1976)	Ratified (1998)		Ratified (1979)	Ratified (2006)	Ratified (1991)	Ratified (1980)
Optional Protocol to the International Covenant on Economic, Social and Cultural Rights (2008)				Ratified (2020)		
Convention on the Elimination of All Forms of Discrimination against Women (1981)	Ratified (1984)	Ratified (1981)	Ratified (1993)	Ratified (1993)	Ratified (1991)	Ratified (1981)
Convention against Torture and Other Cruel, Inhuman or Degrading Treatment or Punishment (1987)	Ratified (1998)		Signed (1997)	Ratified (2004)	Ratified (1991)	Ratified (1994)
Optional Protocol to the Convention against Torture and Other Cruel, Inhuman or Degrading Treatment or Punishment (2006)				Ratified (2006)		Ratified (2017)
Convention on the Rights of the Child (1990)	Ratified (1990)	Ratified (1990)	Ratified (1992)	Ratified (1991)	Ratified (1990)	Ratified (1991)

Human Rights Instrument	Bangladesh	Bhutan	India	Maldives	Nepal	Sri Lanka
Optional Protocol to the Convention on the Rights of the Child on the involvement of children in armed conflict (2002)	Ratified (2000)	Ratified (2009)	Ratified (2005)	Ratified (2004)	Ratified (2007)	Ratified (2000)
Optional Protocol to the Convention on the Rights of the Child on the sale of children, child prostitution and child pornography (2002)	Ratified (2000)	Ratified (2009)	Ratified (2005)	Ratified (2002)	Ratified (2006)	Ratified (2006)
Optional Protocol to the Convention on the Rights of the Child on a communications procedure (2014)				Ratified (2019)		
International Convention on the Protection of the Rights of All Migrant Workers and Members of Their Families (1990)	Ratified (2011)					Ratified (1996)
Convention on the Rights of Persons with Disabilities (2007)	Ratified (2007)	Signed (2010)	Ratified (2007)	Ratified (2010)	Ratified (2010)	Ratified (2016)
Optional Protocol to the Convention on the Rights of People with Disabilities (2008)	Ratified (2008)				Ratified (2010)	
United Nations Declaration on the Rights of Indigenous Peoples (2007)[a]	Abstained (2007)	Abstained (2007)	Adopted (2007)	Adopted (2007)	Adopted (2007)	Adopted (2007)

[a] As a General Assembly declaration, the United Nations Declaration on the Rights of Indigenous Peoples is not a legally binding instrument under international law. UN. Department of Economic and Social Affairs. *United Nations Declaration on The Rights Of Indigenous Peoples.*

Sources: United Nations Office of the High Commissioner for Human Rights. Status of Ratification Interactive Dashboard: Ratification of 18 International Human Rights Treaties (accessed 30 July 2020); and United Nations Department of Economic and Social Affairs, Division for Inclusive Social Development. 2007. *United Nations Declaration on the Rights of Indigenous Peoples.* New York.

APPENDIX 3
DEFINITIONS OF DISABILITY

DMC	Definition
Bangladesh	"A person with disabilities is one who is physically disabled either congenitally or as a result of disease or being a victim of accident, or due to improper or maltreatment or for any other reasons has become physically incapacitated or mentally imbalanced as a result of such disabledness or one to mental impairedness has become incapacitated, either partially or fully and is unable to lead a normal life."[a] A disability is any restriction or lack of ability to perform an activity in the manner or within the range considered normal for a human being.
Bhutan	The Population and Housing Census 2017 defined people with disabilities as people who face difficulty in six functional domains of seeing, hearing, walking, cognition, self-care, and communication.[b]
India	According to the Rights of People with Disabilities Act, 2016, [a] "'person with disabilities' means a person with long term physical, mental, intellectual or sensory impairment which, in interaction with barriers, hinders his full and effective participation in society equally with others."[c]
Maldives	Section 14 (a) of the Disabilities Act, 2010 defines people with disabilities as those "having long-term physical, mental, intellectual or sensory impairments, which in interaction with various barriers may hinder their full and effective participation in society, on an equal basis with others."[d]
Nepal	"'Person with disabilities' means a person who has long-term physical, mental, intellectual or sensory disability or functional impairments or existing barriers that may hinder his or her full and effective participation in social life on an equal basis with others."[e]
Sri Lanka	The Protection of the Rights of People with Disabilities Act, 1996 contains the following definition: "'person with disabilities' means any person who, as a result of any deficiency in his physical or mental capabilities, whether congenital or not, is unable by himself to ensure for himself, wholly or partly, the necessities of life."[f] This is considered the legal definition of disability in the Sri Lankan context, "although the National Policy on Disability, 2003 also notes the International Classification of Functioning, Disability and Health classification model and the need to consider environmental, cultural, and social factors when understanding disability".

[a] Government of Bangladesh, Ministry of Planning, Statistics and Informatics Division, Bangladesh Bureau of Statistics. 2015. *Population Monograph of Bangladesh—Disability in Bangladesh: Prevalence and Pattern.* Dhaka. p. 1.
[b] Government of Bhutan, National Statistics Bureau. 2018. *2017 Population and Housing Census of Bhutan: National Report.* Thimphu.
[c] Government of India, Ministry of Law and Justice, Legislative Department. *The Rights of People with Disabilities Act, 2016.* New Delhi. p. 6.
[d] United Nations. 2019. *Convention on the Rights of People with Disabilities: Initial report submitted by Maldives under article 35 of the Convention, due in 2012.*
[e] Government of Nepal, Law Commission. 2017. *The Act Relating to Rights of People with Disabilities, 2074 (2017).* Kathmandu. pp. 1–2.
[f] Government of Sri Lanka, Parliament of the Democratic Socialist Republic of Sri Lanka. 1996. *Protection of the Rights of People with Disabilities Act, No. 28 of 1996.* Colombo.

Source: Asian Development Bank (South Asia Department).

APPENDIX 4

DEFINITIONS AND POPULATION OF DIFFERENT SOCIAL IDENTITIES

DMC	Social Identity	Definition	Population
Bangladesh	Ethnic and tribal communities	Ethnic and tribal groups in Bangladesh possess their own cultures, ways of life, traditions, and customary laws. They also have major ethnic, cultural, religious, and linguistic distinctions from the majority Bengalis. The Government of Bangladesh uses the term 'Small Ethnic populations.'[a]	The most recent census figures (2011) do not provide ethnically disaggregated data. In the previous census conducted in 1991, the total population is at 1.2 million. Taking into account the average demographic growth rate of the country, their population at present should be around 1.5 million. Bangladesh Adivasi Forum, an apex advocacy and networking organization of the ethnic minorities, has given a figure of 3 million as the total population.[b]
	Religious minorities	Article 2A of the Constitution of the People's Republic of Bangladesh declares that the state religion of the republic is Islam, but the State shall ensure equal status and equal rights in the practice of the Hindu, Buddhist, Christian and other religions. The constitution also stipulates the state should not grant political status in favor of any religion. It provides for the right to profess, practice, or propagate all religions "subject to law, public order, and morality," and states religious communities or denominations have the right to establish, maintain, and manage their religious institutions.[c]	The population share of religious minorities in Bangladesh is Hindu (8.5%), Buddhist (0.6%), Christian (0.3%), and other (0.1%). Dalits, the caste minority, are estimated to have a population of 6.5 million in Bangladesh.[d]

DMC	Social Identity	Definition	Population
India	Scheduled castes	The Constitution of India, Article 366 (24) defines scheduled castes as "such castes, races or tribes or parts of or groups within such castes, race or tribes as are deemed under Article 341 to be Scheduled Castes."[e]	Based on the 2011 census, scheduled castes constitute 16.6% of the total population of India.[f]
	Scheduled tribes	The Constitution of India, Article 366 (25) defines scheduled tribes as "such tribes or tribal communities or parts of or groups within such tribes or tribal communities as are deemed under Article 342 to be Scheduled Tribes."[e]	Scheduled tribes are 8.6% of the total population of India. They are primarily in rural areas, with only 3% in urban areas. Mizoram (94.4%), Nagaland (86.5%), Meghalaya (86.1%), Manipur (37.2%), Tripura (31.8%), Chhattisgarh (30.6%), Jharkhand (26.2%), and Odisha (22.8%) are some of the states and union territories with a high proportion of the tribal population.[g]
	Religious minorities	Under the National Commission for Minorities Act, 1992, Muslims, Sikhs, Christians, Buddhists, Zoroastrians (Parsis) and Jains are notified as minority communities in India.[h] The Constitution of India does not define the word "Minority" and only refers to "Minorities" and speaks of those "based on religion or language." The rights of the minorities have been spelled out in the Constitution in detail.[i]	As per the Census 2011, the percentage of minorities in the country is about 19.3% of the total population of the country. The population of Muslims are 14.2%; Christians 2.3%; Sikhs 1.7%, Buddhists 0.7%, Jain 0.4% and Parsis 0.006%.[j]
Nepal	Janajatis	The National Foundation for Development of Indigenous Nationalities Act, 2002 defines indigenous nationalities (Adivasi Janajati) as distinct communities having their own mother tongues, traditional cultures, written and unwritten histories, traditional homeland and geographical areas, and egalitarian social structures.[k]	Terai constitutes 50.27% (13,318,705) of the total population while Hill and Mountain constitutes 43% (11,394,007) and 6.73% (1,781,792) respectively.[l]
	Dalits	"The National Dalit Commission defined the Dalit community and caste-based untouchability in its bill for an act in 2003. According to this, the 'Dalit community' refers collectively to communities that have been left behind in social, economic, educational, political, and religious spheres; and deprived of human dignity and social justice because of caste-based discrimination and untouchability."[m]	Based on the 2011 census Dalits constitute 14.99% (Hill Dalit 7.11%; Madhesi Dalit 3.24% and Unidentified Dalit 0.76%) of the total national population of Nepal. Some local surveys carried out by Dalits' organizations, in some selected villages revealed Dalit populations higher than in the census (20% to 25% of the total population).[m]

DMC	Social Identity	Definition	Population
	Religious minorities	In 2012 the Government of Nepal constituted a special commission to study the socioeconomic situation of Muslims in Nepal. The new constitution of 2015 acknowledged the Nepali Muslims as marginalized and underprivileged group.[n]	Based on the 2011 census, there are ten types of religion categories reported, Hindu (81.3%); Buddhism (9%), Islam (4.4%), Kirat (3.1%), Christianity (1.4%), Prakriti (0.5%), Bon (13,006), Jainism (3,214), Bahai (1,283) and Sikhism (609).[m]
Sri Lanka	Religious minorities	There is a strong overlap between religion and ethnicity in Sri Lanka, with most of the Buddhist majority estimated in the 2012 Census belonging to the Sinhalese population. Similarly, most of the Hindu and Christian minorities are Tamil. The Muslim community is made up primarily of Sri Lankan Moors, Malays, and smaller religious groups. Other religious minorities, including Parsis and Baha'i, are also present in the country in smaller numbers.[o]	According to the 2012 census, population of ethnicity based groups include Sri Lankan Tamils (11.2%), Indian Tamils (4.2%), Sri Lankan Moors (9.3%), Malays (0.2%), and Burghers (0.2%), amongst others. Muslims (Islam) constituted 9.66% of Sri Lanka's population.[p]
	Wanniyala-Aetto	The Wanniyala-Aetto are an indigenous group from the island's original Neolithic community dating from at least 14,000 BC and distinguished by their hunting and gathering way of life, by their unwritten language, by their beliefs in traditional gods and ancestor spirits, and by the importance of ancestral lands to all aspects of their life.[q]	The 1981 census classified the Wanniyala-Aetto population in the category of "others;" they numbered 2,000 individuals.[q]

DMC = developing member country.

[a] International Labour Organization. 2017. *Building Capacities on Indigenous and Tribal Peoples' Issues in Bangladesh.* Geneva.
[b] Government of Bangladesh, Ministry of Health and Family Welfare. 2017. *Bangladesh Health Sector Support Program, Framework for Tribal Peoples Plan.* Dhaka.
[c] Government of the United States, Department of State, Office of International Religious Freedom. 2021. *2020 Report on International Religious Freedom: Bangladesh.* Washington, DC.
[d] Minority Rights Groups International. World Directory of Minorities and Indigenous Peoples: Bangladesh.
[e] Government of India, National Commission for Scheduled Castes. Special Constitutional Provisions for Protection and Development of the Scheduled Castes and the Scheduled Tribes. p. 9..
[f] Government of India, Ministry of Social Justice and Empowerment. Department of Social Justice and Empowerment.
[g] Government of India, Ministry of Social Justice and Empowerment, Department of Social Justice and Empowerment. 2018. *Handbook on Social Welfare Statistics.* New Delhi.
[h] Government of India, Ministry of Minority Affairs, National Commission for Minorities.
[i] Government of India, Ministry of Minority Affairs, National Commission for Minorities Constitutional Provisions.
[j] Government of India, Ministry of Minority Affairs. 2022. Percentage of Population as Minorities. News release. 10 February.
[k] Indigenous Television. 2017. Role of National Foundation for Development of Indigenous Nationalities (NFDIN) in Changing Context—Episode 25. 12 March.
[l] Government of Nepal, National Planning Commission Secretariat Central Bureau of Statistics. 2012. *National Population and Housing Census 2011.* Kathmandu.
[m] United Nations Development Programme. 2008. *The Dalits of Nepal and a New Constitution.* Kathmandu. p. 22.
[n] iNSAMER. 2020. Nepali Muslims and Their Struggle for Recognition.
[o] Minority Rights Groups International. World Directory of Minorities and Indigenous Peoples: Sri Lanka Tamils.
[p] Government of Sri Lanka, Department of Census and Statistics. 2012. *Census of Population and Housing of Sri Lanka, 2012.* Battaramulla, Sri Lanka.
[q] Minority Rights Groups International. World Directory of Minorities and Indigenous Peoples: Sri Lanka Wanniyala-Aetto (Veddhas).

Source: Asian Development Bank (South Asia Department).

www.ingramcontent.com/pod-product-compliance
Lightning Source LLC
Chambersburg PA
CBHW050042220326
41599CB00045B/7257